Footprint

Antigua

Sarah Cameron

& Leeward Islands

C000252955

Contents

About the author

After a degree in Latin American Studies Sarah Cameron has been travelling and writing on the continent ever since, both as an economist and as an author for Footprint Handbooks. Initially moonlighting for the *South American Handbook* while working for a British bank, in 1990 she parted company with the world of finance and now concentrates solely on the Caribbean and is the author of *Footprint Caribbean Islands* as well as individual island titles such as *Cuba*, the *Dominican Republic, Barbados, St Lucia, Antigua and the Leeward Islands*.

Acknowledgements

Trying to cover so many islands would be impossible without the invaluable help of a team of local correspondents as well as tourism officers who provided information, logistical support and hours of hospitality and fun. Sarah would like to thank Martha Watkins Gilkes and Annette Michael on Antigua and Joyce Fyfe in London, Claire Frank on Barbuda, Richard Aspin and Rosetta West on Montserrat, Maria Vendiese James and Randolph Hamilton on St Kitts and Esther Smith and Jennifer Hensley in London, Mireille Hermans and William Bell on Sint Maarten, Nicole Liburd on Nevis, Elise Magras on St-Barthélemy, Glenn Holm on Saba, Alida Francis, Roland Lopes and Malvern Dijkshoorn-Lopes on Sint Eustatius, Bernadette Davis and Erica Beaujour on St-Martin, Candis Niles in Anguilla and Carolyn Browne in London. In addition, the following hotels are to be thanked for their hospitality: Old Manor (Nevis), Ottley Plantation Inn and Golden Lemon (St Kitts), Anguilla Great House and Carimar Beach Club (Anguilla), Les Alizés (St-Martin), Maho Beach Resort (Sint Maarten), Hawksbill Beach Resort, Treetops and Siboney Beach Club (Antigua), Island Chalet (Barbuda), Montserrat Moments Inn (Montserrat), Golden Era (Statia), Scout's Place (Saba), Le Manoir de Marie (St-Barthélemy).

So many islands, so close yet so different from each other in culture, wealth and attitude. You can live like kings, find enormous live lobsters for sale on a silvery sand beach in Anguilla or stop for a bite when exploring the streets of Basseterre, St Kitts, and try a local salt fish and johnny cake sandwich washed down with cool coconut water. Fishing boats are pulled up on the black sand beach at Dieppe Bay, St Kitts, where cows and donkeys roam, while luxury yachts are moored in Gustavia harbour, St-Barthélemy, outside chic designer boutiques. Splash out and stay in the latest, minimalist hotel in Antigua or try a guest house on Barbuda where facilities are few but the empty 17-mile beach is among the best in the world. Vegetation ranges from scrub to rainforest, from the broad elephants' ears flourishing on a Saban hillside, to the slender sugar cane wafting on the Kittitian breeze. Monkeys chatter in the tree tops of Nevis, land crabs scuttle away from night time hunters on Statia and the huge Montserratian frog, the mountain chicken, is a delicacy.

Island nations

This group of little islands in the northeastern Caribbean share a chequered history of territorial struggles between colonial powers, plantation agriculture and slavery, but despite alternating between the English, French, Spanish, Dutch or Swedish, they have since diverged nationally. French is spoken on St-Barthélemy and St-Martin, Dutch on Sint Maarten, Saba and Sint Eustatius, Spanish by guest workers from the Dominican Republic and English everywhere. Some islands drive on the right, others on the left. St-Barthélemy is unmistakably French, from the smells of croissants and coffee to the Parisian traffic and parking problems, not forgetting the topless sunbathers. Saba's neat and tidy villages are essentially Dutch, even though the landscape is far from flat. Nevis is the quintessential tropical British colony, despite its independence, with its elegant plantation houses, verandas and manicured gardens. Croquet and tea on the lawn would not be out of place. Cricket is followed passionately in the former British islands and both Antigua and St Kitts are looking forward to hosting matches in the 2007 Cricket World Cup.

Water, water everywhere

All the islands are dependent on tourism: huge cruise ships block out the light when they dock at St John's, Antigua, and shopkeepers look forward to a bonanza, while English Harbour at the other end of the island hums with the rigging of hundreds of yachts when a regatta is in full swing. As islands their relationship with the sea is fully exploited and you can choose from a variety of watersports, whether it is sailing, kayaking, fishing, diving, snorkelling, windsurfing, kiteboarding or just mucking about on a range of water toys. On land there is hiking, horse riding and cycling to keep you fit and active, while most of the large hotels offer tennis and there are golf courses of championship standard. Alternatively, of course, you can just laze on the beach with a good book and a rum cocktail, top up the tan or indulge in a massage.

At a glance

Antigua and Barbuda
Antigua has always been a seafaring nation and the coast is full of historical associations with English Harbour, Nelson's Dockyard and the ruins of many defensive fortresses. Now visited by yachtsmen on trans-Atlantic races or cruising the islands, there is always a yacht on the horizon. Blessed also with lovely beaches and bays, the coast is picturesque and an island tour is enjoyable. Its sister island, Barbuda, lives in a bygone age with none of the trappings of the consumer society. The beaches on the west coast are out of this world, vast, empty and natural, while the frigate bird sanctuary is an untouched wilderness of mangroves and breeding birds.

Montserrat
Known principally for its volcano, which still belches out steam, rocks and lava and occasionally covers everything in ash, Montserrat is a laid-back, peaceful island, busy rebuilding itself after the disaster of the 1990s but with a much-reduced population. The hills and forests remain green and lush while underwater the volcano has in effect created a marine park teeming with life.

Sint Maarten/St-Martin
Not everybody's cup of tea, but if you like busy hotels, watersports, nightlife and entertainment and you're not into undisturbed nature and forests, then this might be the place to come. The French half is more attractive than the Dutch, with prettier architecture and excellent food, but both sides have good beaches. Links with neighbouring islands are well-developed and it is easy to organize a two-centre holiday or day trips to Saba, Statia, St-Barth or Anguilla.

Anguilla

A long, eel-shaped, flat island covered with scrub and brush, Anguilla was long neglected by the British and until the 1980s had only one hotel and one guest house. Now, however, developers have discovered the charms of its extensive pale sand beaches and it has been turned into an upmarket getaway destination for the wealthy of the North American east coast. Luxury hotels and villas dot the coast providing every comfort and select entertainment, but it remains friendly, relaxed and unpretentious.

Saba

This charming outpost of the Kingdom of the Netherlands is home to around 1,200 inhabitants who play host to some 25,000 visitors and medical students each year. With only one road and a handful of hotels, not many of them stay overnight, but those that do quickly relax and slow down to the easy pace of life of the islanders. With no beaches this is not a place for the sunbathing crowd, but divers extol the virtues of the marine park and hikers are drawn to the steps up Mount Scenery and other old stone paths around the island.

Sint Eustatius

An island with many historical associations, Statia has seen better days. Much work is now being done to renovate old buildings and restore the island's undoubted charms, but a lot of the island still appears scruffy, with an air of having been forgotten. Nevertheless, there is excellent diving in the waters offshore and plenty of opportunities to beach comb or hike up the Quill, an extinct volcano.

St-Barthélemy

A French outpost in the Caribbean with luxury hotels and villas, designer boutiques and gourmet food to tempt the rich and famous. It is, however, a delightful island with its crumpled, hilly landscape and jagged coastline giving rise to a multitude of bays, coves and glorious beaches. Whenever you come over the brow of a hill you are greeted by glorious views below with horse shoe-shaped bays looking out to sea dotted with islets and rocks. Reached by small plane with a heart-stopping approach over the mountain to the landing strip or by boat with a stomach-churning crossing from Sint Maarten, the islanders make sure you won't want to leave in a hurry.

St Kitts

The cone of Mount Liamuiga rises majestically at one end of the island, its slopes green with sugar cane on the lowlands disappearing into forest at altitude. Old stone sugar mills dot the landscape while a few plantation houses remain as testament to a prosperous past, guarded by the magnificent Brimstone Hill Fortress. The southern end of the island tapers into a narrow peninsula where golden sand beaches are attracting hotels and tourists, although most of this spit of land remains wild and untouched, home to monkeys, goats and deer.

Nevis

Separated from St Kitts by a narrow channel, Nevis climbs steeply out of the sea in a cone to match Mount Liamuiga. There is one good road around this scenic island, but the slopes are criss-crossed with old donkey paths and goat trails through the forest if you want to explore on foot, by bike or on horseback. Nevis' plantation inns have a reputation for gentility but the island is far from dead. Most of the usual watersports are available: fishing, diving, snorkelling, sailing, windsurfing, and you can dine extremely well in either gourmet restaurants or local bars.

★ **Ten of the best**

1 **A Test Match at Antigua Recreation Ground** More than a game, catch the excitement of the crowd and join the party with a whistle, a conch horn and a flag, p225.

2 **Nelson's Dockyard, Antigua** A magnificent Georgian naval dockyard which Nelson visited prior to the Battle of Trafalgar 200 years ago in 1805, p41.

3 **Montserrat Volcano Observatory** All the scientific data you could need and a marvellous view of the active volcano across the valley, p52.

4 **Brimstone Hill Fortress, St Kitts** The best preserved colonial fortress with a commanding view and tremendous atmosphere of military days long gone, p101.

5 **Gourmet St-Barthélemy** From delicious dinners to tasty picnics on the beach, the Creole food and French wine is worth going out of your way for, p176.

6 **Frigate Bird Sanctuary, Barbuda** Thousands of Magnificent Frigate Birds and Boobies nest in the mangroves, undisturbed by human interference, p47.

7 **Rendezvous Bay, Anguilla** A jogger's paradise of 1½ miles of pristine white sand in a huge sweeping bay, empty of crowds, p69.

8 **The Quill, Sint Eustatius** A dormant volcano with lush rainforest and massive trees in its crater where locals hunt for land crabs by flashlight at night, p85.

9 **Dive Saba** The waters around the island are teeming with fish of all sizes and there are reefs, caverns and pinnacles in the beautiful underwater national park, p228.

10 **Cycle Nevis** Take a mountain bike along the goat trails and donkey paths around Nevis Peak for a 360° view of nearby islands, p226.

Trip planner

At any time of year you can get plenty of hot sunshine, but don't expect it to be dry all day every day. The dry season is roughly from January to May with showers to keep things green. The rainy season should start in June lasting almost to the end of the year with occasional hurricanes. However, climate changes have had an effect on rainfall and distinctions between dry and wet seasons are now blurred. Tropical storms are most likely to occur between September and November and can cause flooding and structural damage. The Leeward Islands were badly hit by Hurricane Hugo in 1989, a category four storm which devastated Montserrat with its 150 mph winds, and by Luis in 1995, which sank 500 yachts in Simpson Bay Lagoon, Sint Maarten, causing it to enter the *Guinness Book of Records* for the largest maritime disaster on record. Six more storms followed in 1996-99, but since the millennium hurricanes have veered off and been more considerate to this group of islands. The mean annual temperature is about 26°C, but the northeast trade winds are a cooling influence.

You can time your visit to coincide with Carnival, a national holiday, a music festival or a yacht race or cricket match. There is usually something going on although most outdoor events are planned to catch the best weather. Carnival is celebrated on different islands at different times, from St Kitts' Christmas and New Year Carnival to Anguilla's Summer Festival in August.

A short break

If you have only a long weekend to spare on the islands, then choose a destination you can fly to quickly without wasting time hanging around in airports for connecting flights. The main islands for transport hubs are Antigua, St Kitts and Sint Maarten. A few days relaxing at a beach hotel on Antigua or a plantation inn on St Kitts will soon recharge the batteries, while some prefer the shops and casinos of Sint Maarten for their break.

A week or more

It doesn't take long to explore these small islands and with a week or more to spare a two-centre holiday or some serious island hopping is a good option. Links by air are better than those by sea, but there are several routes worth considering if you don't want to fly. From Antigua to Montserrat, for example, it is fascinating to fly in for a great view of the volcano, but the boat service is excellent with different views of both islands. It is easy to fly one way and return by sea. From Antigua to Barbuda it is better to fly, as most boats are only for day-trippers and the crossing can be rough and time consuming. However, the new government plans a regular ferry and dedicated airline service in the near future. Between St Kitts and Nevis there are frequent flights and ferries and, again, you can fly one way and return by boat. St-Martin/Sint Maartenis a great base for island-hopping. Anguilla is only a short ferry ride away from Marigot with a frequent service all day. There is a good ferry from Sint Maarten to St-Barthélemy for those with sturdy sea legs. The return crossing is better. Flights from Juliana Airport take a few minutes to Saba, Statia or St-Barth and the small planes run like buses. Try to travel light as space for luggage is at a premium.

The best islands for diving and hiking are Saba, Statia and St Kitts and Nevis. Cricket fans should head for Antigua, St Kitts, Montserrat and Anguilla, while sailors will enjoy Antigua, St-Martin/Sint Maarten and St-Barth. Anguilla and Barbuda have the best sandy beaches, although there are also lovely beaches on Antigua, St Kitts, Nevis, St-Martin/Sint Maarten and St-Barth, all of which provide a range of watersports. Historical attractions are greatest on Antigua, St Kitts and Nevis. Food is good on all the islands, particularly the fresh fish and seafood, but it is difficult to beat the Creole cuisine of St-Barth or the fine dining in Grand Case, St-Martin. Night life is most active on St-Martin/Sint Maarten, with its casinos and clubs, although you'll never be short of a lively place to dance until dawn on St Kitts and every island has late night bars for a cold Carib beer or a rum punch.

Contemporary Leewards

The year 2004 was a momentous one for Antigua, when decades of rule by the Bird family were swept aside at the ballot box and the electorate could look forward to a new way of doing things, without the corruption and nepotism endemic under the previous administration. **Vere Cornwall Bird** dominated first the trade union movement and then government from the 1940s until his retirement in 1994 at the age of 84. He was succeeded by his son, **Lester Bird**, while other family members were also in the cabinet despite public condemnation of their activities. Under the Birds, Antigua acquired a reputation for corruption and was frequently implicated in international drugs-running, illegal arms shipments and money-laundering, while at home there were allegations of fraud in the allocation of contracts, in state funded projects and at the ballot box.

Suddenly there is a feeling of optimism in the country and of hope that the new government of **Baldwin Spencer** will sort things out. It faces an uphill struggle, given the scale of its financial and social problems, but it has the support of the people and the crime rate has recently dropped. A new civic pride seems to have taken hold, clean-up programmes are well attended and beautification projects are underway. Even small gestures such as planting goat-proof flowering shrubs in communal areas of outlying villages show a new faith in the future. Special events were to be held around *Independence Day* on 1 November to celebrate not only independence from Britain but freedom from the Antigua Labour Party. Relations between the two islands of Antigua and Barbuda have also improved and the smaller island is to be included in investment projects rather than ignored as a backwater.

Political change is also on the cards elsewhere in the Leeward Islands and qualified **independence** remains a burning issue in certain quarters. Even before independence in 1983, Nevis campaigned to be administered directly from London rather than by St Kitts, and secession is still an electoral issue. No island likes to be governed by another island; the smaller one always thinks it is getting a raw deal, while the larger one resents the financial support it has to provide. In St-Barth, a referendum in December 2003 showed support for a change of political administration with the electorate voting for independence from Guadeloupe. The island will become a *collectivité* with one deputy and one senator being sent to Paris, new elections for local government and a mayor who will become president of the Conseil de Ville. The Dutch islands have been in a constitutional quagmire for 20 years with repeated referenda showing the frustrations the islands feel about the central government in Curaçao, with first Aruba opting for *status aparte* and then in 2000 Sint Maarten voting for similar status. Studies are underway on the whole relationship between the Kingdom of the Netherlands, Aruba and the Netherlands Antilles and it appears that there is a momentum for fundamental change. Two reports have now suggested direct ties of the individual islands with Holland, eliminating the Netherlands Antilles government in Curaçao and expanding the number of Kingdom government responsibilities. It is expected that change will happen within the next five years.

Meanwhile **financial dependence** on tourism becomes ever greater. Few economies have anything else to fall back on and an event like 9/11, a major hurricane or a volcano blowing can have serious repercussions on island incomes if visitors suddenly stop coming. The sugar industry on St Kitts is bankrupt and agriculture elsewhere is at subsistence levels. Statia has an oil-bunkering facility, but there is no significant industry on any of the islands. The pressure of tourism to provide an adequate living for the population and alleviate poverty on such small islands leads inevitably to **environmental concerns**. Hotels have been built in inappropriate places, damaging the local ecology, and a new fashion for building dolphinariums to entertain cruise ship visitors has been greeted with horror by conservationists. Dolphins caught in the wild and under stress from being separated from their pods are trained to perform tricks in return for a diet of frozen fish from Canada and antibiotics. Beaches and reefs are under threat from the pollution and damage of motorized watersports, while huge swathes of land are undergoing species change in the name of golf. Waste management is a constant headache when thousands of visitors pass through each year, whether day trippers off a cruise ship or stayover holidaymakers at hotels.

For the inhabitants of the islands, as tourism takes over, the ugly head of **neo-colonialism** appears. Despite training programmes at home and overseas, the top jobs in running hotels are usually given to foreigners and the investment and subsequent control of tourist projects comes from abroad. Lack of opportunities is leading to a brain drain. Employment outside tourism is limited and young islanders now choose to study and work in the USA or Canada. If they come home at all, they come back full of the ideals of North America and the consumer society.

Nevertheless, for those left behind, **Afro-Caribbean roots** are paramount. There are few American fast-food chains in the Leeward Islands, people still eat the food their forefathers ate, with staples derived from slave rations. They listen to music created in the Caribbean: reggae, zouk, calypso, steel pan and gospel, and they celebrate Carnival more than ever before, with parades and calypso competitions, jump-ups and masquerades, harking back to African and colonial legends, fusing modern-day political and social concerns in the calypso lyrics with centuries of tradition.

The main ports of entry are the VC Bird International Airport on Antigua and the Juliana International Airport on Sint Maarten, which serve as transport hubs for the islands around them: Anguilla, Barbuda, Montserrat, Saba, St-Barthélemy and Sint Eustatius. St Kitts also receives international flights, giving access to its sister island, Nevis. These three islands also have cruise ship ports and can receive very large vessels, but only ferries or small cruise ships can visit the outlying islands. Until the end of 2004 Montserrat could only be reached only by helicopter or ferry; from 2005 one of the small airlines will start to fly in to the new airport.

The easiest way of seeing the islands is to hire a car, particularly on the smallest islands where there are no buses, but if you don't want to drive yourself there are lots of taxis, or water taxis, to take you on an island tour or to the beach.

Getting there

Air

From UK and Europe   The best routes to Antigua are from
London, with direct scheduled services with **British Airways**,
BWIA, **Virgin Atlantic** and, from December 2004, **Excel
Airways**, with introductory flights at £374. There are also many
seasonal charter flights for those on package holidays.
Sint Maarten receives direct flights from Amsterdam with **KLM**
from €500 and from Paris with **Air France** from €590, while
St Kitts has flights from London. Prices vary tremendously
depending on the time of year. Not all airlines have the same dates
for the beginning of high, shoulder and low seasons, so shop
around, as one day can make a huge difference in price.

From North America   There are lots of flights to Antigua and
Sint Maarten from a variety of east coast US cities and from
Toronto, some via Miami, San Juan or Montego Bay, with
American Airlines, **Air Jamaica**, **BWIA**, **Continental**, **Air
Canada** and other airlines. St Kitts has winter services with
Skyservice from Toronto, while **US Airways** flies direct from
Charlotte and Philadelphia, but other North American flights are
via San Juan (**American Eagle**) or you have to change to a
regional airline in Antigua or Sint Maarten.

Caribbean connections   There are dozens of daily flights within
the Leeward Islands and to the rest of the Caribbean and small
aircraft are used like flying buses. The main regional carriers are
BWIA, **LIAT**, **Caribbean Star**, **Air Jamaica**, **American Eagle**
and **Winair**, but there are also many charter fleets for air taxi
services. **LIAT** has two passes called *Explorer tickets*. The *LIAT
Explorer* costs US$225 (peak season, 1 July-31 August, 5 December-
6 January, two weeks around Trinidad Carnival and two weeks
around Easter), or US$199 (off-peak, the rest of the year), valid for

→ **Airlines and travel agents**

Airlines

Air Canada, T 1-888-2472262, www.aircanada.ca
Air France, T 0845-0845111, www.airfrance.com
Air Jamaica, T 1-800-5235585 (North America/Caribbean,
T 44-20-85707999 (Europe), www.airjamaica.com
American Airlines, T 1-800-4337300, www.aa.com
American Eagle/American Airlines, T 1-800-4337300,
www3.aa.com
British Airways, T 0845-7733377, www.britishairways.com
BWIA, T 0870 499 2942 (UK/Europe), T 1-800-538 2942 (North
America/Caribbean), www.bwee.com
Caribbean Star, T 1-800-744STAR, www.flycaribbeanstar.com
Excel Airways, T 0870-1690169, www.excelairways.com
KLM, T 0900-2635556 www.klm.com
LIAT, T 1-268-4805625 (Caribbean), www.liatairline.com
Skyservice, T 416-6795700, www.skyserviceairlines.com
Virgin Atlantic, T 44-1293-450150, www.virgin-atlantic.com
Winair, T 599-545 4237, www.fly-winair.com

Travel agents

http://travel.kelkoo.co.uk
www.opodo.co.uk
www.cheapflights.com
www.travelocity.com
www.ebookers.com
www.startravel.com

21 days, maximum four stops permitted at Tortola, San Juan, Antigua, St Kitts, Nevis, St Thomas, St Croix, Sint Maarten, Guadeloupe, Dominica, St Lucia, Barbados, St Vincent, Grenada, Trinidad and Tobago. The *LIAT Super Caribbean Explorer* costs US$425 (peak season) or US$399 (off-peak), for a 30-day ticket, allowing unlimited stopovers in all its Caribbean destinations except Guyana and the Dominican Republic. **LIAT** also operates an *Airpass* within the Caribbean except Guyana and Santo Domingo, in which each flight costs US$75, valid for 21 days, minimum three stop overs. These tickets may only be issued in conjunction with an international flight to a Caribbean gateway, the itinerary must be settled in advance, with no changes permitted, and no child discounts. A return ticket with stopovers is often cheaper than the airpass. **BWIA**'s Caribbean airpass covers all its destinations including Caracas and Paramaribo, but if you want to include Kingston, Havana, Santo Domingo or San Juan, it will cost more. A first class unlimited mileage pass is US$750 (US$900 including the four cities listed) and the economy pass is US$450 (US$550). There is also a four-stop pass for US$350 (US$450 three stops to/from Havana, Santo Domingo, San Juan), but this can only be bought in the UK, Europe, New Zealand and Australia and you have to travel to the Caribbean with **BWIA**. You can have any number of stopovers, but no destination may be visited more than once (no 'back-calling'), except for making a connection and the entire journey must be fixed at the time of payment; dates may be left open. This airpass is valid for 30 days, no refunds are given for unused sectors. It may not be used between 19 December and 6 January.

Airport information Services at all the airports are limited. The airports at Antigua and Sint Maarten are cramped, uncomfortable and inconvenient but there are plans to improve or replace both of them. **VC Bird airport**, Antigua has an exchange desk but no ATM. There is no bank at **Juliana airport**, Sint Maarten, although

Travel extras

Money In Anguilla, Antigua, Barbuda, Montserrat, St Kitts and Nevis, Eastern Caribbean dollars are used, at a rate of EC$2.70=US$1. On Saba, Statia and Sint Maarten the currency is the florin or Antillean guilder, while on St-Martin and St-Barth the official currency is the euro. However, US dollars are accepted everywhere and it is rarely necessary to change any money if you are carrying dollars. You will often be given local currency if change is due, so on some islands you are likely to acquire lots of local coins.

Safety All the islands are relatively safe and you only need to follow the usual precautions such as not leaving your possessions unattended on the beach. Saba is so safe that the hotels do not even give you room keys, while there are some areas of Antigua that you would not want to wander around after dark.

Vaccinations None required unless you are coming from a yellow-fever infected area.

there is an ATM just outside the arrivals hall where the taxis wait. **Espérance airport**, St-Martin can only take light aircraft for short hops. Montserrat's airport terminal and runway are newly built as part of the relocation to the north of the island. The helicopter service will continue until the end of 2004 (US$60, several daily except Wednesday and Saturday); only one piece of luggage is allowed and credit cards are not accepted. Saba's airport building is new but tiny as only very small aircraft come in, Statia and Anguilla have small, ageing terminals although the latter has an extended runway now, while St-Barth has a large new building on two floors with car hire offices, bank, restaurant and other services. for payment. St Kitts already has a shiny new terminal building with plenty of space, as does Nevis.

Visas All visitors must have a passport except in some cases nationals of the USA, who can enter on a birth certificate with a photograph, a driver's licence with photo, a registration card and/or identification card. Some non-European or non-US nationalities need a visa, check with the relevant Tourist Office. The French islands of St-Barth and St-Martin require the same documentation as mainland France, while the Dutch islands of Saba, Statia and Sint Maarten have the same rules as the Netherlands. Under a 1994 Franco-Dutch immigration accord, visitors to Dutch Sint Maarten have to meet French immigration criteria, even if not visiting the French side. Therefore, many nationalities now have to obtain a French visa before embarking on a shopping trip to Philipsburg. All local immigration officials are particularly concerned that you fill in a tourist card with a hotel address, even if you do not know whether you'll be staying there.

Sea

Cruise ships will sometimes allow you to break your journey on an island, but you must check they will pick you up again on the return voyage. There are ferries between some of the islands, allowing you to island hop by boat. Montserrat has a regular service from St John's, Antigua (unlimited luggage allowance, no credit cards), but Antigua is not connected by sea to any of the other Leeward Islands. From Sint Maarten/St-Martin there are lots of routes and you can go by boat to Saba, St-Barth, Anguilla and sometimes Statia. There are several ferries between St Kitts and Nevis (*Caribe Queen*, *Caribe Breeze*, *Caribe Surf* and *MV Sea Hustler* operate on a regular schedule) and you can sometimes go by sea from St Kitts to Statia on a supply boat.

Departure tax

Antigua and Barbuda Airport departure charges amount to US$30, children half price.

Montserrat US$10 for Caricom residents and US$17 for visitors.

Sint Maarten/St-Martin Departure tax from Juliana airport is US$6 to the Netherlands Antilles and US$20 to international destinations. Espérance airport taxes are included in the airfare. Ferry departure tax to Anguilla is US$2. Passengers staying less than 24 hours are exempt, so keep your ticket as proof, as are French visitors returning to Guadeloupe or France from Juliana airport.

Anguilla US$20 by air and US$3 by sea.

Saba US$5 to the Netherlands Antilles, US$20 elsewhere.

Sint Eustatius US$5.65.

St-Barthélemy Airport taxes are included in the airfare.

St Kitts and Nevis Four different taxes amount to a total of US$22.

Getting around

Bus

Buses are cheap and fun but they do not run everywhere. There are no buses on Anguilla, Barbuda, Saba, Statia or St-Barth.

Antigua has a good bus network for the south of the island but they are banned from north of the line from the airport to St John's. They run frequently between St John's and English Harbour EC$2.50. There are no buses to the airport and very few to beaches though two good swimming beaches on the way to Old Road can be reached by bus. Bus frequency can be variable, and there are very few after dark or on Sunday. Buses usually go when they are full, ask the driver where he is going. They are numbered and destinations are on display boards at the West Bus Station.

On **Montserrat**, the standard fare in minibuses is EC$2. Outside the fixed times and routes they operate as taxis and journeys can be arranged with drivers for an extra fee.

On **Sint Maarten/St-Martin** there is a fairly regular bus service from 0700 until 2400 between Philipsburg and Marigot (US$1.50), French Quarters and St Peters, and from Marigot to Grand Case on the French side. After 2000 there are few buses. The best place to catch a bus is on Back Street, Philipsburg. Buses run along Back Street and Pondfill and only stop at bus stops. Outside towns, however, just wave to stop a bus. Fares are usually US$1 in town, US$1 for short trips, US$2 for long trips. There is no regular bus service between Philipsburg and the airport although the route to Mullet Bay Resort passes the airport. Buses on this route run mostly at the beginning and the end of the working day (although there are a few during the day) and drivers may refuse to take you, or charge extra, if you have a lot of luggage.

On **St Kitts**, minibuses do not run on a scheduled basis, but follow a set route (more or less), EC$1-3 on most routes, EC$3 from Basseterre to the north of the island. There is a frequent service from the bus terminal close to the market area on the Bay Road from where buses go west to Sandy Point. To catch a bus east, wait off Bakers Corner at the east end of Cayon Street. You can get a bus to the airport from the bus stop at the roundabout northeast of Independence Square, EC$1.25, and walk the last five minutes from the main road; some buses might go up to the terminal. There are no minibuses to Frigate Bay and the southeast peninsula.

On **Nevis** buses start outside *Foodworld Cash & Carry* and run to all points, until about 2300 – look for the green H registration plate, EC$1-3.50; an island tour is possible, if time consuming.

Car
Drive on the left in Anguilla, Antigua and Barbuda, Montserrat, St Kitts and Nevis; drive on the right in Saba, St-Barth, St Maarten/St-Martin and Statia.

On **Antigua** watch out for pot holes, narrow streets and animals straying across the street in the dark. Renting a car is probably the best way to see the island's sights, as the bus service is inadequate, but be aware that roads are very bumpy and narrow and speed bumps are poorly marked. Finding your way around is not easy: there are no road signs and street names are rarely in evidence. There are car hire companies in St John's and some at the airport; most will pick you up. Be careful with one-way streets in St John's. At night people do not always dim their headlights. Watch out for pedestrians in the dark. A local driving licence, US$20, valid for three months, must be purchased on presentation of a foreign (not international) licence. There is a 24-hour petrol station on Old Parham Road outside St John's.

Roads are paved and fair on **Montserrat**, but narrow and twisty. Drivers travel fast, passing on blind corners with much use of horns.

On **Sint Maarten/St-Martin** there can be a shortage of cars or jeeps for hire in high season. It is advisable to request one from your hotel when you book the room. Out of season car rental is inexpensive. Traffic is very heavy, not just at rush hour, and there are frequently traffic jams, so allow plenty of time for a journey. Foreign and international driving licences are accepted. The speed limit is 40 kph in urban areas, 60 kph outside town, unless there are other signs. Many car hire companies have offices at the airport or in the hotels; free pick-up and delivery are standard and you can leave the car at the airport on departure.

On **Anguilla** the speed limit is 30 mph. Hired cars cannot be picked up from the airport because of local regulations; they have to be delivered to your hotel, but can be dropped off at the airport. Watch out for loose goats and sheep on the roads.

Roads on **Saba** are few, narrow and twisty and you should take care. Goats wander across the road on the way down to Fort Bay.

On **Statia** you have to watch out for cows, donkeys, goats and sheep roaming around freely. They are a traffic hazard. To hire a car you need a driving licence from your own country or an international driver's licence. The speed limit is 50 kph and 30 kph in residential areas.

The roads on **St Barth** are extremely narrow and congested. As a result there are an extraordinary number of Smart cars, quite a sight parked in a row at the beach or outside a restaurant. Parking is very difficult everywhere. Hiring a car for just one day in high season can be difficult but your hotel can sometimes help.

The main road on **St Kitts** is, for the most part, very good and motorists, especially bus drivers, can be very fast.

On **Nevis** the paved road round the island is good except in the northeast, but storm ditches frequently cross it, so drive slowly and carefully. Parking in both Basseterre and Charlestown is difficult. If visiting at Carnival time, book your car-hire a long time in advance.

Cycling

The state of the roads makes cycling potentially dangerous, with pot holes, wandering animals and car drivers exceeding the speed limits, but several of the islands have good off-road cycling. It is hot work so take lots of water and sun screen.

Nevis is possibly the best island for cycling, with a network of back roads and tracks as well as a quiet main road round the island. **Anguilla** is nice and flat, so bikes are available from lots of hotels as well as rental companies. **Antigua** has its own cycle club, the *Antigua & Barbuda Amateur Cycling Association*.

▸▸ *See Sports p226 for details of tours, tracks and bike hire on the islands*

Taxi

All the islands have plenty of taxis, which are often minibuses. They are rarely metered so you have to check the fare in advance. The tourist offices usually have lists of fares; they are sometimes on display at the airports, or your hotel can help you. Taxis will take you to a beach and pick you up later, or offer island tours for a fixed price depending on the number of people, see p30.

On **Antigua** taxis have TX registration plates. They should all have an EC$ price list so ask to see it to avoid overcharging. From the airport to Falmouth Harbour is US$24/EC$64, to the Dickenson Bay area US$13/EC$34.

Juliana airport to Philipsburg on **Sint Maarten/St-Martin** is US$12 for two passengers, US$4 for additional passengers, 25% extra if it is after 2200 and 50% extra between 2400-0600, not forgetting further charges for a lot of luggage.

On **Anguilla** only taxis are allowed to ferry passengers from the airport, costing US$6 to The Valley and US$22 to the western end of the island, with US$2 extra between 1800-0600.

On **St Kitts** taxis have a yellow T registration plate. The ride from the airport to Basseterre is US$7, to Frigate Bay US$11. On **Nevis** a taxi from the airport to Charlestown costs US$14 and an extra 50% is charged on both islands for taxi rides between 2200-0600.

Walking

Walking on the roads is not recommended on any of the islands where there is fast traffic, such as Antigua and Sint Maarten, but there are several excellent tracks and paths. There are some good walks on **Antigua**, such as up Boggy Peak and on the east coast, and 40 km of trails for hiking on **Sint Maarten/St-Martin**. Several islands have volcanoes up which you can hike, such as Saba and Statia and St Kitts. **Saba** is a hiker's dream, with the stone steps of old trails around the island and up Mt Scenery dating from before the road was built. **Statia** is quiet without much traffic and walking on the roads is safe. The tourist office has a guide leaflet describing 11 trails. **St Kitts** has comparatively clear trails including Old Road to Philips, the old British military road. As with cycling, **Nevis** has many tracks and small, quiet roads which are good for walking.

▶▶ *See Sports p238 for details of hiking on all the islands*

Tours

Air tours

Helicopter tours of Montserrat and the still-active volcano are well worth doing. A charter helicopter service is offered by **Caribbean Helicopters**, Jolly Harbour, Antigua, **T** 268-4605900, helicopters @candw.ag. They do a 45-minute aerial Montserrat Volcano Tour from Jolly Harbour, for US$190 per person, around and over the cone. Even a regular flight to Montserrat will give you a good view of the smoking volcano and the destruction down the sides. There are several helicopter flights daily except Wednesday and Saturday from Antigua, US$60 one way. Check with an agent for times, which are always changing, and make sure you book well in advance otherwise it can be hard to get on. Agents in Antigua are **Carib Aviation**, VC Bird International Airport, **T** 268-4623147, caribav@candw.ag. Agents in Montserrat are **Montserrat Aviation Services**, Nixons, **T** 664-4912533, **F** 664-4917186.

Boat tours

Excursions by boat can be arranged nearly everywhere, whether by motor launch, catamaran, yacht or dive boat. In Antigua, trips around the island with stops at smaller islands such as Bird Island, Prickly Pear Island, or even Barbuda or Montserrat, can be arranged for US$60-90. There are many day sails offered by boat charter companies in Sint Maarten/St-Martin, with sailing boats and motor boats, with or without a crew. You can find most of them around Bobby's Marina, Philipsburg, or around Marina Port La Royal, Marigot, about US$360 per day for four people on a yacht with crew. There are some 40 boats offering different trips around the islands, some just going out for snorkelling on the reefs or taking cruise ship passengers around. Sailing trips with lunch and snorkelling to beaches around the island or smaller islands such as Tintamarre, Sandy Island or Prickly Pear (Anguilla), cost about US$70 per person. Day trips to St-Barth are for those with good sea legs; the crossing is normally quite rough and unpleasant on the way there, but better on the return journey. Check the weather; the swell and the waves can be up to 3½ m even on a nice day. A popular trip is to Nevis for the day from **St Kitts**. On St Kitts there are several boats doing fishing trips (US$60 per person), moonlight cruises (US$25), party cruises (US$25), sunset cruises (US$35), Nevis day tours (US$60) and snorkelling trips (US$35).

▸▸ *See Sports p243 for more details and listings*

Bus tours
There are many tour operators on all the islands offering island tours by minibus including pick up and drop off at your hotel. These vehicles are usually also taxis and can be hired for tours at any time, see below. It is cheaper to book a taxi driver direct than to go through a tour operator and pay commission, although tour operators will often include lunch or other refreshments as a package deal.

Taxi tours
The tourist offices usually have lists of fares for tours. Taxis will take you to a beach and pick you up later, or offer island tours for a fixed price depending on the number of people. Prices vary consderably between islands. On **Antigua** a day tour for one-four people normally costs about US$70, US$76 for five-seven people. Taxi excursions advertised in hotels are generally overpriced. A two-hour tour of **Anguilla** is US$40 for two people, US$5 for additional passengers. Taxis on **St-Barth** charge €45 for a one-hour island tour, although you can hire them for longer if you wish. On **St Kitts** an island tour is US$60, while on **Nevis** it is US$50.

▸▸ *See Sports p226 and p238 for cycling and walking tours*

Tourist information

Antigua and Barbuda Tourist Office is on Nevis St/Friendly Alley, St John's, close to the cruise ship dock and all the shops, **T** 268-4620480, www.antigua-barbuda.org, *Mon-Fri 0830-1600, Sat 0830-1200*. They have a list of official taxi charges and hotel information. Barbuda has a separate Tourism Department here, too. The Antigua Tourist Office at the airport helps book accommodation mainly at the more expensive resorts. The Antigua Hotels and Tourist Association is at Lower Newgate St, St John's, **T**268-4620374, www.antiguahotels.org.

Montserrat Tourist Board is at Brades, **T**664-4912230, www.visitmontserrat.com.

Sint Maarten Tourist Office is at Vineyard Office Park, 33 WG Buncamper Rd, Philipsburg, **T**599-5422337, www.st-maarten.com, *Mon-Fri 0800-1200, 1300-1700*, with information desks on Front St, Philipsburg. **St-Martin's Tourist Office** is on Route de Sandy Ground, 97150 Saint-Martin, **T**590-(0)590-875721, www.st-martin.org, *Mon-Fri 0830-1300, 1430-1730*.

Anguilla Department of Tourism, PO Box 1388, Coronation Av near the roundabout, The Valley, **T**264-4972759, www.anguilla-vacation.com, *Mon-Fri 0800-1700*. The office at the airport is closed at lunchtime, but the customs officers will often phone to reserve a hotel for you. **Anguilla National Trust** welcomes members in the Museum Building, The Valley, **T**264-4975297, axanat@anguillanet.com. The map of archaeological and historical sites of Anguilla is worth getting if you want to explore. Contact them or the Anguilla Archaeological and Historical Society.

Saba Tourist Board (Glenn Holm, Zuleyka and Desiree) is in Windwardside, PO Box 15, **T**599-4162231-2,www.sabatourism.com *Mon-Fri 0800-1200, 1300-1700*. Plenty of leaflets and maps and the staff are friendly and helpful.

St Eustatius Tourism Development Foundation is in Fort Oranjestraat, **T/F**599-3182433, *Mon-Fri 0800-1700*. There are tourism information booths at the airport, **T**599-3182620 and at the Harbour Office, **T**599-3182205, www.statiatourism.com. **The St Eustatius Historical Foundation**, at Wilhelminaweg 3, PO Box 71, Oranjestad A255, **T**599-3182288, publishes a quarterly newsletter and runs the Museum and the Tourist Information Centre and Gallery, 'Little House on the Bay', a replica gingerbread house *(Mon-Sat 0930-1200, Sun 1500-1700)* staffed seasonally by volunteers so opening times are approximate. Local artists and artisans sell their work here. **STENAPA**, Jan Faber, President, White Wall Rd, St Eustatius, Netherlands Antilles, **T/F**599-3182661, has information on walks, trails and conservation at the office by the dock.

St-Barthélemy, Quai de Gaulle, Gustavia, **T**590-(0)590-278727, odtsb@wanadoo.fr. *Mon-Thurs 0830-1230, 1400-1730, Fri 0830-1230, 1400-1700*. Very helpful staff and lots of leaflets.

St Kitts Tourism Authority is in Pelican Mall, Basseterre, **T**869-4652620, www.stkitts-tourism.com. *Mon-Fri 0800-1600*, with information, maps and leaflets available.

Nevis Tourism Authority is in the Old Treasury Building, Main St, Charlestown, **T**869-4697550, www.nevisisland.com. Extremely helpful. *Mon-Fri 800-1700, Sat 0830-1200*.

Maps

Plenty of maps with advertising are distributed by the tourist offices, hotels and other organizations. These are adequate for navigating on such small islands but give little geographical information. Many are produced by *Skyviews*, www.skyviews.com.

Antigua and Barbuda, 35 A beach for every day of the year on the sugar island of Antigua; deserted sands and an enormous frigate bird colony on Barbuda.

Montserrat, 51 The unforgettable experience of a very active volcano.

Sint Maarten/St-Martin, 57 Half Dutch, half French, with its beach hotels, casinos, shops, marina and cruise ship dock.

Anguilla, 66 Quiet and relaxing, a place to come for the beaches.

Saba, 73 No beaches but immaculate Dutch villages, strenuous hiking and fabulous diving.

Sint Eustatius, 80 So laid back it might just fall over, 'Statia' has wonderfully unspoilt diving.

St-Barthélemy, 87 France in the Caribbean, buy croissants and camembert and dine in style.

St Kitts and Nevis, 96 Two islands joined at the hip: St Kitts, a sugar island with a history from its glory days and the stunning Brimstone Fortress; Nevis, small and precious, with delightful plantation inns and good walking.

Antigua

Sandy beaches, quiet coves, blazing sun and refreshing trade winds are what make a seaside holiday in Antigua. Its rolling hills can be parched and brown at certain times of the year, but a bit of rain will quickly transform them into green and lush pastures, reminiscent of the sugar plantations of old. No sugar cane is grown now, but the history of the days of slavery remains, with the ruins of more windmills per square mile than any other island. Its strategic position for the British navy in the 18th century is evident in the well-preserved buildings of Nelson's Dockyard and the harbour is still a great attraction for seafarers on more modern craft.

Antigua, pronounced Anteega, is the largest of the Leewards, at 108 square miles, and also one of the most popular, being easy to reach and with good communications with neighbouring islands. Boggy Peak, its highest elevation, rises to over 405 m (1,330 ft) and the rolling hills and flowering trees are picturesque. Its coastline however, curving into coves and graceful harbours with 365 soft white-sand beaches, many of them fringed with palm trees, is among the most attractive in the West Indies. Antigua is the jumping-off point for exploring many of the other Leeward Islands. Its dependencies are nearby Barbuda and Redonda.

Barbuda *is like many of the islands were in the 1950s: quiet, unhurried and undeveloped. It does, however, have one of the most fantastic beaches in the Caribbean: miles and miles of uninterrupted and deserted sand along the west coast. In addition, there is a frigate bird sanctuary, where thousands of birds come to breed and nest in the mangroves on the edge of Codrington Lagoon.*

Redonda *is uninhabited but has more than its fair share of kings and the aristocracy.*

▸▸ *See Sleeping p119, Eating and drinking p154, Entertainment and nightlife p187, Sport p225*

Sights

St John's
Map 1, B3, p280 and Map 2, p281

Built around the largest of the natural harbours is St John's, the capital, formerly guarded by Fort Barrington and Fort James either side of the entrance to the harbour. The town is a mixture of the old and the new, with a few historical sites such as the cathedral and a good museum. The **Antigua Recreation Ground** alongside the cathedral contains the main cricket pitch, used for Test matches, but this is to be replaced for the 2007 Cricket World Cup by moving the prison and building a new ground. There are still some slum areas but the area around the cruise ship docks has been developed for tourism: boutiques, duty-free shops and restaurants compete for custom. Most activity now takes place around the two quay developments. **Redcliff Quay** is a picturesque area of restored historical buildings now full of souvenir shops. **Heritage Quay** is a duty-free shopping complex with a casino, strategically placed to catch cruise ship visitors. When a cruise ship is in dock (*Dec-May*) it becomes very crowded. There is a vendors' mall next to Heritage Quay, selling souvenirs.

St John's Cathedral
Newgate St and Long St, **T** 268-4624686. *Donations requested. Map 2, B4, p281* Some of the old buildings in St John's, including the Anglican cathedral, have been damaged several times by earthquakes, the last one in 1974. A cathedral in St John's was first built in 1681 of wood. Today its twin towers, now in stone, can be seen from all over St John's. It has a wonderfully cool interior lined with pitch pine timber intended to secure it against hurricanes and earthquakes. The bronze figures of *St John the Baptist* and *St John the Divine* (painted white) are on top of the pillars of the iron south gates, which date from 1789.

Museum of Antigua and Barbuda

Long St and Market St, **T** 268-4624930, www.antiguamuseums.org
*Mon-Fri 0830-1600, Sat 1000-1400, free although donations
requested. Map 2, B1, p281* The museum and former courthouse is
worth a visit. There is an exhibition of pre-Columbian and colonial
archaeology and anthropology of Antigua, Viv Richards' cricket bat
– with which he scored the fastest century – naval history,
plantation history and slavery, frequently changing exhibitions
relating to Carnival, sailing week or other local events as well as a
gift shop with local items. The **courthouse building** itself was
first built between 1747-50 using yellow stone quarried from the
islands off the northeast coast. Damaged by earthquakes in 1843
and 1974, it is now restored. The Court of Justice was on the
ground floor with the Council and Assembly upstairs. The *Historical
and Archaeological Society* (HAS), based at the museum, publishes a
useful newsletter; the *Environmental Awareness Group* is also here.

⬤ *Antigua was first inhabited by the Siboney (stone people),
whose settlements date back to at least 2400 BC. Island Arawaks lived
here between about AD 35 and 1100. Columbus landed in 1493 and
named it Santa María de la Antigua, but initial Spanish and French
attempts to settle were discouraged by the absence of freshwater
springs and attacks by Caribs.*

Fort Barrington

Goat Hill. *West of St John's. Map 1, B1, p280*

The ruins of Fort Barrington are on a promontory at Goat Hill
overlooking Deep Bay and the entrance to St John's Harbour. It
was erected by Governor Burt, who gave up active duty in 1780
suffering from psychiatric disorders; a stone he placed in one of the
walls at the fort describes him grandly as 'Imperator and
Gubernator' of the Carib Islands. The previous fortifications saw the
most action in Antigua's history, with the French and English
battling for possession in the 17th century.

Beaches west of St John's
Map 1, p280

There are several pleasant beaches on the peninsula west of St John's. On **Trafalgar Beach** condominiums have been built on the rocks overlooking the small, sheltered bay. If you go through Five Islands village you come to **Galley Bay**, a secluded and unspoilt hotel beach which is popular with locals and joggers at sunset. The four **Hawksbill beaches** at the end of the peninsula are crescent shaped, very scenic and unspoilt. Hotel guests tend to use the second beach, leaving the other three empty. Take drinks to the furthest one (clothes are optional) as there are no facilities.

Fort James
Head north out of St John's, turn west by Barrymore Hotel to the sea, follow the road parallel to the beach to the end. Map 1, A2, p280

At the other side of the harbour are the ruins of Fort James, from where you can get a good view of St John's. There was originally a fort on this site dating from 1675, but most now dates from 1739. By 1773 there were 36 guns with barracks for about 75 men. Eleven men and a powder man were needed to fire each 2½-tonne cannon. Fort James is the nearest beach to St John's. It can be pleasant, with its palm trees and a few boulders. However, it gets crowded at weekends, and at times it becomes rough and so has a milky appearance, lots of weed and is not good for swimming.

The northwest and north
*This is a popular area for a beach holiday with a long stretch of hotels, restaurants, bars and nightlife, plenty of watersports and easy access to the **Cedar Valley Golf Course**. St John's is a few minutes away by taxi. **Dickenson Bay** and **Runaway Bay** are the two main beaches, separated from the main road by McKinnons Salt Pond. Windsurfing and kitesurfing are good off the coast north of the airport.*

Dickenson Bay/Runaway Bay
North of St John's. Map 1, A2, p280

Dickenson Bay and Runaway Bay are adjacent long stretches of
white sand, separated by a small promontory and the
dolphinarium, making it impossible to walk the length of the two.
Dickenson Bay is wall-to-wall, low-rise hotels, starting with *Rex
Halcyon, Sandals, Antigua Village, Siboney Beach Club* and *Marina
Bay*, with watersports outlets, bars and restaurants on the beach.
The sea is calm and perfect for children, with roped off areas to
prevent motor boats and jet skis getting in with swimmers. The
further you get from *Sandals* the quieter the beach becomes,
although its beauty is marred by ruined beach houses at the far
end. Much of the southern beach has also been eroded by storms.

Huge controversy surrounds the former Government's approval
of a captive dolphin programme (the company involved is being
investigated in the USA for illegal purchase of dolphins from Cuba)
and legal action is pending from conservation groups. Dolphins
have allegedly been caught in the wild and taught to perform
tricks, in the name of education and conservation, in return for
frozen fish and antibiotics. The building of the **dolphinarium** has
also interfered with drainage from the swamp, which now floods in
heavy rain and makes the road impassable to Runaway Bay.

Dutchman's Bay and Jabberwock Beach
North of the airport. Map 1, A5, p280

The north coast is idea for **windsurfing** and **kitesurfing**. The
Lord Nelson Hotel at Dutchman's Bay has been a windsurfing mecca
for decades but the new sport of kitesurfing was banned because
of its proximity to the airport. Jabberwock Beach is now 'kite
beach' and conditions are excellent with cross-onshore winds, a
long sandy beach and shallow water. The best season is
January-July when winds are in the 20-knot range, see p247.

The southwest

*A pleasant circular route can be taken by car from St John's, passing by the **marina at Jolly Harbour**, stopping to swim at one of several beaches some of which, such as **Dark Wood Beach** (good snorkelling) and **Cades Bay**, have restaurants and/or beach bars, turning inland at Old Road to see Antigua's last remaining patch of rainforest at **Fig Tree Drive** before returning to the capital. On the way round the coast, between Urlings and Old Road, you can test your legs with the hike up **Boggy Peak**, Antigua's highest point, for a spectacular view across the sea to the smoking volcano on Montserrat.*

Boggy Peak

From Urlings walk (or take minibus) about ½-¾ mile in the direction of Old Town. Map 1, D2 p280

Boggy Peak rises to 405 m (1,330 ft) and the views from the top over to Guadeloupe, St Kitts, Nevis and Montserrat are wonderful. It is a good walk up, or you can take a car. There is a clear track on the left (ask the bus driver to drop you off there) which is very straight then ascends quite steeply. At the top, walk round the fence surrounding the *Cable and Wireless* buildings to get a good view in all directions. It takes over an hour to walk up (signs say it is a private road) and you are advised not to wander around alone.

Fig Tree Drive

Between Old Road and the Catholic church on the road going north from Liberta. Map 1, E3, p280

Fig Tree Drive is a steep, winding road, through a patch of hilly rainforest. It is greener and more scenic than most of the island with lots of fruit trees, but the rainforest is scanty. If travelling by bicycle make sure you go down Fig Tree Drive from the All Saints to Liberta road, heading towards Old Road; the hill is very steep. At weekends fruit and vegetable sellers set up stalls outside their homes.

The southeast

*The southeast is the area of most historical interest, with the old **naval dockyard** which was of such strategic importance in the 17th and 18th centuries. Now a leading **marina**; it is a mecca for yachts from all over the world and many world-class yacht races are held here. Yachtsmen need entertainment and there are several good hotels, lots of restaurants, bars and nightlife in both **Falmouth Harbour** and **English Harbour**, which are also the best places to arrange a wide range of watersports. Former military buildings cover the hillsides up to the top of **Shirley Heights**, from where you get a spectacular view of the coastline, popular with visitors on Sunday for a barbecue, steel band and reggae.*

English Harbour and Nelson's Dockyard

*Parks Commissioner, **T** 268-4601379. US$1.60, children under 12 free. Souvenirs and T-shirts on sale at the entrance. Map 1, F5, p280*

On the other side of the island from St John's, **English Harbour**, has become one of the world's most attractive yachting centres and is now a hot spot at night for tourists. Here **Nelson's Dockyard**, the hub of English colonial maritime power in the region, has been restored and is one of the most interesting historical monuments in the West Indies. It is the only existing Georgian naval dockyard in the world and was designated a national park in 1985. The TV film *Longitude*, starring Jeremy Irons, was filmed here, standing in for Jamaica and Barbados. The **Nelson's Dockyard Museum** has been renovated to give the complete history of this famous Georgian naval yard and the story of famous English Harbour. See *Admiral's Inn*, with its boat and mast yard, slipway and pillars still standing, but which suffered earthquake damage in the 19th century. The *Copper and Lumber Store* is now a hotel, bar and restaurant. On the quay are three large capstans, showing signs of wear and tear. Boat charters can be arranged from here; also a 20-30-minute cruise round the historic dockyard for US$6 on *Horatio*, from outside the *Copper and Lumber Store*, depending on seasonal demand. A footpath leads round the bay to **Fort Berkeley** at the harbour mouth, well grazed by goats, and wonderful views. Built in stages in 1704-45 it predates the dockyard and once had 29 large cannon to defend the harbour. Near the dockyard, **Clarence House** still stands where the future King of England, William IV, stayed when he served as a midshipman.

On the left of the road from English Harbour to Shirley Heights are the remains of the British Navy's magazines and a small branch road to the **Dow Hill Interpretation Centre**, which offers an interesting 15-minute multimedia show every 15 minutes on the history of the island. There is a gift shop, restaurant and small museum with shell display. Local guides are also available.

Near English Harbour is **Galleon Beach**, which is splendid, (water taxi from English Harbour, EC$2). It has an excellent hotel and restaurant. There is a cave on **Windward Beach**, which is good for a moonlight bonfire (go in a group, not just as a couple). Follow the road past the Antigua Yacht Club leading to Pigeon Beach and turn left to Windward Beach on a bumpy track, best with a 4WD. Also excellent is **Pigeon Point**; turn left at the *Last Lemming* restaurant and follow the path up and over the hill.

Shirley Heights
Map 1, F6, p280

Overlooking English Harbour, are the ruins of fortifications built in the 18th century, with a wonderful view. Buildings, such as the officers' quarters, are still standing, restored but roofless, which

!   Nelson served in Antigua as a young man for almost three years, and visited it again in 1805, during his long chase of Villeneuve which was to end with the Battle of Trafalgar. Look out for bicentenary celebrations of the event.

★ Attractions for kids

Best

- **Shirley Heights**, Antigua, p42 The hilltop 18th-century fortifications and a Sunday barbecue and party.
- **Sting Ray City**, Antigua, p45 Snorkel with the rays, touch them and feed them under the water.
- **Montserrat Volcano Observatory**, Montserrat, p52 See boulders tumbling down as explosions continue.
- **Butterfly Farm**, Baie L'Embouchure, St-Martin, p64 Hundreds of tropical butterflies fluttering.
- **Brimstone Hill Fortress National Park**, St Kitts, p101 One of the best preserved and biggest fortresses.
- **Under the Sea**, Oualie Beach, Nevis, p248 Touch-and-go, an educational snorkelling experience.

give an idea of their former grandeur. At the lookout point, or **Battery**, at the south end is a bar and restaurant. On Sunday a steel band plays (*1600-1900*), followed by reggae (*1900-2200*) – very popular, and can be heard all the way to the dockyard below. **Great George Fort**, on Monk's Hill, above Falmouth Harbour (a 30-minute walk from the village of Liberta, and from Cobb's Cross near English Harbour) is less well preserved. Off the coast below Shirley Heights is one of the deeper dives up to 110 ft.

East to Half Moon Bay
On the way to Mill Reef. Map 1, E8, p280

At Half Moon Bay, there is plenty of room on a lovely long, white-sand beach; the waves can be rough in the centre of the bay, but the water is calm at the north end. There is a beach bar serving drinks and local food, but it is not always open.

The northeast and islands offshore

*Parham is the site of the first settlement on the island and the area is full of secluded bays offering safe harbour for shipping, shielded by numerous **islands offshore**, now either protected as nature reserves or used as exclusive resorts for the wealthy. You can go **kayaking** in the mangroves or visit **the stingrays** kept in a shallow area at the mouth of a bay off Seatons. Evidence of past dependence on sugar can be seen by visiting **Betty's Hope**, where the mill has been restored and opened to visitors. Good spots for birdwatching include **Potworks Dam** a little further south, noted for the great blue heron in spring and many water fowl. **Harmony Hall** is an excellent place for lunch and a visit to the art gallery see p155. A car is essential for visiting the villages in the northeast and east, as there are no buses.*

Parham

Take the road out to the airport from St John's. Do not enter the airport, but take the right fork which runs alongside it. After about 1½ miles take a right turn down a small road to St George's Church then follow the rough road round the coast to Parham. Map 1, B5, p280

On your way to Parham, take a look at **St George's Church**, on Fitches Creek Bay, first built in 1687 as the parish church of St Peter's in a beautiful location, and with the marble tombstone of the first English settler to be buried within a place of worship in 1659. It was remodelled in 1735. From there, a rough coast road leads to Parham, the first British settlement on the island, which has an attractive octagonal church, **St Peter's**, surrounded by flamboyant trees. Designed by Thomas Weekes in the Palladian style, it dates from the 1840s. Parham was once the main port, exporting sugar from some 20 sugar estates, but after 1920 it ceased to be a port of entry and its fortunes declined along with those of sugar. On Market Street are the remains of imposing Georgian buildings.

Betty's Hope

Visitors' centre, *0830-1600 (except Tue , Sun). Guided tour:* Antigua Museum, **T** 268-4624930, or Lionel George, **T** 268-4601356. *South from Parham, east at petrol station through Pares to Willikies. Past Pares village is a sign to Betty's Hope.* Map 1, C6, p280

Betty's Hope is a ruined sugar estate built in 1650 and owned by the Codrington family from 1674 to 1944. Restoration was carried out by the Antigua Museum in St John's. One of the twin windmills can sometimes be seen working. The visitors' centre tells the story of life on a sugar plantation and is well worth a visit.

Sir Christopher Codrington established the first large sugar estate in Antigua in 1674 and leased Barbuda to raise provisions for his plantations. Forests were cleared for sugar cane production and slave labour was imported. Today many Antiguans blame frequent droughts on the island's lack of trees to attract rainfall, and ruined towers of sugar plantations stand as testament to the barrenness.

Sting Ray City

Seatons, **T** 268-5627297, stingray@candw.ag Map 1, C6, p280

Here a boat takes you into a shallow area at the edge of a bay where stingrays are confined in a spacious pen on a sandbank in the sea (there are also a few huge lobsters). You are given snorkelling gear to get into the water with the rays, which come up to be fed. You can hold them under the water: they are quite harmless.

Devil's Bridge

After Willikies the road is signed to the Pineapple Beach Club at Long Bay, but before you get there, turn right down a small road, then a bumpy track to Devil's Bridge at Indian Town Point. Map 1, C8, p280

The area on the Atlantic coast is a national park where rough waves have carved out the bridge and made blowholes, not easily visible at first, but quite impressive when the spray breaks through. There is a good view of Long Bay and the headland.

● *It is said that African slaves from the nearby plantations threw themselves off the bridge with locals saying "the devil made them do it".*

Long Island
EAG **T** 268-4626236, eag@candw.ag *Map 1, A5/6, p280*

Long Island is occupied by the exclusive hotel, *Jumby Bay*, a 300-acre property managed by Rosewood Hotels. At Pasture Bay, the hawksbill turtle lays its eggs from late May to December. The *Environmental Awareness Group (EAG)* organizes turtle watches.

Great Bird Island
Map 1, A6, p280

The Antiguan Racer Conservation Project was set up in 1995 to save the harmless Antiguan racer snake (*Alsophis antiguae*) which had been devastated by mongooses and black rats. The 60 remaining snakes were living on Great Bird Island and a campaign to eliminate the rats helped their numbers to increase. Racers have now been reintroduced to other islands. Great Bird Island is also home to the red-billed tropic bird. Tour operators and boat captains bring visitors and snorkelling is good in the bay.

Barbuda

Some 30 miles to the north of Antigua is Barbuda, a flat coral island 68 miles square, one of the two island dependencies of Antigua. A visit here is like stepping back in time: there are few paved roads, no crime and the people are friendly – life is slow and simple. Barbuda has one of the most spectacular beaches in the West Indies, a 17-mile stretch of uninterrupted sand, and the world's largest frigate bird colony.

▸▸ *See Sleeping p124, Eating and drinking p160, Nightlife p192.*

Sights

Codrington
Map 3, D6, p281

Most residents live in the only village on the island, Codrington, on the edge of a large lagoon. Barbuda has a fascinating history, having been privately owned in colonial times by the Codrington family, who used it to supply their sugar estates on Antigua with food and slaves. This caused problems after emancipation as all property belonged to the Codringtons and the freed slaves were trapped with no jobs, no land and no laws. After several years and court cases, Antiguan law was applied to the island, but while Barbudans may own their own houses, all other land is generally held by the government. In places you can see the remains of the stone wall used to demarcate the limit of the village within which everybody had to live until 1976, when the creation of a local government inspired people to move further afield. You can also see the village well which was used to draw water until the 1980s.

Frigate Bird Sanctuary
*Boats can be arranged at the dock when you get there, US$2 per person. For further information contact the Barbuda Tourism Desk in Antigua, **T** 268-4620029. Map 3, D6, p281*

This is one of the few islands in the area where there is still abundant wildlife, although much of it has been introduced by man: duck, guinea fowl, plover, pigeon, wild deer, pigs, goats, sheep, horses and donkeys, left over from the Codrington era. There is an impressive Frigate Bird Sanctuary (the largest colony in the world) in the mangroves in Codrington Lagoon, particularly on Man of War Island where thousands of birds mate and breed betweenSeptembert and January. The sanctuary is definitely worth a visit and the sight of some 10,000 frigates raising their young is

▶ Frigate birds

Fregata magnificens are indeed magnificent when seen soaring high in the air, using the thermals to suspend themselves on their huge wings for days at a time, and travel great distances.

Frigates are one of the oldest known birds, with a history spanning 50 million years, and during that time they've picked up a trick or two. One of them, piracy, has earned them the nickname of Man-O'-War bird. Their fishing technique relies on finding fish or squid close to the surface which they can just skim off, but failing that they have developed a method of hassling other seabirds, encouraging them to regurgitate whatever they have just caught. In an amazing display of aerobatics, the frigate birds manage to catch the food before it hits the water and get a free meal.

The breeding colony on Barbuda is believed to be the largest in the world, larger even than that of the Galapagos. Locals will tell you that there are some 10,000 birds, having recovered from the effects of Hurricane Luis in 1995, but numbers are anyone's guess. The breeding season is roughly September-January, although even later you can still see males displaying their bright red pouches, blowing them up like balloons to attract a mate. It is the male who chooses a nest site, and when he is sure he has found a long-term partner, he builds a precarious nest of twigs in the mangroves alongside all the other males. The female lays a single egg, which the male incubates and initially cares for once it is hatched. The chick is born white and fluffy and sits on the twiggy nest, suspended above the water, for 8-10 months until it is fully fledged. It takes a lot longer to be fully proficient at flying and feeding itself.

stunning (see box, p48). Visitors are taken to only one or two spots to view the birds, and ropes keep the boats from getting too close. The rest of the birds are left entirely at peace. There are also brown boobies nesting alongside the frigates and pelicans can be seen in the lagoon. An endemic warbler (*Dendroica subita*) lives on Barbuda and although DNA studies have been carried out, numbers and habitat requirements are so far unknown.

● *Around 150 different species of birds have been observed in Antigua and Barbuda, of which a third are year-round residents and the rest seasonal or migrants.*

Palaster Reef
Map 3, off the map, p281

Palaster Reef is a marine reserve to protect the reef and the shipwrecks (there are around 60 ships documented and the Codringtons made a healthy income from wrecking). The seas are rich with impressive formations of elkhorn and staghorn coral, all types of crustacean and tropical fish. Lobster is plentiful and a mainstay of nearly every meal. Diving is extremely rewarding but you will need to take a guide, see p231. Snorkelling equipment is available but is more expensive than on Antigua.

Palmetto Point
Map 3, F5, p281

The beaches are an outstanding feature of Barbuda and are arguably the most magnificent in the whole Caribbean. The longest beach is a swathe of white sand stretching for 17 miles down the west side, while the most spectacular is the pink sand beach at Palmetto Point, made up of zillions of tiny pink shells. There are no beach bars or vendors, you will probably be the only person for miles. There is no shade except around Palm Beach where a few palm trees survived past hurricane damage.

Caves
Map 3, C7, p281

The Gunchup Caves near Two Foot Bay are interesting to explore. People have used them for shelter since the days of the Amerindians. Dark Cave is home to a blind shrimp (*Typhlatya monae*) found only in these pools and at Mona Island off Puerto Rico, but access is difficult. A road is planned.

Martello Tower
Map 3, E6, p281

The Martello Tower and fort is the most complete historical site on the island. The tower is 20 m (56 ft) high and once had nine guns to defend the southwest approach. From Codrington, River Road runs three miles to Palmetto Point, past Cocoa Point and on to Spanish Point, a ½-mile finger of land that divides the Atlantic from the Caribbean Sea. There is a small ruin of a lookout post here and the most important Arawak settlements found in Barbuda.

Redonda

Antigua's second dependency, 35 miles to the southwest and half a mile square, is little more than a rocky volcanic islet and is uninhabited. Goats, lizards and seabirds live an undisturbed life apart from the occasional birdwatcher who might come to find the burrowing owl, now extinct on Antigua. Columbus sighted the island on 12 November 1493 and named it after a church in Cadiz, Santa María la Redonda. He did not land, however, and thus did not formally claim the island. Neither did anyone else until 1865 when Matthew Dowdy Shiell, an Irish sea-trader from Montserrat, celebrated the birth of a long-awaited son by leading an expedition of friends to Redonda, claiming it as his kingdom. In 1872, the island was annexed by Britain and came under the jurisdiction of the colony of Antigua, despite protests from the Shiells. The title of King was not disputed and has survived to this day. The island was never inhabited, but guano was extracted by the Redonda Phosphate Company until the works were blown away by a hurricane.

In 1880 MD Shiell abdicated in favour of his son, Matthew Phipps Shiell, who became King Felipe of Redonda, but emigrated to the UK where he was educated and became a prolific and popular novelist. His best-known novel was *The Purple Cloud* (1901), later made into a film, *The World, the Flesh and the Devil*, starring Harry Belafonte. On his death in 1947, he appointed as his literary executor and successor to the throne his friend John Gawsworth, the poet, who became Juan, the third King of Redonda, but continued to live in London. His reign was notable for his idea of an 'intellectual aristocracy' of the realm of Redonda and he conferred titles on his literary friends, including Victor Gollancz, the publisher, JB Priestley, Lawrence Durrell and Dorothy L Sayers. This eccentric pastime hit a crisis when declining fortunes and increasing time spent in the pub sparked a rash of new titles to all and sundry, and a number of abdications in different pubs. The succession was, and still is, disputed.

Montserrat

Montserrat is incomparable. The Irish-influenced 'Emerald Isle' is totally unspoiled by tourism but its volcano has put it on the map, having wiped out the southern part of the island. Here you can enjoy volcanic moonscapes and views of a glowing volcano, deserted black sand beaches, a network of challenging mountain trails, historic sites, waters teeming with fish, coral and sponges, and perhaps the friendliest people in the region. Only the northern third of the island is populated because of the volcano and the 4,500 inhabitants are developing the area in style.

▸▸ *See Sleeping p125, Eating and drinking p160, Diving p227*

◉ Sights

Montserrat Volcano Observatory

T 664-4915647, www.mvo.ms *Mon-Fri 1530-1600. US$4 adults, US$2 children. Map 4, E2, p282*

The volcano is now a tourist attraction and can best be viewed from the Montserrat Volcano Observatory, where visits are also possible on weekday afternoons when volcanic activity permits. If the volcano is dangerously active visitors are excluded. Video shows of volcanic activity and a tour of the monitoring rooms and equipment are available, and an expert guide from the scientific community will be available to show you around. Spectacular views of the volcano and its damage can also be viewed in safety from Jack Boy Hill in the east, close to the start of the Exclusion Zone. (Do not attempt to enter the Exclusion Zone as it is very dangerous and hefty fines are levied on anyone caught in there.) From here you can see the grey, ash-covered flanks of what was Chances Peak, in stark contrast with the Centre Hills, which are still green, forested and fertile. Another vantage spot is from the top of Garibaldi Hill near to the communications tower – a long drive up a twisting, winding road. A 4WD vehicle is recommended.

Little Bay

Map 4, A2, p282

Plymouth, the former capital, was flooded with ash up to the roofs of the colonial buildings and completely destroyed. A great vantage point for looking out over Plymouth is the site of the old museum on Richmond Hill, but there is no access to Plymouth as the site is quite dangerous and further mudflows have occurred as recently as June 2004. Administrative offices have now moved to the new Government Headquarters at **Brades** in the north of the island. There are plans to develop the **Little Bay area** as a future capital. The port is here and a state-of-the-art performance centre/convention centre is being built, to open in 2005, with an adjacent open-air performing area to replace the Festival Village.

Centre Hills trail and the Silver Hills

Centre Hills in the middle of the island between Soufrière Hills and the Silver Hills in the north Map 4, D3 and A3, p282. For information and guides contact Montserrat National Trust, North Main Rd, Olveston, **T** 664-4913086, www.montserratnationaltrust.com *Mon-Fri 0830-1630, Sat 0900-1300.* Natural History Centre and Botanical Garden *Map 4, E1, p282*

Natural vegetation is confined mostly to the summits of hills, where elfin woodlands occur. At lower levels, fern groves are plentiful and lower still, cacti, sage bush and acacias. Flowers and fruit are typical of the Caribbean with many bay trees, from which bay oil (or rum) is distilled, the national tree, the mango, and the national flower, *Heliconia caribaea* (a wild banana known locally as 'lobster claw'). There are 34 species of bird resident on the island and many more migrants. Unique to Montserrat is the Montserrat oriole, *Icterus oberi*, a black and gold oriole named the national bird. The British FCO is funding a project to study the effect of the volcano on the oriole. There are also the rare forest thrush, the bridled quail dove, mangrove cuckoo, trembler and purple-throated carib.

Many of these can be seen along the **Centre Hills trail** in the middle of the island between the ash-covered Soufrière Hills and the Silver Hills. The vegetation here is biologically diverse and supports a variety of wildlife. Montserrat cannot boast many wild animals, although it shares the terrestrial frog, known as the

! Caribs called the island Alliouagana, which means 'land of the prickly bush'.

▶ Volcanic violence

In 1995 the lives of Montserratians were turned upside down when the 'dormant' volcano erupted. The residents of Plymouth and villages in the south were evacuated to the north as lava, rocks and ash belched from the Soufrière Hills for the first time since the 1930s. Activity increased in 1997; during March and April pyroclastic flows reached 2miles down the south side of the volcano, the former tourist attractions of the Great Alps Waterfall and Galways Soufrière were covered, there was a partial collapse of Galways Wall and lava flowed down the Tar River Valley. In May the volcanic dome was growing at 3.7 cubic metres per second, and in June a huge explosion occurred when a sudden pyroclastic flow of hot rock, gas and ash poured down the volcano at 200 mph. It engulfed 19 people, destroyed seven villages and some 200 homes. The flow, which resulted from a partial collapse of the lava dome, came to within 50 yards of the sea, close to the airport runway, which had to be closed. The eruption sent an ash cloud 6 miles into the air and people were forced to wear ash masks. In August another bout of activity destroyed Plymouth, which

mountain chicken, only with Dominica. Agoutis, bats and lizards, including iguanas which can grow to over 1½ m in length (they used to take the balls on the golf course, mistaking them for eggs), can be found and tree frogs contribute to the island's 'night music'.

A walk around the **Silver Hills** in the extreme north reveals a dramatic coastline where you can find lots of seabirds. There is a fabulous vantage spot from the communications tower on Silver Hills which can be reached after a 30-minute walk from Drummonds Village.

caught fire under a shower of red-hot lava. It now looks like a lunar landscape, completely covered by grey ash. In December 1997 there was a huge dome collapse which created a 600-yard amphitheatre around Galways Soufrière and destroyed several deserted communities. The White River delta was increased to about 1 mile and the water level rose by about 3 ft. During 1998-99 dome collapses continued, with ash clouds at times up to 8 miles high, but scientists reported that the dome, while still hot, was gradually cooling and entering a quieter phase.

In 2000 there was further activity and in July 2003 the dome of the volcano collapsed again and a thick cloud of ash and rocks spread across the island. Since then activity has been extremely quiet and on 1 May 2004 former areas making up the Day Time Entry Zone (DTEZ) reopened for 24-hour access. A small portion of the Exclusion Zone at St Georges Hill has now been made a Day Time Entry Zone allowing entry from 0600-1800 every day. A programme to rehabilitate the former DTEZ is currently being planned.

Rendezvous Bay
In the north of the island. Map 4, A2, p282

Montserrat's beaches are volcanic 'black' sand, which in reality means the sand may be a silvery grey or dark golden brown colour. The single white coral beach is at Rendezvous Bay in the north. It is a stiff hike from Little Bay along a very steep mountainous trail (not suitable for small children). Take food and water, it is a long hot walk until you reach your refreshing swim. There is no shade on

▶ The Emerald Isle and its Irish-African heritage

Montserrat was settled by the English Thomas Warner, who brought English and Irish Catholics from their uneasy base in the Protestant island of St Kitts. Once established as an Irish-Catholic colony, the only one in the Caribbean, Catholic refugees fled there from persecution in Virginia and, following his victory at Drogheda in 1649, Cromwell sent some of his Irish political prisoners to Montserrat. By 1648 there were 1,000 Irish families on the island. An Irishman brought some of the first slaves in 1651 and the economy became based on sugar. Slaves quickly outnumbered the original British indentured servants and today the vast majority of the people are of African descent. A slave rebellion in 1768, appropriately enough on St Patrick's Day, led to all the rebels being executed and today they are celebrated as freedom fighters.

The Irish influence is still seen in national emblems. On arrival your passport is stamped with a green shamrock, the island's flag and crest show a woman, Erin of Irish legend, complete with harp. There are many Irish names, of both people and places, and the national dish, goat water stew, is supposedly based on a traditional Irish recipe, although some historians claim it is of African origin. A popular local folk dance, the *Bam-chick-a-lay*, resembles Irish step dances and musical bands may include a fife and a drum similar to the Irish bodhran. The new Government House at Woodlands has a shamrock fixed to its roof.

the beach; avoid the poisonous manchineel trees and the spiny sea urchins among the rocks at the north end. You can also take a boat, and it is quite a good idea to walk there and arrange for a boat to come and pick you up at an agreed time.

Other beaches
All on the west of the island. Map 4, p282 See also Diving p227

The best of the rest of the beaches, all black sand, are **Woodlands** (National Trust, beach house, washrooms), where you can safely swim through caves, **Lime Kiln Bay**, tiny **Bunkum Bay, Carr's Bay** and **Little Bay** in the north. An interesting beach to visit is the one at **Old Road Bay**, below the *Vue Pointe Hotel*, which has been impacted by volcanic mudflows, creating strange patterns. Be careful in rainy weather as mud can flow very quickly down the valley behind the beach. **Foxes Bay** is a deserted beach in a zone which at the height of the volcanic crisis was a no-go area. The area has now reopened and the beach is a delight. Danny Sweeney in Olveston can take you fishing or organize watersports, see p235.

Sint Maarten/St-Martin

Shared amicably between Holland and France, this island is the smallest in the world to be divided by two nations and offers you two cultures within easy reach of each other. Dutch Sint Maarten is the hub of air and sea transport and most people pass through here on their way to the other islands. Good international air links have encouraged the construction of large resort hotels with casinos and duty-free shopping. There are few traces of Dutch influence and it is overwhelmingly US in its outlook. French St-Martin is more attractive, with more stylish architecture, and although increasingly Americanized, is considered more 'chic' and packed with restaurants, dedicated to the serious business of eating well. There are no border formalities, only a modest monument erected in 1948, commemorating the division of the island three centuries earlier. Both sides have good harbours and marinas and are popular with the sailing crowd. Heavily populated, this is not somewhere to come to get away from it all, but it is ideal for a beach holiday, perhaps in combination with a quieter island nearby. Island hopping is easy.

Popular legend has it that the division of the island was settled with a race starting from Oyster Pond: the Frenchman went north and the Dutchman went south, but the Frenchman walked faster because he drank only wine while the Dutchman's penchant for genever (a drink similar to gin) slowed him down. Since 23 March 1648 and the Treaty of Mount Concordia which officially divided the island, however, Sint Maarten has changed hands 16 times, including brief occupations by the British, but the Dutch-French accord has been peaceably honoured since it was last revised in 1839. The Dutch have the southern 37 sq km of the island and the French have the northern 52 sq km.

The population of at least 62,000 (33,459 in Sint Maarten and 28,518 in St-Martin) has mushroomed with the tourist boom: the 1950 Sint Maarten census gave the total population at 1,484. A large proportion have come from other Caribbean islands to seek work. Few people speak Dutch, the official language of Sint Maarten, although Papiamento has increased with the migration of people from the Dutch islands of Aruba, Bonaire and Curaçao. Nearly everybody speaks English and there is a large Spanish-speaking contingent of guest workers from the Dominican Republic. The French side is noticeably Gallic and fewer speak English.

▸▸ *See Sleeping p128, Eating and drinking p163, Nightlife p194*

 ## Sights

Philipsburg
Map 6, p283

Philipsburg, the capital of Dutch Sint Maarten, is built on a narrow strip of sandy land between the sea and a shallow lake which was once a salt pond. It has two main streets, Front and Back, and a ringroad built on land reclaimed from the salt pond, which all run parallel to beautiful **Great Bay Beach**, perhaps the safest and cleanest 20-m wide city beach anywhere with a new boardwalk running along it. **Front Street** is full of shops offering duty-free goods. **Back Street** contains low-cost clothes shops and low-budget Chinese restaurants. The historic **Courthouse** dating from 1793, on De Ruyterplein, better known as Wathey Square, faces the pier. In the past it has been used as a council hall, a weigh station, jail and, until 1992, a post office. Now renovated, it is exclusively a courthouse. The **harbour** is frequented by cruise ships and a host of smaller craft. Captain Hodge's Wharf can handle 1,800 passengers per hour and has a tourist information desk, telephones, toilets, taxis and live entertainment, but in 2001 a new cruise ship harbour was opened outside Philipsburg. There are two **marinas**, Bobby's and Great Bay, at the east end of town where you can organize fishing or sailing trips. For details on outdoor concerts, choirs, theatre and art exhibitions, ask at the **Cultural Centre** of Philipsburg on Back Street (**T** 599-5422056).

Fort Amsterdam was the first Dutch fort in the Caribbean, built in 1631, captured by the Spanish in 1633 and partly pulled down before they left the island in 1648. It was still used for military purposes until the 19th century and as a signalling and communications station until the 1950s. You reach it through the grounds of a private timeshare development. The guard allows visitors to park outside and walk to the fort. **Fort Willem**, started by the British at the beginning of the 19th century, has a television transmitting tower and there is a good view from the top.

Sint Maarten Museum

Museum Arcade, 7 Front St, Philipsburg, **T** 599-5424917, www.speetjens.com/museum *Mon-Fri 1000-1600, Sat 1000-1400. Free, but donations requested. Map 6, G6, p283* The museum is upstairs in a restored 19th-century house, exhibiting the history and culture of the island. There is a little bit of everything, making an extensive collection, from Arawak artefacts, slave paraphernalia, household items, furniture, china, minerals, geology and marine life. The display stretches to other islands where relevant, with lots of photos and prints. There is a museum shop downstairs.

South coast beaches
Map5, p283

The bays on the south and west shores are excellent for swimming, diving and fishing, and the beaches are of fine white sand. **Great Bay** is home to Philipsburg and visiting cruise ships with a lovely clean beach lined with restaurants and bars. The peninsula of Fort Amsterdam protects **Little Bay**, the next bay west, which has the only shore dive site, with shipwrecks. Little Bay is accessible via the *Divi Resort* and is good for kayaking and snorkelling as well as diving, but beware of the motorized as well as non-motorized watersports. You get a good view of Philipsburg, the cruise ships, Statia, St Kitts and Saba on a clear day. **Cay Bay** is isolated and generally visited only by horse riders and mountain bikers because of its inaccessibility. **Simpson Bay beach** is a large sweep of sand with very few hotels on it, partly because of its proximity to the airport, sandwiched between the sea and the lagoon. **Maho Beach**, at the end of the runway, has regular Sunday beach parties with live music competitions; don't forget to duck when planes arrive and hang on to your towel before it is blown into the sea. It is home to the *Sunset Beach Bar*, see p197, which has a happy hour with live music every evening. The most popular beach is **Mullet Bay**, where you can rent umbrellas, beach chairs, etc. It can get crowded in season and at weekends. It is good for surfing when the swell comes from the north, local swimmers and triathletes train here. The most westerly beach on the Dutch side of the island is **Cupecoy**, where rugged sandstone cliffs lead down to a narrow sandy beach, providing morning shade and a natural windbreak. This beach changes according to the seasons and is the only beach on the Dutch side where nudity is more or less tolerated. **Baie Longue** lives up to its name as the longest beach on the

! The Amerindians who originally settled on the island named it *Sualiga*, meaning land of salt.

island, stretching away from the luxury hotel, *La Samanna*, on the cliff at the east end to **Pointe du Canonnier**, the most western point on the island. There are no facilities outside the hotel.

Simpson Bay
Map 5, C3, p283

A large part of the island is occupied by Simpson Bay Lagoon which straddles the international boundary and is fringed by a narrow strip of land round its southern, western and northern shores. There are two bridges allowing an outlet to the sea. The main one, just east of Juliana Airport, on Simpson Bay, opens for a maximum of 20 minutes at 0900, 1130 and 1730 to allow large boats to enter the lagoon. Just inside the lagoon by the bridge is a new harbour for mega yachts, an amazing sight. Allow extra time to get to the airport if coming from the east of the island at these times. The other bridge doesn't open. It is a much smaller affair on the north side at Sandy Ground, just west of Marigot, used by fishing vessels and small craft. Lots of watersports are based at Simpson Bay including boats for deep-sea fishing, see p235.

Marigot
Map 5, B4, p283

The capital of French St-Martin lies between Simpson Bay Lagoon and the Caribbean sea. Despite new building works, Marigot still has charm and the modern architecture is in keeping with the traditional style. **Rue de la République** has 19th-century Creole houses with gingerbread fretwork and **rue du Général de Gaulle** is in the same style, though it dates only from the 1980s. Recent development includes the upscale Marina Fort-Louis in the bay in the shadow of the 18th-century fort on the hill, and the West Indies Shopping Mall overlooking the marina and the ferry.

For shopaholics, boutiques offer French *prêt-à-porter* fashions and St-Barth batiks, and gift shops sell liqueurs, perfumes, and cosmetics at better duty-free prices than on the Dutch side. At the **Marina Port La Royale** complex there are chic shops, cafés and bistros where you can sit and watch the boats. Rue de la République and rue de la Liberté also have good **shopping** with fashion names at prices below those of Europe or the USA. There is a **market** every morning in the market place on the waterfront next to Marigot harbour. It is a colourful affair with clothing and souvenirs available every day as well as the usual fruit and vegetables and best on Wednesday and Saturday. On the right-hand side of the market (as you face the sea) is the taxi stand and the ferry departures to Anguilla and St-Barth.

It is a 10-minute climb to **Fort-Louis** overlooking Marigot and Marigot Bay. It was built in 1767-89 by Chevalier de Durat, who oversaw the construction of a prison (now fire station) and a bridge, the Pont de Durat, which opened up Marigot village to the north of the island. The fort was used to defend the settlement, its cotton, indigo and tobacco from pirates but fell into disuse after 1820.

'On the trail of the Arawaks' Museum

Route de Sandy-Ground, Marigot, **T** 590-(0)590-292284. *Mon-Fri 0900-1600. US$5 (US$2 children). Christophe Henocq, curator and president, leads tours to Hope Estate archaeological dig, 3 hrs, US$30. Map 5, B4, p283* Beside the tourist office, this historical and archaeological museum has an exhibition from the first settlers of St-Martin around 3500 BC to 1960. There are sections on pre-Columbian, colonial and 20th-century history and geology, with lots of information on the salt industry, photos and a gift shop. Most of the archaeological exhibits came from the Hope Estate Plantation, which grew sugar cane and cotton in 1750-1850.

! Marigot' is a French West Indian word meaning a spot from which rainwater does not drain off but forms marshy pools.

West coast beaches
Map 5, p283

Round the point is **Plum Beach**, popular with surfers but also lovely for snorkelling around the points at each end. The popular **Baie Rouge** has cliffs at the eastern end and if you swim along the point you will find a private beach and cave you can swim through. Schools of small fish dart among the boulders and snorkelling is good. **Baie Nettlé** is a long strip of sand within easy reach of Marigot, but a number of hotels have made access to the whole length of it difficult. North of Marigot is **Friar's Bay**, a sheltered bay down a bumpy road with a couple of restaurants, from where you can walk along a path to **Happy Bay**. You get a good view of Anguilla, the water is calm and good for children and beach loungers are available as well as inexpensive food. **Grand Case** beach has been eroded by storms but the sand is coming back with each new swell. The sea reaches the foot of the buildings lining the shore in places. Sandy **Petite Plage** at the end of Grand Case beach is dominated by the *Grand Case Beach Club*. You can rent kayaks from Petite Plage and paddle out to **Creole Rock** for excellent snorkelling, but it is further than it looks. Try hiring a boat to drop you off and pick you up. It is visited daily by dive boats. **Anse Marcel**, north of Grand Case, is a shallow beach, ideal for small children, but packed with guests from *Le Meridien*. On the extreme north of the island is **Petites Cayes**, a strip of sand fringed by reefs, a 25-minute walk along the coast from Cul de Sac.

Grand Case
13 km east of Marigot. Map 5, A5, p283

Grand Case (pronounced 'grand cars') is a quaint town by an old salt pond (which has been partially filled in to provide the Espérance airstrip). Grand Case boasts it is the gastronomic centre of the island and the main street is lined with restaurants.

Pic du Paradis
Turn off at Rambaud on Marigot-Grand Case road. Map 5, B5, p283

Pic du Paradis (424 m, 1,391 ft) is a good lookout point from where, on a fine day, you can see Anguilla, Saba, Sint Eustatius, St Kitts, Nevis and St-Barth. By 4WD you can reach the top on the track used to access the radio-television transmitting tower. There are footpaths from Colombier (1½ km) and Orléans (1 km). **Colombier** is a small, sleepy village with wonderful gardens – well worth a visit.

Loterie Farm
Pic du Paradis, **T** 590-(0)590-878616, loteriefarm@powerantilles.com
Daily, sunrise to sunset. US$5, children under 5 free. Bar open all day, restaurant Tue-Sat 0930-1500, 1800-2100, Sun 0930-1800. Great menu from Canadian chef, under US$17, kids US$5. Map 5, B5, p283

This 150-acre farm at the foot of Pic du Paradis is a private nature reserve of humid forest. It is being restored by BJ Welch, who discovered it after damage by Hurricane Luis revealed a farmhouse (believed haunted by ghosts from a dispute and murder between the Gumbs and Fleming families) and stone walls. Trails once used by slaves have been marked in the forest up the mountain and in the fields for serious hiking or a gentle stroll. This is one of the few places left on the island where mature forest remains – a delight.

Butterfly Farm
Le Galion Beach Rd, Baie L'Embouchure, **T** 590-(0)590-873121, www.thebutterflyfarm.com *Daily 0900-1530. US$10 adults, US$5 children, reusable ticket. Just before you get to the riding centre and animal rescue. Map 5, B6, p283*

The butterfly farm was opened in 1994 but has been rebuilt five times because of hurricanes. Best in the morning and in full sun when the butterflies are most active. All the larvae are imported.

Sarongs for sale
Shopping on the sand for beachwear.

1 The plume of steam from Montserrat's volcano rises into the sky, but activity is quieter now. ►► See page 52.

2 St-Barthélemy is characterised by picture-book houses and shops with red roofs and colourful paintwork. ►► See page 87.

3 Standing firm against invasion from the sea, magnificent Brimstone Hill Fortress is a UNESCO World Heritage Site. ►► See page 101.

4 The Harmonites Steel Band entertains visitors to St John's, the capital of Antigua. ►► See page 188.

5 Regattas and races for yachts, windsurfers and kitesurfers take advantage of the constant winds and excellent sailing conditions in this part of the Caribbean. ►► See page 243.

6 Carnival on St-Martin is a multi-coloured affair; catch a festival on any island for a cultural blast. ►► See page 207.

Photo finish
Horse racing is a major social event on Nevis, held on a spectacular seaside course.

Duck!
Sunworshippers on Maho Beach are undeterred by aircraft landing at Juliana Airport, Sint Maarten.

Fish and dips
Scuba diving into the deep blue sea is rewarding around any of the Leeward Islands.

Who's a pretty boy then?
A male frigate bird displays his scarlet pouch among the mangroves of Barbuda.

Island haven
Sailing boats find shelter in English Harbour and Falmouth Harbour, Antigua, as they have done for centuries.

Sunset cocktail
Sugar-mill buildings have been converted into a luxury setting for Ottley's Plantation Inn, St Kitts.

Sint Maarten Park

Arch Rd, Madam Estate, **T** 599-5432030, www.stmaartenpark.com
*Daily 0900-1700. US$10, children 3-12 years US$5. Close to New
Amsterdam shopping centre. Map 5, C5, p283*

Formerly called the zoo, the park has a small exhibition of the
fauna and flora from the islands. All the animals were born in
captivity and the emphasis is on conservation of endangered
species. There is a monkey island housing squirrel monkeys, a bat
cave and night safaris on Saturdays to see the nocturnal animals.
Work is now being undertaken to develop the botanical aspect of
the park with open and natural exhibits.

East coast beaches
Map 5, p283

On the east side, **Grandes Cayes** is popular for family picnics.
Cul-de-Sac is a traditional village, with calm sea and fishing boats.
It is the departure point for boats to the **Île de Tintamarre** (take
all food and water with you) and **Îlet Pinel** (US$5 per person
return, five minutes) just offshore. Pinel is a protected nature
reserve and the beach is very sheltered, with shallow, crystal-clear
water, great for small children. Snorkelling is rewarding along both
sides of the island. Lunch, beach chairs and umbrellas are available.
Baie Orientale (Orient Bay) is beautiful but rough (beware of its
undertow). Several new developments along the beach mean the
area is often overrun with day visitors. At the southern end is a
clothes-optional resort. Windsurfers and kitesurfers can be hired,
with a good protected area for beginners and more open waters.
You can also rent wave runners, jet skis or go parasailing, see p247.
From here you can find boats to **Caye Verte**, just offshore. Round
the point is **Le Galion**, a good beach for families with protected
water, and then **Baie de l'Embouchure**, a long strip of sand
separating the Étang aux Poissons from the sea. The outer reef

creates good conditions for surfers and shelters the bay for windsurf beginners. When the winds pick up the kitesurfers and experienced windsurfers come out to play. The next bay, **Baie Lucas** is good for snorkelling. **Oyster Pond** is a landlocked harbour which is difficult to enter because of the outlying reefs, now home to a yacht club and bare-boat charter. **Dawn Beach** nearby is popular with bodysurfers and snorkelling is good in calm weather because of the shallow reef offshore. **Guana Bay**, next to Dawn Beach, is the bodysurfers' best beach. Private and rugged, it is for strong swimmers only as it has an undertow. Although it is in a residential area there are no umbrellas and little shade.

Anguilla

Anguilla is flat, dry and unappealing, until you hit the beaches. These are some of the most spectacular in the Caribbean: 33 beaches, 12 miles of fine white coral sand to bury your toes in and crystal-clear water protected by a ring of coral reefs and offshore islands are the main attractions of this tiny island. Anguilla is only 16 miles long and 3 miles across at its widest point. The most northerly of the Leeward Islands, it is just 11 miles from St-Martin. It is a British island, everyone speaks English and the currency is the US and EC dollar, making it popular above all with American visitors seeking rest and relaxation.
▸▸ *See Sleeping p132, Eating and drinking p169, Nightlife p197*

 Sights

The Valley
Map 7, B4, p284

The Valley is the island's administrative centre, with a population of 500. The tourist office is here, as are banks, shops, sporting facilities and schools. The Methodist church is the oldest church, dating from 1830, a pretty building of stone and timber.

Wallblake House

The Valley, **T** 264-4972759, www.website.com *Tue-Fri 1000-1200. US$5 tour.* *Map 7, B4, p284* This restored, 18th-century plantation house is where the priest from St Gerard's Roman Catholic Church lives. It is not a Great House as you might find on other islands where plantation agriculture was more profitable, but it is the oldest and only surviving plantation house on Anguilla, dating from 1787 and restored in 2002. The church itself is worth a visit to see the unusual ventilation and extraordinary crazy paving on the three arches at the main door. Several resident artists exhibit work on Saturday mornings during the winter season in the grounds.

Beaches near The Valley
Map 7, p284

Crocus Bay is the nearest beach to The Valley. The rocks on both sides have attractive underwater scenery. There is a bar/restaurant and toilets. **Little Bay**, with crystal-clear water and dramatic cliffs, is very difficult to reach but eagle rays, turtles and lots of fish can be seen and, as well as excellent snorkelling, it is a birdwatcher's and photographer's dream; turn right in front of the old cottage hospital in The Valley; after about ½ mile some trails lead down the cliff to the water; fishermen have put up a rope for the last bit down the rock face. Glass-bottom boats and cruise boats also come here or you can get a boat ride from Crocus Bay. At the end of **Limestone Bay**, just north of Little Bay, is a small beach with wonderful snorkelling, but be careful, the sea can be rough here.

Road Bay/Sandy Ground
Map 7, C2, p284

Known for its **nightlife** and **restaurants,** Road Bay/Sandy Ground is the starting point for most day trips, dive tours and a popular anchorage for visiting yachts with races usually starting from here. At

Sandy Ground village, you can see the **salt pond**, around Great Road Pond, although it is not in operation. There is a mini museum at the **Pump House bar**, Sandy Ground, **T** 264-497515, once part of the salt factory and equipment used in salt-making is on display.

Islands offshore
Boats go from Road Bay, Shoal Bay or Island Harbour. Map 7, B2,A6 and off the map, p284

Day trips can be arranged to neighbouring islands or to the offshore islands and cays. **Sandy Island**, a pleasant desert island for swimming or snorkelling, is only 15 minutes from Sandy Ground harbour. Motor boats or sailing boats cross over hourly (*1000-1500, US$8 per person*); lunch or drinks are from a beach bar under coconut palms, **T** 264-4976395. There are trips to **Prickly Pear**, 6 miles from Road Bay, where you can snorkel if you are not a scuba diver, or to other cays for fishing or a picnic. **Scrub Island**, 2 miles long and 1 mile wide, off the northeast tip of Anguilla, is a mix of coral and scrub, uninhabited except by goats. There is a lovely sandy beach on the west side and ruins of an abandoned tourist resort and airstrip. There can be quite a swell in the anchorage, so anchor well.

Blowing Point
Map 7, D2, p284

Blowing Point is where the ferry comes in from St-Martin and the docks are the focal point of the village. You can see Marigot across the channel and it is an easy crossing to get to the shops. The ferry starts at 0730 from Anguilla and 0800 from Marigot and continues every 30-40 minutes, pay on board, US$10 one way, children under 12 half price. The last ferry from Anguilla is at 2215 and from Marigot at 2300 costs US$25 (inc. tax). Put your name and passport number on the manifest before boarding and pay departure tax of

US$3/EC$8 leaving Anguilla, US$2/€2 leaving Marigot.

Before the British

The earliest known Amerindian site on Anguilla is at the northeast tip of the island, where tools and artefacts made from conch shells have been recovered and dated at around 1300 BC. Saladoid Amerindians settled on the island in the 4th century AD and brought their knowledge of agriculture, ceramics and their religious culture based on the god of cassava. By the 6th century large villages had been built at Rendezvous Bay and Sandy Ground, with smaller ones at Shoal Bay and Island Harbour. Post Saladoid Amerindians from the Greater Antilles arrived in the tenth century, building villages and setting up a chiefdom with a religious hierarchy. Several ceremonial items have been found and debris related to the manufacture of the three-pointed zemis, or spirit stones, associated with fertility rites. By the 17th century, Amerindians had disappeared from Anguilla: wiped out by enslavement and European diseases.

Artefacts and petroglyphs have been found in caves at The Fountain national park and at Big Spring Cave, a ceremonial centre near Island Harbour.

Rendezvous Bay
Map 7, C2, p284

If you like to walk or jog along a beach, then Rendezvous is near perfection. Stretching for 1½ miles along the south coast, it is a broad sweep of fine white sand with *Rendezvous Bay Hotel* (see p134) at one end and Bankie Banx' Dune Preserve at the other. There is very little in between apart from a couple of hotels and it is quiet with not much in the way of watersports. You get a good view of St-Martin and all the boats going between the two islands.

Mead's Bay
Map 7, C1, p284

Mead's Bay is popular, with a couple of small bars, top-class hotels and watersports, but there is plenty of room to stroll along the bay. The sand is powder soft and almost white. A controversial **dolphin lagoon** has been built here, stocked with dolphins from Cuba, allegedly caught in the wild, which have been trained and are giving performances. Conservationists have protested against keeping dolphins in captivity for the amusement of tourists. For information, contact the *Whale and Dolphin Conservation Society*, Alexander House, James St West, Bath, BA1 2BT, www.wdcs.org.

Heritage Collection Museum
Pond Site, East End, **T** 264-2357440. *Mon-Sat 1000-1700. US$5, children under 12 US$3. In the northeast.* Map 7, B5, p284

A local historian, Mr Colville Petty OBE, collects traditional household artefacts and nostalgic old photos. Boat building, fishing, salt raking and house building are all documented as a vivid reminder of how hard life used to be and the innovation of local people. The 1967 Anguilla Revolution and its leaders are also preserved for posterity with newspaper cuttings and photos. Until then, when Anguilla was under the jurisdiction of St Kitts, there were no paved roads, no electricity, no piped water, no phones and no proper education or health care. Most young people with any ambition left the island to seek employment elsewhere. A breakaway movement was led by Ronald Webster of the People's Progressive Party (PPP). In 1969 British forces invaded the island to install a British Commissioner after negotiations had broken down. The episode is remembered locally for the unusual presence of the London Metropolitan Police, who remained until 1972 when the Anguilla Police Force was established. There are several photos preserving the image of the British Bobby on the beach.

Shoal Bay
Map 7, A4, p284

Beautiful Shoal Bay is the most popular beach and very busy at weekends: island bands play here on Sundays until the evening. There are villas, guesthouses, casual restaurants and beach bars (*Uncle Ernie's* has the cheapest drinks) for lunch and dinner. The snorkelling is good, with the closer of two reefs only 10 m from the shore. You can rent snorkelling and other watersports equipment, and lockers, beach umbrellas, loungers, rafts and towels. There may even be someone to sell you live lobster. Northeast of The Valley, by Shoal Village, is **The Fountain national park**, closed at present. Its focus is a cave which has constant fresh water and Amerindian petroglyphs. Artefacts have been found and it is hoped they will be housed in a museum at the site. Anguilla awaits detailed archaeological investigation, but it is thought that the island had several settlements and a social structure of some importance, judging by the ceremonial items which have been found. **Big Spring Cave** is an old Amerindian ceremonial centre where you can see petroglyphs. It is near Island Harbour, a fishing village with Irish ancestry.

Scilly Cay/Island Harbour
Map 7, A5, p284

Scilly Cay is a small cay off Island Harbour with good snorkelling. Chartered yachts and motor boats leave from Road Bay or from Island Harbour for Scilly Cay, privately owned by Eudoxie and Sandra Wallace and also named *Gorgeous Scilly Cay*. They have their own boat with a free ferry service, which takes you to the bar (*1000-1700*) on a palm-fringed beach where walls are made from conch shells – a good place to come for lunch, see p198. *Smitty's Bar*, across the water at Island Harbour, is less sophisticated, with tables made from old cable barrels, TV and a pool room, popular

Natural Anguilla

Although you will see colourful gardens, the island appears mostly covered with scrub. Nevertheless, there are 523 recorded species of flora, of which around 60% are native and the rest naturalized but introduced. The **north coast** has the most unspoilt open areas which have not been cultivated or built on. There are steep cliffs of over 100 ft high, with caves and sink holes, and inland are areas of dense vegetation. The most common plants are the white cedar, pigeonwood, manchineel, frangipani, five-finger trees, bromeliads and cacti.

In this area you can find lizards, iguanas, snakes, bats and birds. The tiny ground lizard (*Ameiva pleei*) is endemic to Anguilla and you can often see their ribbon-like trails in the sand on the dunes and along the pond shores.

Katouche Valley has a beach, a mangrove pond and a forest where you can find orchids and bromeliads and some patches of bamboo among the pepper cinnamon, mawby, sherry and turpentine trees. The valley ends at **Cavannagh Cave**, which was mined for phosphorous in the 19th century, but now is home to bats, birds, crabs and lizards. Birdwatching is good at **Little Bay**, Crocus Bay's north point, and at the many ponds and coves. Anguilla has 136 recorded species of bird, including the blue-faced booby, kingfisher and the great blue heron. The national bird is the turtle dove.

with the locals. Seafood comes straight off the boats. Beach chairs and umbrellas are complimentary and snorkelling is good just off the beach. **Captain's Bay**, northeast of Island Harbour, is rougher but the scenery is dramatic and not many people go there. The dirt road is full of potholes and goats, and may be impassable with a low car.

Saba

This tiny Dutch island, Saba, pronounced 'Say-bah', shoots out of the sea, green and lush, with no beaches, only cliffs. Diving and hiking are the attractions here, a destination for the fit and active. It is the smallest of the three Netherlands Antilles in the Leewards group, and despite some development it is still deserving of its official title, the 'Unspoiled Queen'. An extinct volcano, its peak is aptly named Mount Scenery. Neat and tidy villages cling to hillsides and picture-book cottages perch on any vaguely flat land. Underwater, the landscape is equally spectacular and divers treasure the marine park, noted for its 'virginity'. When not under water, visitors find walking rewarding. Ancient trails weave their way around the island, the most stunning being the 1,064 irregular steps up Mount Scenery through different types of tropical vegetation according to altitude. Lodging is in small, friendly hotels, guesthouses and cottages, where you won't need a key – there is no crime.

There are four picture-book villages on Saba, connected by a single spectacular 10½ km road which begins at the airport and ends at the pier. The road itself is a feat of engineering, designed and built in the 1940s by Josephus Lambert Hassell (1906-83), who studied road construction by correspondence course after Dutch engineers said it was impossible to build a road on Saba.

▸▸ *See Sleeping p136, Eating and drinking p173, Sports p228 , p239*

Sights

Juancho E Yrausquin Airport
Map 8, E5, p284

Saba's airport is famed for having the shortest runway in commercial use in the world, 478 m (1,312 ft) long and 47 m (130 ft) above sea level. It is built at Flat Point, rightly named for being the only flat part of the island, with steep cliffs dropping down to the sea at both ends. Only Twin-Otter, 19-seater, short take-off and landing aircraft can land here. A French pilot, Remy F de Haenen, who had previously used seaplanes, landed a single-engine plane in 1959 watched by most of the population who had previously cleared the area of rocks and stones. Regular air services from Sint Maarten began in 1963 and a connecting road was built to Hell's Gate. There are lots of photos showing the arrival of the first plane.

Also on display in the airport is a replica of a pre-Columbian snuff inhaler (the original is on loan in the Netherlands). A Dutch archaeologist found it during excavations in 1988-92 on Kelbey's Ridge near the airport. It is carved from manatee bone in the shape of a large-headed fish with its mouth open. Shamans or political leaders would inhale their hallucinogenic powders by placing two bones into the gills of the fish, dipping the fish mouth into a shallow dish spread with the finely ground snuff, then inserting the bones, like straws, into the nostrils. It is believed that they snorted the ground seeds of the spineless cohoba shrub, *Adadenathera peregrine*, which is still used by shamans in the Amazon basin.

Windwardside
Map 8, G4, p284

From the airport, the road rises to Hell's Gate and then on past tiny vegetable plots on any patch of level land which can be cleared of rocks up to Windwardside, where most of the hotels and shops are situated. There is a small museum, a bank and post office. **Lambee's Place**, originally the home of Josephus Lambert Hassell, has been redeveloped into a little shopping precinct and now houses *Sea Saba Dive Shop*, *Peanut Art Gallery*, *El Momo Folk Art* and *Y2K Café* (bakery, bar and grill).

All the houses on the island are painted white with red roofs and most have green outlines on the shutters. Heleen Cornet's book, *Saban Cottages* (1994), gives watercolour portraits and information on some interesting houses. A walk around Windwardside will give you a good idea of their traditional way of life, the houses walled in with a small garden, neatly tended, and the family burial plot in the yard. A pleasant lookout point is from Booby Hill, up the 66 terraced steps to the **Booby Hill Peak** above Windwardside.

Harry Luke Johnson Museum
Mon-Fri 1000-1200, 1300-1600. US$2. Map 8, G3, p284
This was once a sea captain's house, built around 1840, a typical, tiny, four-room Saban house on one floor. Harry Luke Johnson (1914-72) started Saba's first museum in 1970 with his own personal collection and paintings. When he died he requested that a larger setting be found for a national museum and this property was purchased for that purpose. It is now filled with antique furniture and memorabilia donated by local families, including a wonderful antique Saba lace christening gown. The kitchen is in its original state with old cooking implements and an oven built into the stone hearth. There are a few Amerindian relics, but most of the best pieces are now in the Netherlands. Croquet is played on Sunday afternoon in the museum grounds.

Mount Scenery
Register at the Saba Trail Shop in Windwardside, **T** 599-4162630. *Tue-Fri 0930-1530, Sat-Sun 1000-1400. US$3 fee for park maintenance, you receive a disk entitling you to hike on any trail. US$1 for hire of walking stick, recommended. In places a guide is recommended as interpretative and directional signs are variable because of weather damage. Map 8, G3, p284 See also p239*

Before the road was built people got about Saba by donkey or on foot, and there are still numerous steep trails and stone steps linking villages which make strenuous, yet satisfying, walking. The *Saba Conservation Foundation* (SCF) preserves and marks trails. All of them are accessible from the road and many can be done without a guide. However, they are all on private land and you are requested not to stray off the tracks. The most spectacular hike is probably the one from Windwardside up 1,064 steps of varying sizes and intervals to the crest of Mount Scenery, best done on a clear day otherwise you end up in the clouds. It is a hard slog, 1½ hours each way at least, unless you cut out the first third by driving along the Mountain Road above the village. The summit has now been cleared (Cable & Wireless have built a telecommunications tower there by helicopter drops) and there is a spectacular view down to Windwardside and the surrounding isles if it is not cloudy. There are lots of birds, lizards, snakes and land crabs, and the botanical changes are noticeable as you climb.

There is also a five-hour walk through a variety of ecosystems (see Saba's flora and fauna, p78) circling Mount Scenery. Starting from Windwardside, walk up the road to Upper Hell's Gate, then take the **Sandy Cruz trail**. This wanders through rainforest on the northern slopes of Mount Scenery, where you can see yellow heliconia (*Heliconia bihai*), tree ferns, giant elephant ears (*Philodendron giganteum*) and orchids, with several viewpoints down to the sea. There are lots of birds, butterflies, frogs, lizards and snakes sunning themselves on rocks. Proceed on the Sandy Cruz trail extension to Troy Hill, where you meet the road which takes you to The Bottom. A short walk up the road out of The Bottom towards Windwardside brings you to the start of the **Crispeen Track**, which is followed back to Windwardside.

For the **Sulphur Mine** take the Sandy Cruz trail. Walk for about 20 minutes until you get to a sign for a turning to the right on the **All Too Far trail** leading down to the remains of the old mines and the cliffs of the north coast, with splendid scenery. There is a shorter route starting in Lower Hell's Gate following part of the **North Coast trail**. In 1988 all the land formerly owned by the Sulphur Mining Company was donated to the SCF on condition that it should be a national park and remain wild. The land was

bought by the company in 1875, but mining was discontinued as unprofitable in 1915. The **Saba National Park** covers 43 ha (100 acres) stretching from the edge of the airport, west along the north coast to the sulphur mines and up almost to the peak of Mount Scenery through several ecosystems. It is possible to carry on along the North Coast trail to Mary's Point and Wells Bay. However, the SCF does not recommend you go far along this old path as several people have got lost – best to take a guide. There are magnificent views of the northern coastal cliffs, but there is a danger of rock falls set off by feral goats which may be above you.

● *Mount Scenery, at 887 m, is the highest point in all the Netherlands, while Willards of Saba is the highest hotel.*

The Bottom
Map 8, H2, p284

The road goes on past Kate's Hill, Peter Simon's Hill and Big Rendezvous to St John's, where the schools are perched on a cliff top, and which has a wonderful view of Sint Eustatius, then climbs over the mountain and drops sharply down to The Bottom, the island's seat of government. The Bottom is on a plateau, 245 m above the sea. It can be hot as there is little breeze. The **Medical University** trains postgraduate students from abroad, who study here for about two years and swell the local population by 300, or around 25 %. The **Governor's House** is a modern replica of a traditional Saban two-storey house, built in 1972 in the same style as the wooden house which preceded it. The **Wilhelmina Park** alongside was designed by Lt Gov Willem F M Lampe in the 1930s for musical events, discontinued after his term of office.

The **Sacred Heart Roman Catholic Church**, built in 1935, is the third on this site, the earliest being in 1877. It is notable for the magnificent mural painted around the altar by Heleen Cornet. It is a very cheerful Adoration scene, the bright sun above the altar, and Mary and Jesus surrounded by local plants, architecture and the portraits of local children depicted as happy, multi-ethnic cherubs.

▶ **Natural Saba**

Vegetation on Saba changes according to altitude, and a walk up Mount Scenery is a sightseeing highlight for the many different types of tropical vegetation. At an altitude of 490-610 m there is **secondary rainforest** with trees of between 5 and 10 m tall. Further up there are **tree ferns** of 4-5 m, then **palm trees**, then at 825 m the **cloud forest** begins (known as Elfin forest), where you find the **mountain mahogany tree** (*Freziera undulata*). Since Hurricane Lenny, however, the forest remains only in protected pockets. Wildlife on the island is limited to: the endemic **anole lizard** (*Aanolis sabanus*, widespread); **iguanas** (the green iguana, *Iguana iguana*, the island's largest, can be seen sunbathing on Old Booby Hill in the afternoon); a harmless **red-bellied racer snake** (*Alsophis rufiventris*) can be seen on the Sandy Cruz and Mary's Point trails if you are quiet); and over **60 species of bird** have been recorded, with many migratory birds coming to nest here. The **trembler** and the **purple-throated hummingbird** can be seen in the Elfin forest and the Sandy Cruz rainforest, where you can also find the **wood hen**.

The Saba Conservation Foundation (SCF), PO Box 501, Windwardside, Saba, T/F 599-4162709, preserves the environment on land and underwater, developing protected areas, maintaining trails and promoting nature conservation.

The cobblestone street outside was left as it is at the request of the Queen. Nearly all others have been covered with concrete. The **Wesleyan Holiness Church**, built in 1919, is currently being restored after hurricane damage. It used to be one of the prettiest on the island with graceful white fretwork and efforts are being made to return it to its former grandeur.

Fort Bay
Map 8, J2 , p284

Leaving The Bottom, the road makes its final descent to Fort Bay, where small cruise ships, yachts and the ferry from St Maarten arrive at the 85-m pier, built in 1972. At the top the road is lined with flamboyant trees in a range of different shades of scarlet and orange. As you descend, the landscape becomes more arid and the population of goats increases dramatically. Work began on the cement road from Fort Bay to The Bottom in 1938; in 1947 the first automobile arrived and in 1951 the road was extended to St John's and Windwardside. Extensive work is being done at the port to repair storm damage, with funding from the Netherlands for the protection of the dock. All the **dive shops** are here and there are a couple of bars and the **Marine Conservation Office**.

Ladder Bay
Map 8, G1, p284

Before the construction of the port at Fort Bay, Ladder Bay was the main port of entry for commercial shipping. However, there was no road and everything had to be carried up 400 steps by donkey or on people's heads. Even a grand piano came up this way, as did all furniture and goods bought overseas. The steps still survive and you can walk down them from The Bottom.

Wells Bay
Map 8, F1, p284

A road continues up the west side of the island with excellent views of Diamond Rock to Wells Bay, where Saba's only **beach** can be found. Diving is excellent here and there are moorings so that yachts can tie up without anchor damage to the reef. The bay is also good for snorkelling. **Torrens Point** at the end of the bay has a cave you can snorkel through. The bay is surrounded by huge cliffs and is very dramatic with black sand on the beach. Sometimes, however, storms sweep away the sand leaving only rocks on the shore. The cliffs are not stable and are constantly eroding. A village on top of the hill at Mary's Point was evacuated in 1934 when the cliffs started to collapse and everyone was relocated to an area known as the Promised Land adjoining The Bottom. Houses were moved piece by piece and floated round the coast on boats, bringing them up the Ladder to be reassembled.

Sint Eustatius

Very few tourists make the effort to visit this Dutch outpost, but Sint Eustatius has a rich colonial history and a prosperous past. Having made its fortune in the 18th century out of the slave trade and commerce in plantation crops, it lost it in the 19th century with the abolition of slavery and has never really recovered. The main town, Oranjestad, still has the fortifications and remains of warehouses from its heyday, when around 3,500 ships used to visit each year and the island was known as the Golden Rock. This is an off-the-beaten-track destination, a little scruffy but worthy of investigation, particularly by divers. There are walking trails up into the rainforest of the extinct volcano, the Quill, and diving is good in the marine park.

The name 'Statia' comes from St Anastasia, as it was named by Columbus, but the Dutch later changed it to Sint Eustatius. Unofficially it is known as 'the historic gem'. Statia is the poorest of the three Dutch islands, with only 2,100 people living on the 30.6 sq-km island. A variety of nationalities are represented, the island having changed hands 22 times in the past, but the majority are of black African descent. Everybody speaks English, although Dutch is the official language and is taught in schools.

▸▸ See Sleeping p139, Eating and drinking p175, Sports p229

Sights

Oranjestad
Map 10, p285

Oranjestad is the capital, set on a cliff overlooking the long bay below and divided between Upper Town and Lower Town. It is possible to walk round the village and see the sights of Upper Town in a morning. The museum or tourist office will provide you with a *Walking Tour* brochure listing the historical sites. Many private houses have been or are being restored to their former glory as part of the Historic Core Development Plan, but with modern conveniences such as glass windows, bathrooms, kitchens and even air conditioning, under a scheme by which the owner pays 10% of the cost and the government funds the balance. This is improving the look of the historical core and some houses may soon be used as tourist rental homes. The rest of the town is still scruffy, littered and unattractive, although on the very outskirts some smart new houses have been built.

Fort Oranje
Map 10, C/D6, p285 The town used to be defended by Fort Oranje (pronounced Orahn'ya) perched on a rocky bluff. Built by the Dutch when they arrived in 1636, on the site of a 1629 French fortification, the preserved ruins of the fort have now been restored following a fire in 1990, and large black cannon still point out to sea. Cannon were rarely fired from here, for fear of the cliffs disintegrating. Some administrative buildings of the island's government are here including the tourist office. You can see the old prison cells and walk around the battlements for a good view of the harbour below.

The island still celebrates 16 November 1776 when the cannon of Fort Oranje unknowingly fired the first official salute by a foreign nation to the American colours. At that time, Statia was a major trans-shipment point for arms and supplies to George Washington's troops. The arms were stored in the yellow ballast brick warehouses built all along the Bay and then taken by blockade runners to Boston, New York and Charleston. However, the salute brought retaliatory action from the English, and in 1781 the port was taken without a shot being fired by troops under Admiral George Brydges Rodney, who captured 150 merchant ships and £5 million of booty before being expelled by the French the following year.

Sint Eustatius Historical Foundation Museum

Wilhelminaweg, **T** 599-3182288. *Mon-Fri 0900-1700, Sat, Sun and holidays 0900-1200. US$2, children US$1. Map 10, C6, p285* The 18th-century Doncker/De Graaff House, once a private merchant's house and also where Admiral Rodney lived, has been restored as a museum. On the ground floor and upstairs is a reconstruction of 18th-century rooms at the height of Statia's prosperity. It is worth a visit for the graphic descriptions of the slave trade. There is a pre-Columbian section in the basement which includes an Amerindian skeleton. Archaeological excavations at Golden Rock near the airport have uncovered a large Amerindian village with the only complete floor plan of Indian houses found in the Caribbean. All the houses are round or slightly oval, vary in size and accommodate up to 30 people. Large timbers up to 8 m high were set in deep holes for the framework of the biggest houses. The museum contains pottery buried in the ceremonial area of the village next to a grave. The curator normally explains the history of the exhibits.

Honen Dalim Synagogue

Breedeweg, *Map 10, C7, p285* Other places of historical interest include the ruins of this synagogue built in 1739 and the nearby cemetery. Statia once had a flourishing Jewish community and was a refuge for Sephardic and Ashkenazi Jews, but with the economic decline after the sacking of Oranjestad by Admiral Rodney, most of the Jewish congregation left. The walls of the synagogue have been restored with yellow bricks imported from Holland just like the originals, which came over as ballast in the ships. However, the upper floor used as the women's gallery and the roof have not yet been replaced.

Dutch Reformed Church
Kerkweg, *Map 10, D6, p285* The church, consecrated in 1755, suffered a similar fate to the synagogue when its congregation fled. The square tower has been restored but the walls are open to the elements. Weddings and events are held here in the open air. Legend has it that Admiral Rodney found most of his booty after noticing that there were a surprising number of funerals for such a small population. A coffin, which he ordered to be opened, was found to be full of valuables and further digging revealed much more.

Lower Town
In its heyday Lower Town stretched for 3 km along the bay, with warehouses, taverns and slave markets attracting commercial traffic. The ruins are still visible along the shore line, where they collapsed into the sea. There is not much of a beach since storms removed the sand, but at one end a small patch has returned and it is hoped that further swells will bring in more black sand. Being on the leeward side of the island it is safe for swimming. If you like beachcombing, blue, five-sided slave beads over 200 years old can occasionally be found along the shore. The port is at one end of the bay and STENAPA, the three main hotels, dive shops and a restaurant are also on the waterfront. Lower Town and Upper Town are linked by a road but also by an old slave road, a mixture of cobblestones and concrete for pedestrian use only.

Berkels Family Museum
Lynch Plantation, **T** 599-3182338. *Map 9, D3, p285*

The Berkels family museum is a collection of household utensils
and antiques housed in two wooden replica buildings on the
Lynch Plantation. One is a replica of the original family home,
about the size of a garden shed although it is referred to as the
plantation house, and the other is a replica of the three-room
house in town, recently restored and renovated. It is kept exactly as
Mr Berkels' mother had it, with the family photos displayed on the
walls. They were a numerous family and it is a wonder they all
fitted in the house. You can see the original house in town, on the
corner close to where the old slave road descends to Lower Town.

Windward beaches
Map 9, p285

On the Windward side are two fine beaches, but there is a strong
undertow and they are not considered safe for swimming.
Zeelandia Beach is 3 km of off-white sand with heavy surf and
interesting beachcombing, particularly after a storm. It is safe to
wade and splash about in the surf but not to swim. **Lynch Beach**,
also on the Atlantic side, is small and safer for children in parts, but
ask local advice.

Miriam C Schmidt Botanical Garden
STENAPA, **T** 599-3182884. *Mon-Fri 0700-1200, weekends if anyone
is there. On the southeast side of The Quill. Map 9, F4, p285*

STENAPA is developing the 5.6-ha gardens in the area called
'Behind the Mountain'. Still in its initial phase, the aim is to make
the gardens educational, for the benefit of local children, and they
will eventually include an ecolodge. So far a sensory garden has
been built and a nursery is being developed for future planting.

The Quill

The tourist office has a guide leaflet describing 11 trails. Quill hikes with local guides are available with a voucher system from the tourist office or participating hotels. Some of these trails are in bad condition, overgrown and sometimes difficult to follow. Map 9, F3, p285

STENAPA, the St Eustatius National Parks Foundation, was founded in 1996 and is responsible for the marine park, The Quill, Boven, Gilboa Hill, Signal Hill, Little Mountain and the Botanical Garden (above). In 1998 The Quill was declared a national park, consisting of the volcano and the limestone **White Wall** to its south, a massive slab of limestone which was once pushed out of the sea by volcanic forces and is now clearly visible from miles away across the sea. The Quill is protected above 250 m, but the White Wall is protected down to the high water line. Dutch settlers first called it *Kuil*, meaning pit or hole, but later English settlers dubbed it Quill. At the crater of The Quill are many species usually found in tropical rainforest: huge tree ferns, mahogany, giant elephant ears, figs, begonias, plantains, bromeliads, the balsam tree and more. The Quill's southern slope has not been fully explored by botanists.

STENAPA has built a clearly marked trail from Rosemary Lane to the rainforest crater at the top of The Quill, which is remarkable for its contrast with the dry scrub of the rest of the island. After about 20 minutes' walk there is a left turn to The Quill. Carry on if you want to overlook the White Wall. The walk up to the lip of the crater is easy but you will need walking boots or good trainers. You will see butterflies, lizards, hundreds of hermit crabs and, if you go quietly, the red-bellied racer snake. At the top in one direction is the panorama trail. The other direction leads to the highest point, called **Mazinga**, which affords a magnificent view. The first 10 minutes of the walk to the Mazinga is easy, then there is a turn to the left marked where it becomes a scramble because of hurricane damage. The last 20 m up to the summit is only for the very experienced. Plant life in the crater includes mahogany and

Natural Statia

Despite the small size of the island, in the 17th and 18th centuries there were more than 70 plantations, worked intensively by slaves. As a result, most of the original forest has disappeared except on the most inhospitable parts of the volcano. Nevertheless there are 15 different kinds of **orchid** and 54 species of **bird**, of which 25 are resident and breeding, 21 migrants from North America and 12 species of seabirds. There are iguanas, land crabs, tree frogs and lots of butterflies. Unfortunately there are lots of goats too, which eat everything in sight. The **Antilles iguana** (*Iguana delicatissima*) is rare and threatened and has now been protected by law. It lives mostly in the northern hills such as Boven. The young and females vary from bright green to dull grey, while the large males can be nearly black. The population is stronger on Sint Eustatius than on neighbouring islands because the mongoose was never introduced here. Neither was the green iguana, with which it has interbred on some islands. The **red-bellied racer** (*Alsophis rufiventris*) is a small snake found only on Statia and Saba. It is brown with black markings on its back and a pink belly. It is not poisonous and kills its prey (small reptiles and baby rats) by strangulation.

breadfruit trees, arums, bromeliads, lianas and orchids. From the rim, hikers can scramble down a poor path. The vegetation is dense, forming the breeding ground for land crabs, which Statians catch at night. Their camp and litter is an eyesore. A local guide is recommended as once you are in the crater it is difficult to get your bearings. The new trail to the **Boven**, the highest peak on the north side of the island, is a strenuous, steep, four-hour hike (round trip) but well worth it for the view.

St-Barthélemy

Saint-Barthélemy, also known as St-Barth or St-Barts, a piece of France picked up and put down in the tropics, has a well-deserved reputation as a holiday heaven for the rich and famous. Pop stars and film stars have been seen here, but mostly they hide away in their luxury villas or exclusive hotels where management understands the meaning of privacy. Gourmet French restaurants, Creole bistros and chic designer boutiques all enhance the image of expensive indulgence, but in fact prices are no higher than in France, and that includes the wine. It is a beautiful island of only 24 sq km, with rugged volcanic hills and 22 splendid white sandy beaches, most of which are protected by both cliff and reef.

St-Barth is attached administratively to the Département de Guadeloupe and is administered by the sub-prefect in St-Martin who resides here two to three days a week. The island has its own mayor, who is elected for a six-year term of office.

▸▸ *See Sleeping p140, Eating and drinking p176, Nightlife p201*

 Sights

Gustavia
Map 12, p286

For most of its colonial history, St-Barth was French, but between 1784 and 1878 it belonged to Sweden, traded by France in return for shipping rights in Göteburg. In 1852 a fire severely damaged the capital, although the Swedish influence is still evidenced in the city hall, the belfries, the forts (Karl, Oscar and Gustave), the street names and the trim stone houses which line the harbour. The **harbour**, or Carénage, was renamed Gustavia after the 18th-century Swedish king, Gustavus III. Today, however, the atmosphere is thoroughly French. Since the 1980s a huge amount of restoration and rebuilding has taken place to enhance the

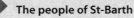

▶ The people of St-Barth

St-Barth is inhabited mostly by people of Breton, Norman, and Poitevin descent who live in quiet harmony with the small percentage of blacks. Norman dialect is still widely spoken, while many islanders also speak English, but French is the dominant language. A few elderly women still wear traditional costumes (with their characteristic starched white bonnets called *kichnottes*); they cultivate sweet potato patches despite the dry, rocky soil, also weaving palm fronds into hats and bags which they sell in the village of Corossol. The men traditionally smuggled rum among neighbouring islands and now import liqueurs and perfumes, raise a few cattle, and fish for lobsters offshore. Immigrants from France have taken most of the best jobs in hotels and restaurants though and relations there are sometimes strained. Twice as many tourists as the island's population pass through each month. St-Barth has become a very chic and expensive holiday destination; the Rockefellers and Rothschilds own property on the island, while the rich, royal and famous stay in the luxury villas dotted around the island.

harbour and make it a tourist attraction. There are branches of several well-known French and other designer shops (such as *Cartier, Hermès, Armani, Louis Vuitton*). The small crowd of town habitués is mostly young, chic and French. The food, wine and aromas are equally Gallic. The town is a **free port** and the harbour is always full of yachts of all sizes, ferries and cargo ships berthed a little further out. It is a delightful town, very pretty and very clean, as is the whole island, thanks to daily collections of rubbish. The tourist office has a leaflet for a **walking tour** of the main stone buildings dating from the Swedish period and other attractions.

In the southeast corner of the harbour by the promenade is a truly massive **anchor**. Probably from a British Royal Navy frigate, and dating from the late 18th century, it weighs 10 tonnes. Marked 'Liverpool...Wood...London', it came to Gustavia by curious means in 1981. The cable of a tug towing a barge across from St Thomas fouled on something at the entrance of the harbour. A man dived down to have a look and found the anchor. It is thought that the cable dragged it up as the tug left St Thomas and, suspended below water, it got carried across. Opposite the anchor is **St Bartholomew's Anglican Church**, in a prime position overlooking the harbour. It dates from 1855 and is of simple construction with shuttered windows. The walls are of local stone, but the bricks for the steps came from France and the dark lava corner stones came from Sint Eustatius. Round the corner and up rue Gambetta is a stone **bell tower** of an old Lutheran church destroyed by a hurricane. The bell is named after a Swedish princess, Sofia Madgalena, and was cast in 1799 in Stockholm. It was used for celebrations, to announce the death of local citizens and to ring the curfew (2000) until the 1920s. In 1930 a clock was added to take the place of children, who tolled the bell at sunrise and sunset. The Roman Catholic Church, **Notre Dame de L'Assomption**, was built in 1822, destroyed in 1837 and rebuilt in 1842, unusually of Hispanic design rather than French or Swedish. Its bell tower is higher up the hill to allow the sound to carry further and prevent damage if the bells should fall during a hurricane.

Anse des Grands Galets, in Gustavia, three or four minutes' walk from the harbour front, is also known as Shell Beach. It is a small bay, with cliffs and rocks at either end and patches of pink shells washed up on the sand. Swimming is safe although the sand shelves quite steeply in the water and it is good for snorkelling. There is a beach bar here, *Dō Brazil*, and boulders among which you can settle yourself for the day, but no shade.

St-Barth's Municipal Museum

La Pointe, **T** 590-(0)590-297155. *Mon 1430-1800, Tue-Fri 0830-1230, 1430-1800, Sat 0900-1300. €2. On the western side of the harbour entrance. Map 12, A6, p286* The museum has a fair cross-section of historical material including clothing, household items, fishing tools and Amerindian archaeological finds, old photos and models of traditional houses. However, the items are not well labelled and there is little method in the displays. The museum is located on the ground floor of the **Wall House** which is believed to date from the end of the 18th century. In ruins, it was restored using traditional techniques with materials imported from St Kitts and completed in 1995. Upstairs is a library and outside, at the back, an old baker's oven. The square outside on the waterfront was named Place Vanadis in 1996 after the last Swedish military vessel to leave the harbour when France repossessed the island in 1878. Sweden donated a trident and a sundial for the square.

St-Jean
Map 11, D2, p286

The main resort area is Baie de St-Jean. There are several small and medium-sized hotels here, many restaurants, bars, shopping plazas and other entertainment, strung along the coast. It is also very close to the airport runway and if you walk along the beach you may feel you need to duck when the small planes come over. The large bay is divided by Eden Rock, upon which is a luxury hotel (under renovation 2004). The sand extends quite a way out but the beach is protected by a shallow reef and swimming is safe, ideal for families. It is breezy, making it good for **windsurfing**. Motorized watersports are only allowed 300 m off the beach.

> **!** Called *Ouanalao* by the Caribs, the island was renamed in honour of Christopher Columbus' brother after he spotted it in November 1496.

Lorient
Map 11, D3, p286

Another large and popular bay, although quieter than St-Jean, there are a couple of paths down to the beach in between the villas along the shoreline. The left side of the beach as you look at the sea is good for **surfing**, although be careful of the rocks at the water's edge as you enter and leave the waves. The right side is fine for **swimming** and there are picturesque fishing boats at anchor. There is no shade except under the trees hanging over from someone's garden. The **village** is pleasant, with a couple of good supermarkets stocked with French cheeses and delicacies. In the centre is a very pretty cemetery, the graves all picked out with white wooden crosses and white picket fencing, decorated with flowers. Above the cemetery is the Roman Catholic Church, **Eglise de Notre Dame de L'Assomption**. Founded in 1724, it was burned by pirates and reconstructed in 1820 with the help of the Swedish government. Restored after subsequent earthquake damage, it has the appearance of a large stone barn with wooden rafters, a semicircular altar where there are two modern stained-glass windows and a separate square bell tower alongside.

● *The name Lorient has nothing to do with the orient. It is a corruption of Quartiers d'Orléans, the old administrative name.*

Marigot
For the Réserve Naturelle, contact the harbour front office in Gustavia, T 590-(0)590-278818, www.reserve-naturelle-stbarthelemy.com. The tourist office distributes leaflets with a map. Map 11, C4, p286

A small bay with crystal-clear water of many colours and a rocky beach with small patches of sand and outcrops of rocks, this is a good beach for snorkelling. It is in the high protection area of the marine reserve, so no fishing, motorized watersports or scuba diving are allowed and it is very quiet.

Grand Cul de Sac
Map 11, C5, p286

This bay is so protected from the sea by the peninsula and reef that it is almost like a lagoon, with very tranquil, shallow water in a variety of blues and greens with patches of rocks and weed as well as sand. Although it is in the **marine reserve**, Réserve Naturelle, mooring with buoys is allowed and the beach is fringed with small craft at anchor, used by pelicans as launching pads for fishing activities. **Windsurfing, kitesurfing** and other non-motorized watersports are available at the *St Barth Beach Hotel* and there is a dive shop on the road leading to the beach. For surfing you have to paddle right out to the reef to find any waves. There is a nice beach bar, *Cocoloba*, with shade under the sea grape (cocoloba) trees, but there is no other shade unless you are a guest at one of the hotels.

Petit Cul de Sac
Map 11, C5, p286

Hardly anyone comes here other than local families at weekends for picnics. There are a few villas around the bay but it is very quiet and calm. The sea is protected by cliffs and a reef at the mouth of the horseshoe shaped bay. There is plenty of sand for sunbathing on, but no shade. There are rocks at the waterline but sandy patches once you get into the water. No fishing, diving or mooring is allowed as it is in the nursery zone of the Réserve Naturelle.

Anse de Toiny/Anse du Grand Fond
Map 11, E4/5, p286

Anse de Toiny and Anse du Grand Fond are on the Atlantic side of the island and unprotected from the currents. Swimming is not advised here, although **surfing** is popular. This is a wild, rugged part of the island, with rocky mountains tumbling into the sea and bracing winds coming off the ocean. Beachcombing is rewarding and a walk along the beach will make you feel you've had plenty of exercise. The luxury hotel, *Le Toiny*, is on the hillside overlooking the beach of the same name, otherwise this area has a few villas.

Anse de Grande Saline
Map 11, E3/4, p286

Park your car at the end of the road and walk down the rocky and sandy path to the wide expanse of beach with beautiful white sand. Backed by sand dunes and protected by cliffs and rocks at either end, this is one of the **most beautiful beaches** in St-Barth, if not the Caribbean. There is no shade and nothing on the beach apart from a few sunbathers. Behind the beach is the salt pond, from which the area gets its name, and here there are three restaurants where you can get lunch and/or dinner.

Gouverneur
From Gustavia take the road to Lurin, a high point on the island marked by a satellite mast. Map 11, E3, p286

A sign will direct you to the very steep road leading down to the beach, with a lovely panoramic view over to the neighbouring islands and parking at the end of the road. There is soft, pale golden sand and very few rocks at the water's edge, although there are cliffs at either end to give interest to the view and good snorkelling. The beach shelves steeply into the sea and the water deepens quickly. Only one large sea grape tree provides any shade and is usually occupied by picnicking local families who knew they had to get there early. There are a few villas at sea level and up on the hill to catch the breeze, but the bay is quiet and undeveloped.

● *Legend has it that the 17th-century pirate, Montbars the Exterminator, hid his treasures in a cove at Gouverneur and they have never been found.*

Public
Just outside Gustavia, beyond the commercial docks.
Map 11, D1, p286

Public is a small bay with not much beach. The **sailing school** is here and lots of small craft can be seen flitting about on the water. A pretty Swedish cemetery takes up most of the waterfront, rather than housing, although there is *Maya's* restaurant at one end.

Corossol
Northwest of Gustavia.   Map 11, D1, p286

Corossol is a typical **fishing village** and maintains an air of days gone past. There are many old wooden houses here, mostly neatly kept and brightly painted. There are lots of yachts, dinghies and fishing boats in the bay and tied up along the jetty. The **beach** is small but safe, with tiny children splashing happily at the edge of the water. Car parking is available on the seafront.

If you turn left as you meet the sea, you come to the **Inter Oceans Museum** (**T** 590-(0)590-276297, *Tue-Sun 0900-1230, 1500-1700. €3*), an absorbing private collection of 9,000 seashells, corals and stuffed fish from all around the world. The owner, M Ingenu Magras, is enthusiastic about his collection and will introduce you to the 100,000 species distributed around the oceans of the world, of which some 1,600 species are found in the Caribbean.

Colombier
At the northwestern tip of the island.   Map 11, B0 off the grid, p286

Colombier Beach is one of the most **unspoilt beaches** on the island. It cannot be reached by car but is well worth the 20-30 minutes' walk for the majestic views of the island. There are two trails going down to the beach. One is a steep one down from

Colombier on top of the hill, but a nicer one with spectacular views of all the little islands offshore starts from La Petite Anse just beyond Anse des Flamands. The path is stony and rocky and good shoes are advised, but it is not difficult. You will see wild flowers, butterflies, cactus and lizards scuttling about in the undergrowth while sea birds soar overhead. As you round the headland you will see the beach below you, a pretty stretch of sand with yachts in the bay. The sea is beautifully clear with a full range of colours looking across to St-Martin. There is no shade and no facilities. There are also several day tours by boat from Gustavia.

Anse des Flamands
Northwest coast. Map 11, C1, p286

Flamands beach is of very clean white sand with three hotels and numerous villas. The sea is very changeable, being calm and clear one moment and then rough with lots of surf the next. The bay is not in the marine reserve, so watersports are available.

● *From April to August, female sea turtles come to Colombier, Flamands and Corossol to lay their eggs.*

Anse des Cayes
North of the airport Map 11, C2, p286

One access to the beach is beside the *Manapany* hotel but there is no parking so it is best to leave your car in the village, where there is a small shopping area with grocery and café. There is a fair amount of sand on the beach but also lots of rocks at the water's edge, some of which are quite sharp and house sea anemones, so you have to pick your spot to enter the water. When the wind gets up **surfing** is good. If you turn left on entering the village and follow the signs to Anse des Lézards, you come to the end of the road at a rocky cove where waves crash against the rocks when it is rough. There are a couple of small hotels and lots of villas in the area.

St Kitts and Nevis

The islands of St Kitts (officially named St Christopher) and Nevis are slightly off the beaten track and neither island is overrun with tourists. St Kitts is developing its southern peninsula, where there are light sandy beaches, but most of the island is untouched. Rugged volcanic peaks, forests and old fortresses produce spectacular views.Two miles away, the conical island of Nevis is smaller, quieter and very desirable. While one federation, the sister islands are quite different in atmosphere. St Kitts is more cosmopolitan and lively, particularly for nightlife, while Nevis is tranquil and sedate. Wherever you go on these two small islands there are breathtaking, panoramic views of the sea, mountains, cultivated fields and small villages.

St Kitts

St Kitts is made up of three groups of rugged volcano peaks split by deep ravines and a low-lying peninsula in the southeast where there are salt ponds and fine beaches. The dormant volcano, Mount Liamuiga (1, 156 m, 3,792 ft), pronounced Lie-a-mee-ga) occupies the central part of the island. The mountain was previously named Mount Misery by the British, but has now reverted to its Carib name, meaning 'fertile land'. The foothills of the mountains, particularly in the north, are covered with sugar cane plantations and grassland, while the uncultivated lowland slopes are covered with forest and fruit trees. St Kitts is the last 'sugar island' in the Leewards group, but the industry operates at a loss.

A clockwise route around the island will enable you to see most of the historical sites. A cheap way of touring the island is to take a minibus from Basseterre (Bay Road) to Dieppe Bay Town, then walk to Saddlers (there might be a minibus if you are lucky, but it is only half a mile up the road) where you can get another minibus back to Basseterre along the Atlantic coast. Evidence of sugar cane is everywhere on the comparatively flat, fertile coastal plain. You will drive through large fields of cane and glimpse the narrow-gauge railway used to transport it from the fields. Disused sugar mills are also often seen.

▸▸ *See Sleeping p143, Eating and drinking p179, Nightlife p203*

 Sights

Basseterre
Map 14, p287

The port of Basseterre is the capital and largest town. It was founded some 70 years later in 1727. Earthquakes, hurricanes and finally a disastrous fire destroyed the town in 1867 and consequently its buildings are comparatively modern. There is a complete mishmash of architectural styles from elegant Georgian buildings with arcades, verandas and *jalousies*, mostly in good condition, to hideous 20th-century concrete block houses.

The **Circus**, styled after London's Piccadilly Circus (but looking nothing like it), is the centre of the town. It is busiest on Friday afternoon and comes alive with locals 'liming' (relaxing). The clock tower is a memorial to Thomas Berkely, former president of the General Legislative Council. In recent years, the development of tourism has meant a certain amount of redevelopment in the centre. An old warehouse on the waterfront has been converted into the **Pelican Mall**, a duty-free shopping and recreational complex. It also houses the Ministry of Tourism and a lounge for guests of the *Four Seasons Hotel* in Nevis awaiting transport.

A new cruise ship berth has been built on the waterfront between Bramble Street and College Street in the heart of Basseterre, capable of accommodating the largest ships afloat, together with a sailing and powerboat marina, and berthing facilities for the inter-island ferries.

Kim Collins, the Quiet Man

Market Street is the home of Kim Collins, the sprinter who won the 100 metres in 9.98 seconds at the Commonwealth Games in Manchester in 2002 and again in 10.07 seconds at the World Track and Field Championships in Paris in 2003, putting St Kitts firmly on the map. Although he ran faster in the Olympic Games in Athens in 2004, with a speed of 10.00 seconds, he was beaten into sixth place by a strong US team, with Justin Gatlin winning in 9.85 seconds.

After his Paris triumph, St Kitts honoured him by naming a highway after him, putting his image on a postage stamp, giving him a diplomatic passport and giving him a house worth US$150,000.

Born in 1976 and the sixth of 11 children, he still spends three months of the year in St Kitts, where he is treated as a national hero. The rest of the time he lives in the USA, where he graduated in sociology from Texas Christian University, in Fort Worth.

St George's Church

Cayon St, **T** 869-4652167 at the Rectory. *Map 14, D7, p287*
Head north up Fort Street, turn left at the main thoroughfare (Cayon Street) and you will come to St George's church, set in its own large garden, with a massive, square buttressed tower. The site was originally a Jesuit church, Notre Dame, which was razed to the ground by the English in 1706. Rebuilt four years later and renamed St George's, it suffered damage from hurricanes and earthquakes on several occasions. It, too, was a victim of the 1867 fire. It was rebuilt in 1869 and contains some nice stained-glass windows. There is a fine view of the town from the tower.

Museum of National Culture and Arts

At the south end of Fort St on Bay Rd, **T** 869-4655584. *Mon-Tue, Thu-Fri 0830-1300, 1400-1600, Wed, Sat, 0830-1300. Free. Map 14, F7, p287* On the outside is the imposing façade of the Old Treasury Building, with a dome covering an arched gateway. It has been converted into a museum of national culture and arts, and also houses the St Christopher Heritage Society, which has a small, interesting display of old photographs and artefacts. They work on conservation projects and are grateful for donations.

Independence Square

Map 14, E8, p287 Surrounded now by a low white fence, eight gates let paths converge on a fountain in the middle of this square (it looks like the Union Jack when seen from the air) which was built in 1790. There are gaily painted muses on top of the fountain. Originally designed for slave auctions and council meetings, the square now contains many plants, spacious lawns and lovely old trees. It is surrounded by 18th-century houses and, at its east end, the Roman Catholic **cathedral** with its twin towers. Built in 1927, the Immaculate Conception is surprisingly plain inside. At 10 North Square Street you can visit the very attractive building housing the **Spencer Cameron Art Gallery**. See Rosey Cameron-Smith's paintings and prints of local views and customs, as well as an impressive selection of the work of other artists, **T/F** 869-4651617. On West Independence Square, the impressive Courthouse in the colonial style reflects the original which burnt down in 1867. The **Bank of Nova Scotia** houses interesting paintings of Brimstone Hill by Lt Lees of the Royal Engineers, *c.1783.*

International House Museum

Central , **T** 869-4650542. *Mon-Fri 1000-1700, Sat 1000-1300, Sun 1300-1700. US$5 for visitors, EC$5 for locals. Map14, E6, p287* The museum was designed by Winston Zack Nisbett, a cultural preservationist and friend of the previous owner of the property, Edgar Challenger, a well-known trade unionist and historian, who died in January 2001. Challenger's residence was a gold mine of traditional utensils and equipment used in 1920-40, as well as books on the history of the Federation.

The west coast
Map 13, p287

The west coast is guarded by no less than nine **forts** and the magnificent Brimstone Hill Fortress. Taking the road out of Basseterre, you will pass the sites of seven of them: Fort Thomas, Palmetto Point Fort, Stone Fort, Fort Charles, Charles Fort, Sandy Point Fort and Fig Tree Fort. The remaining two are to the south of Basseterre: Fort Smith and Fort Tyson. Little remains of any of them.

At Old Road Town turn right to visit **Wingfield Estate**, home to *Caribelle Batik*, **T** 869-4656253, www.caribellebatikstkitts.com *Mon-Fri 0830-1600. Map 13, D1, p287* You drive through a sugar mill and the edge of rainforest. Unfortunately, Romney Manor was destroyed by fire in 1995, but the gardens remain with views over the coast and a 350-year-old saman tree. Apart from a well-stocked shop you can watch the artists producing the colourful, attractive material for *Caribelle Batik*. A guide will explain the process.

At the village of **Middle Island**, you will see, on your right and slightly up the hill, the church of St Thomas at the head of an avenue of dead or dying royal palms. Here is buried Sir Thomas Warner who died on 10 March 1648. The raised tomb under a canopy is inscribed 'General of y Caribee'. There is also a bronze plaque with a copy of the inscription inside the church. Other early tombs are of Captain John Pogson (1656) and Sir Charles Payne, 'Major General of Leeward Caribee Islands', who was buried in 1744. The tower, built in 1880, fell during earth tremors in 1974.

Brimstone Hill Fortress National Park

T 869-4652609, www.brimstonehillfortress.org *Daily 0930-1730.
Entrance EC$13 or US$5 for foreigners, EC$2 for nationals, children
half price. Allow up to 2 hrs. Turn right off the coastal road just before
J's Place (drink and local food, open from 1100, the caged green vervet
monkeys are very aggressive). The local minibus from Basseterre to
Brimstone Hill is EC$2.25, then walk up to the fortress, less than 30
mins but extremely steep. Map 13, C1, p287*

Brimstone Hill Fortress was inaugurated as a national park by the
Queen in October 1985 and made a UNESCO World Heritage Site in
October 2000. One of the 'Gibraltars of the West Indies' (a title it
shares with Les Saintes, off Guadeloupe), the fortress sprawls over
38 acres on the slopes of a hill 800 ft above the sea. It commands
an incredible view of St Kitts and Nevis and on clear days, Anguilla
(67 miles), Montserrat (40 miles), Saba (20 miles), Sint Eustatius (5
miles), St-Barts (40 miles) and St-Martin (45 miles) can be seen. The
English mounted the first cannon on Brimstone Hill in 1690 in an
attempt to force the French from Fort Charles below and the
fortress was not abandoned until 1852. It has been constructed
mainly out of local volcanic stones and was designed along classic
defensive lines. The five bastions overlook each other and also
guard the only road as it zigzags up to the parade ground. The
entrance is at the Barrier Redan where payment is made. Pass the
Magazine Bastion but stop at the **Orillon Bastion** which contains
the massive ordnance store (165 ft long with walls at least 6 ft
thick). The hospital was located here and under the south wall is a
small cemetery. You then arrive at the **Prince of Wales Bastion**
(note the name of J Sutherland, 93rd Highlanders 24 October 1822
carved in the wall next to one of the cannon) from where there are
good views over to the parade ground. Park at the parade ground;
there is a small snack bar and good gift shop near the warrant
officer's quarters with barrels of pork outside it. Stop for a good
video introduction at the **DL Matheson Visitor Centre**. A

Defence of the realm

Sir Thomas Warner landed at Old Road Bay in 1623 and was joined in 1625 by the crew of a French ship badly mauled by the Spanish. They were initially befriended by the local chief Tegreman, but the Caribs became alarmed at the rapid colonization of the island. 3,000 Caribs tried to mount an attack in 1626. 2,000 of them were massacred by the combined French and English forces in the deep ravine at **Bloody Point** (the site of Stone Fort). An amicable settlement meant that the English held the central part of the island roughly in line from Sandy Point to Saddlers in the north to Bloody Point across to Cayon in the south. French names can be traced in both of their areas of influence (Dieppe Bay Town in the north, the parishes are called Capisterre and Basseterre in the south). The southeast peninsula was neutral. This rapprochement did not last long as, following the colonization of Martinique and Guadeloupe, the French wished to increase their sphere of influence. St Kitts became a target and in 1664 they squeezed the English from the island. For 200 years the coast was defended by troops from one nation or another.

narrow and quite steep path leads to **Fort George**, the Citadel and the highest defensive position. Restoration continues and several areas have been converted to a most interesting museum. Barrack rooms now hold well-presented and informative displays (pre-Columbian, American, English, French and Garrison). Guides are on hand to give detailed explanations of the fortifications.

● *The green vervet monkey was introduced by the French some 300 years ago and Kittitians used to eat them. They can be seen in many areas including Brimstone Hill but can be a pest to farmers. To keep down numbers, many have been exported for medical research.*

Mount Liamuiga
Map 13, C1, p287

The island is dominated by the southeast range of mountains and the higher northwest range which contains **Mount Verchilds** (1,069 m, 2,931 ft) and the crater of **Mount Liamuiga** (1,383 m, 3,792 ft). To climb Mount Liamuiga independently, get a bus to St Paul's. After the village entrance sign is a track leading through farm buildings which you follow through canefields. After 20 minutes take a left fork; ask people working in the fields if you are unsure. At the edge of the forest, the track becomes a path, which is easy to follow and leads through wonderful trees – if you hear something in the upper branches, look up before the monkeys disappear; on the steady climb from the end of the road note the wild orchids in the forest. At 948 m (2,600 ft) is the crater into which you can climb, holding onto vines and roots. You need a full day for this climb which is really only for experienced hikers. To get beyond the crater to the summit will require a guide. You can reach the attractive, but secluded, **Dos d'Ane pond** near Mount Verchilds from the Wingfield Estate; a guide is recommended.

The north coast
Map 13, D1-2, p287

Rawlins Plantation, reached up a long drive through canefields, has magnificent gardens full of tropical plants and flowers and is an excellent place to stop for lunch on a tour of the island, see p145. Alternatively, there is a black sand beach at **Dieppe Bay** with the excellent *Golden Lemon Inn*, see p144. The beach is not what it was because of hurricanes moving the sand around, but it is still a good place to stroll, with a view of The Quill on Sint Eustatius in the distance and lots of sandpipers and herons. Pass through Saddlers to the **Black Rocks**. Here lava has flowed into the sea, providing interesting rock formations.

▶ The sugar train

The sugar industry was revolutionized in St Kitts when first the estates moved from wind to steam power in 1870 and then a central sugar factory was built in Basseterre in 1912. A narrow-gauge railway was built in 1912-26 to deliver cane from the fields to the central sugar mill – the beginning of the end for all the small estate-based sugar mills dotted round the island. Many sail-less windmills still stand, relics of the old ways. Although the track initially ran as two spurs either side of the island, planters soon saw the sense of abandoning other delivery systems and it was extended to be a circular route round the coast. With the decline in the sugar industry at the end of the 20th century, the track fell into disrepair until the **St Kitts Scenic Railway** opened in 2003 – the perfect way to see the island, as you can see above the sugar cane.

The locomotive originated in Romania and was sold to Poland for sugar beet transport before coming to St Kitts for sugar cane. The power car was built in Colorado, USA, while the 'island series' carriages, the first of their kind, were built in Seattle, Washington, USA. The rails were brought from the UK, Belgium, the USA and abandoned sugar track in Cuba, the sleepers are hard wood from Guyana. An Alaskan engineer is always on board to answer questions and a Kittitian choir will serenade you.

St Kitts Scenic Railway departs 0820 and 1310 from Needsmust station near the airport, three hours 10 minutes. It is expensive, at US$89 per adult, US$44.50 per child, or break your journey with a tour of Brimstone Hill Fortress for US$123, returning by bus. A maximum of 28 guests per carriage have a seat on both levels, the upper open-air deck and the lower, enclosed, a/c carriage. Reservations essential, **T** 869-4657263, www.stkittsscenicrailway.com

The southeast peninsula

*To visit the southeast peninsula, turn off the roundabout at the end of Wellington road (opposite the turning to the airport) and at the end of this new road turn left leading to the narrow spit of land sandwiched between **North and South Frigate bays**. The 6-mile Dr Kennedy A Simmonds Highway runs from Frigate Bay to Major's Bay along the backbone of the peninsula and around the salt pond. From the top there is a lookout with a great view of **North Friars Bay Beach** on the Atlantic and **South Friars Bay Beach** on the Caribbean Sea, with Nevis at the end.*

Frigate Bay
Map 13, E3, p287

This area is being heavily developed with large hotels and condominiums, the natural lagoons providing an additional attraction. It is dominated by the *Marriott Hotel* and adjacent golf course. Breakers have been built on the Atlantic side so that guests of the *Marriott* can get into the water, but generally beaches on the Atlantic side are not safe for swimming. **South Frigate Bay** is on the Caribbean Sea and good for swimming, very popular with locals as it is the closest beach to the capital. There are several beach bars here and *Mr X's* watersports. Friday night is the night to come for dancing and partying on the beach.

Friars Bay
Map 13, E3, p287

North Friars Bay beach is very open and sandy but swimming is dangerous. There are no facilities, no shade and no beach bar. Access is best at the far end. **South Friars Bay** is a long stretch of sand with access at the north and south ends. Take the right fork in the track to the north end, where there are beach bars and nice sand which is cleaned regularly. What appear to be shacks quickly spring into life as bars according to demand, such as when a cruise ship is in port, and it can get very busy at weekends. Two sunbeds and an umbrella rent for US$10. The left fork leads to the southern end and *Shipwreck Beach Bar* (*1000-sundown*). There are some grungy old sun loungers to rent on the beach and a portacabin toilet as well as scruffy thatched umbrellas for shade. The sand here is quite dark and the beach is changing shape because of storms. There is a step down into the water and a platform you can swim to offshore where snorkelling is good (snorkelling gear for rent). Pelicans dive for fish and the view of cliffs and mountains is attractive. Keep an eye out for monkeys in this area.

White House Bay
Map 13, E4, p287

White House Bay, on the Caribbean side, is good for snorkelling, but a hurricane took away a lot of the sand. It is a popular anchorage for yachts and a great dive site with wrecks in the bay. Research is taking place underwater. The Anglo-Danish Maritime Archaeological Team (ADMAT) set up a field school in 2003, to record two pre-1760s shipwrecks uncovered by recent hurricanes.

● *There are some wild deer on the southeast peninsula, imported originally from Puerto Rico by Phillip Todd in the 1930s.*

Sand Bank Bay
Halfway round the Great Salt Pond turn left down an unmarked dirt road. Park near the road and walk to the beach. *Map 13, E4, p287*

Sand Bank Bay is a lovely secluded beach. The bay is horseshoe-shaped backed by sand dunes with hills at each end. There is a small gazebo but no facilities, just a wild, windy and empty beach apart from a few cows. Kite flying is good and it is a great place for picnics, but don't swim: there is an undertow and drownings have occurred.

Cockleshell Beach

Continue on the main highway and turn left for Cockleshell Bay and Turtle Beach. Map 13, F4, p287

Cockleshell Beach is the closest point to Nevis and there is a stunning view across the water. The ruins of an old hotel are expected to be dismantled to make way for a new hotel as Hyatt has bought the land. At present, the large open bay with dark golden sand is home to chickens and there is a beach bar which only comes to life for special occasions in high season.

Turtle Beach

Map 13, F4, p287

Turtle Beach (no turtles nowadays) on Mosquito Bay is the main tourist beach in the area as it has a bar and restaurant, see p180, offering sun loungers and a jetty for motor boats, while villas and a guesthouse (ask bar staff for information) are springing up on the hillside behind. There is even a raised dance floor where you can dance under the stars. In high season there are parties and steel pan, but the cows and a large pig continue to rummage under the coconut palms and along the shore. Weed comes in if the wind is in the wrong direction and is cleaned off the sand fairly haphazardly. You can get a boat to Nevis from here.

Major's Bay

The main road ends at Major's Bay. Map 13, F4, p287

On this thin strip of land between the sea and the pond, the sand is mostly at the far end and it is rocky where the cars stop. There is an old barge in the bay and a lovely view of Nevis. During a hurricane the barge was brought here for shelter, but it was wrecked on the shore. It is now a breeding ground for fish. The water is calm but a bit smelly and there are goats and cows everywhere.

Nevis

Across the 2-mile Narrows Channel from St Kitts is the beautiful little island of Nevis. The circular island covers an area of 36 square miles and the central peak, 1,178m (3,232 ft), is usually shrouded in white clouds and mist. It reminded Columbus of Spanish snow-capped mountains and so he called the island 'Las Nieves'. For the Caribs, it was Oualie, the land of beautiful water. Smaller than St Kitts, it is also quieter. The atmosphere is low-key and easy-going; all the same, it is an expensive island. The delightful plantation inns have long been a favourite with the well-heeled British but the construction of the Four Seasons Hotel now attracts golfing Americans.

▸▸ *See Sleeping p148, Eating and drinking p182, Nightlife p206*

 Sights

Charlestown
Map 15, E1, p288

The main town is Charlestown, one of the best preserved old towns in the Caribbean, with several interesting buildings dating from the 18th century. It is small and compact, on **Gallows Bay**, guarded by Fort Charles to the south and the long sweep of Pinney's Beach to the north. Nevis had the only court in the West Indies to try and hang pirates. Prisoners were taken from the courthouse across the swamp to where the gallows were set up, hence the name, Gallows Bay. There are plans for a national park to protect the swamp, a habitat for many birds, animals and plants.

D R Walwyn's Plaza is dominated by the balconied **Old Customs/Treasury House** built in 1837 and restored in 2002. The tourist office is here. **Memorial Square** is larger and more impressive than D R Walwyn's Plaza; the **War Memorial** is in a small garden. The **courthouse and library** were built in 1825 and used as the Nevis Government Headquarters, largely destroyed by fire in 1873 and subsequently rebuilt. The building still houses the library upstairs and the Nevis High Court and Registrar below. The little square tower on top of this building was erected in 1909-10. It contains a clock which keeps accurate time with an elaborate pulley and chain system. In the library you can see it, together with the weights, among the roof trusses. The courthouse is closed to the public except when a case is in progress.

Along Government Road is the well-preserved **Jewish Cemetery**. The earliest evidence of a Jewish community on the island dates from 1677-78, when there were four families. By the end of the century there were 17 households, a thriving synagogue and part of the main street was known as Jew Street, but invasion by the French in 1706 and 1783, hurricanes and the decline of the sugar industry in the 18th century led to an economic downturn and emigration. By the end of the 18th century only three Jewish households remained. Now there is no evidence of their presence except for the cemetery where 19 stones date from 1679-1730.

Charlestown **market** has a wide range of island produce and crafts (*Mon-Sat 0730-1500*). Market Street to the right houses the **Philatelic Bureau** (*Mon-Fri 0800-1600*). The **Cotton Ginnery** was, until 1994, in use during the cotton-picking season (February-July). In 1995 it was moved out to the New River Estate, Gingerland, in a renovated building next to the sugar mill ruins there. As part of the Nevis Port upgrade, the original Cotton Ginnery building was converted to house 10 gift shops and a restaurant. On Chapel Street the **Wesleyan Holiness Manse**, built in 1812, is one of the oldest stone buildings surviving on the island, while the **Methodist Manse** (next to the prominent church) has the oldest wooden structure; the second floor was built in 1802.

● *Nevis is divided into five parishes, each with its own Anglican church, a tiny fraction of the 80 churches for other denominations. On Sunday church bells ring from 0600, calling the faithful to services lasting three hours or more, and it is a quiet day everywhere.*

The Museum of Nevis History

Between Main St and the sea, **T** 869-4695786. *Mon-Fri 0900-1600, Sat 0900-1200. US$5. Map 15, E1, p288* The museum at the birthplace of Alexander Hamilton is next to the sea and set in an attractive garden. The original house was built around 1680 but destroyed in the 1840s, probably by an earthquake. This house was rebuilt in 1983 and dedicated during the Islands' Independence celebration in September of that year. The Nevis House of Assembly meets in the rooms upstairs, while the rather cramped museum occupies the ground floor. Alexander Hamilton, Nevis' most famous son, was born in Charlestown on 11 January 1757. He lived on Nevis for only five years before leaving for St Croix with his family. About half of the display is given over to various memorabilia and pictures of his life. The rest contains examples of Amerindian pottery, African culture imported by the slaves, cooking implements and recipes, a rum still, a model of a Nevis lighter, the ceremonial clothes of the Warden which were worn on the Queen's Birthday and Remembrance Day and a section on nature conservation. A small shop sells local produce and some interesting books. All proceeds go to the upkeep of the museum.

Fort Charles

Take the road south out of Charlestown, fork right at the Shell station and again at the mini roundabout, keep right along the sea shore (rough track), past the wine company building and through gates at the end of the track. Map 15, F1, p288

The rather unkempt Fort Charles was built before 1690 and altered many times before being completed between 1783-90. Nothing much remains apart from the circular well and a small building (possibly the magazine). The gun emplacements looking across to St Kitts are being badly eroded by the sea; some cannon have been moved to hotels. The Nevis Council surrendered to the French here in 1782 during the siege of Brimstone Hill on St Kitts.

Bath Hotel and Spring House

Bath. *On the main road about half a mile outside Charlestown.*
Map 15, F1, p288

The largely ruined Bath Hotel and Spring House was built by the
Huggins family in 1778. It is reputed to be one of the oldest hotels
in the Caribbean. The **Bath Hotel** was under restoration in 2004
and there are plans to develop the entire Bath Spring area as a
massage/therapeutic centre. Work is in progress on two thermal
dipping pools. The **Spring House** lies over a fault which supplies
constant hot water at 108°F. Most locals bathe further
downstream, often stark naked.

Horatio Nelson Museum

Bath, **T** 869-4690408. *Mon-Fri 0900-1600, Sat 0900-1200. US$5.*
Gift shop. Map 15, F1, p288

The museum is in a building dedicated in 1992 to commemorate
the 205th anniversary of the wedding of Admiral Nelson to Fanny
Nisbett. Based on a collection donated by Mr Robert Abrahams, an
American, it contains memorabilia including letters, china,
pictures, furniture and books (request to see the excellent
collection of historical documents and display of 17th-century clay
pipes). A replica of Nelson's military uniform was unveiled at the
museum and presented to the local government by the British
High Commissioner in January 2001. Nelson was not always
popular, having come to the island to enforce the Navigation Acts
which forbade the newly independent American states trading
with British colonies. In his ship *HMS Boreas*, he impounded four
American ships and their cargoes. The Nevis merchants
immediately claimed £40,000 losses against Nelson, who had to
remain on board his ship for eight weeks to escape gaol. It was
only after Prince William, captain of *HMS Pegasus*, arrived in
Antigua that Nelson gained social acceptability and married the

widow, Fanny Woodward Nisbett (reputedly for her uncle's money; he promptly left the island and spent his wealth in London). The museum also contains some pre-Columbian artefacts and displays on local history, including sugar and slavery. Outside, behind the museum rests the *Pioneer*, a Nevis lighter and the last sugar boat sailing to St Kitts. There are plans to renovate it, but to get a better idea of what it looked like, there is a model in the museum.

St John's Fig Tree Anglican Church
About 2 miles on from the Bath House. Map 15, F2, p288

Originally built in1680, the church was rebuilt in 1838 and 1895. A copy of the marriage certificate of Nelson and Fanny Nisbett is displayed here. There are interesting memorials to Fanny's father William Woodward and to her first husband Dr Josiah Nisbett. Many died of the fever and if you lift the red carpet in the central aisles you can see old tombstones, many connected with the then leading family, the Herberts. The graveyard has examples of tombstones in family groups dating from the 1780s. Slightly off the main road to the south lies **Montpelier Great House** where the marriage of Nelson and Mrs Nisbett took place; a plaque is set in the gatepost. The plantation house is now a hotel with pleasant gardens – a great place for lunch or a drink. Enormous toads live in the lily ponds formed out of old sugar pans.

Saddle Hill
Beyond Montpelier House. Map 15, G4, p288

Saddle Hill (455 m,1,250 ft) has the remains of a small fort, Saddle Hill Battery, and is reputedly where Nelson would look out for illegal shipping. Nevisians had a grandstand view from here of the siege of Brimstone Hill by the French in 1782. You can follow goat/nature trails on the hill dotted with giant aloes. A track starts at Clay Ghaut, but most trails beyond the fort are overgrown.

Botanical Gardens

Montpelier, **T** 869-4693509. *Gardens open Nov-Mar Mon-Sat 1000-1630, other months phone ahead. US$10/EC$25, children half price. Tea house, **T** 869-4693399, 1000-1700. Map 15, F3, p288*

Among 7 acres of plants from around the world are cactus, bamboo, orchids, flowering trees and shrubs, heliconias and rose gardens, a mermaid fountain, a greenhouse with bridges, ponds, waterfall and tea house with English high tea and gift shop. The landscaping is beautiful and it is the perfect spot for relaxation, picnics, small gatherings, weddings, but not wheelchair friendly.

Gingerland

About 3 miles further on. Map15, F4, p288

The rich soils of the small parish of Gingerland made it the centre of the island's ginger root production (also cinnamon and nutmeg), but it is noteworthy for the very unusual **octagonal Methodist church** built in 1830. The **Eva Wilkin Gallery**, Clay Ghaut, **T** 869-4692673, *Mon-Fri 1000-1500, or by appointment*, is in an old windmill. Started by Howard and Marlene Paine, it has a permanent exhibition of paintings and drawings by Nevisian Eva Wilkin MBE (whose studio it was until her death in 1989), prints of which are available, also antique maps, etc.

White Bay Beach

Turn right in Gingerland along Hanleys Rd. Map 15, F6, p288

Go right down to the bottom and turn left at the Indian Castle experimental farm, past the racecourse (on Black Bay) and Red Cliff. There is a small shelter but no general shade. Beware: on the Atlantic coast, the sea can be rough and dangerous. On quieter days, the surf is fun and you can see Montserrat. On the way back watch the deep storm drain crossing the road near the church.

Eastern Nevis
Map 15, p288

After Gingerland the land becomes more barren and this side of
the island is much drier. Several sugar mills were built here
because of the wind, notably **Coconut Walk Estate**, **New River
Estate** (fairly intact) and the **Eden Brown Estate**, built around
1740. A duel took place between the groom and the bride's
brother at the wedding of Julia Huggins. The brother was killed
and the fiancé fled the island to escape trial and execution. Julia
became a recluse and the great house was abandoned. It has the
reputation of being haunted. Although government owned and
open to the public, the ruins are in a poor condition and care
should be taken.

The island road continues north through Butlers and Brick Kiln
(known locally as Brick Lyn), past St James' Church (Hick's village),
Long Haul and Newcastle Bays (with the *Nisbet Plantation Inn*) to
the small fishing community of **Newcastle** and the airport. You
can visit the Newcastle Pottery where distinctive red clay is used to
make, among other things, the traditional Nevis cooking pot.

Northwestern Nevis
Map15, p288

The road continues through an increasingly fertile landscape, and
there are fine views across the Narrows to the southeast peninsula
of St Kitts, with **Booby Island** in the middle of the channel, the
latter being mostly inhabited by pelicans (all birds are referred to
as boobies by the local population). It offers good diving. The small
hill on your left is **Round Hill** (370 m,1,014 ft). It can be reached
on the road between Cades Bay and Camps Village. Turn off the
road at Fountain village by the Methodist church. There are good
views from the radio station at the top over Charlestown, across to
St Kitts and beyond to Antigua.

Horse racing Nevis-style

The Nevis Turf and Jockey Club meets at least six times a year to race island thoroughbreds on the racecourse on Black Bay: New Year's Day, Tourism Week (February), Easter, May Day, August during Culturama, Independence Day and Boxing Day.

Facilities include a grandstand seating 200, washrooms, a pari-mutuel booth, good food and dancing well into the night; this is part folk festival, part carnival, with no social barriers.

There is a minimum of five races on the seaside track, from where you can see Redonda, Montserrat and Antigua in the distance and often whales spouting or breaching. Races start mid-afternoon and end at dusk. There is an average of four horses in each race, run clockwise over a distance of 5½-8 furlongs (1 mile), with a hill up to the home stretch.

Contact Richard Lupinacci, who resurrected racing in the 1980s, at the *Hermitage Inn* for details, **T** 869-4693477.

You should also look out for the more amusing donkey races. Nevis is known for its large number of donkeys.

There is a small beach at **Mosquito Bay** and some good snorkelling can be had under the cliffs of Hurricane Hill. At **Oualie Beach**, the watersports on offer include scuba diving, windsurfing and the enchanting Touch and Go snorkelling run by Babara Whitman, *Under the Sea,* see p.248 for details.

Under Round Hill lies **Cottle Chapel**, built in 1824. It was the first Anglican place on Nevis where slaves could be taught and worship with their masters. Under restoration, its beautiful little font can be seen in the Museum of Nevis History.

Fort Ashby
Just off the island road. Map 15, C1, p288

Fort Ashby is on long-term lease from the government to a private owner who has rebuilt it in its original form with four cannon remaining in their original positions. It is occasionally used as a restaurant/beach bar and is open to the public. It protected Jamestown, the original settlement and former capital, which was supposedly destroyed by an earthquake and tidal wave in1690, and was originally called St James's Fort. Nearby are the **Nelson springs**, where the barrels from *HMS Boreas* were filled, and **St Thomas's Church**, built in 1643, one of the oldest surviving in the Caribbean.

Pinney's Beach
Map 15, D1, p288

Beautiful 4-mile Pinney's Beach is only a few minutes' walk north from Charlestown. There are many tracks leading down to the beach, often with a small hut or beach bar at the end of them, but it is never crowded. The 218-room *Four Seasons Hotel* lies in the middle of the beach. The sun loungers are for guests only, but the public has access to the beach and there are watersports available. Huge amounts of sand were imported after Hurricane Lenny and breakwaters were built to protect the beach by the hotel, but much of the beach has remained stony since the hurricane. Behind the resort is the **Robert Trent Jones II golf course** which straddles the island road. The manicured fairways and greens are in marked contrast with the quiet beauty of the rest of the island but the hotel's considerable efforts at landscaping have lessened its impact.

All the Leeward Islands depend heavily on tourism earnings for a major part of their income and offer a wide variety of places to stay. These range from all-inclusive resorts on Antigua and the massive 648-room Marriott hotel on St Kitts to the elegant plantation inns of Nevis, the height of chic luxury on St-Barthélemy and intimate guest houses offering simple accommodation on all the islands. Whether you want to be upmarket with your every need catered for, or relaxed and casual on a more do-it-yourself basis, there will be something to suit your requirements and your budget. The top hotels, such as Carlisle Bay, in Antigua, Le Toiny, on St-Barth, or the Altamer fully-staffed villas on Anguilla, will charge an arm and a leg, with suites costing thousands of dollars, but there is always plenty of comfortable accommodation in our A-C range and usually several guest houses offering basic rooms in the D-E range. Tourist offices can provide lists of approved hotels, villas and guest houses which have facilities of an adequate standard.

Sleeping codes

Price

LL	US$201 and over	**C**	US$41-60
L	US$151-200	**D**	US$31-40
AL	US$101-150	**E**	US$21-30
A	US$81-100	**F**	US$20 and under
B	US$61-80		

Price of a double room based on two people sharing. See below for details of tax and service charges.

Antigua

There is a 10% service charge and 8.5% tax at all hotels. The greatest concentration of developments is in the area around St John's, along the coast to the west and also to the north in a clockwise direction to the airport, taking advantage of some of the best beaches. You would only want to stay in St John's if you were there on business or for a cricket match. A second cluster of hotels is around English Harbour and Falmouth Harbour in the southeast of the island. These are very pleasant with lovely views of the harbours and yachts at anchor. Many may be closed during September and October. There are several all-inclusives, most of which are not included here, and lots of self-catering apartments, but a common complaint is that sufficient provisions are not available locally and you have to go into St John's for shopping, requiring a taxi or car hire. Camping is illegal.

▸ *See also Chez Pascal and Harmony Hall under Eating p155*

LL Blue Waters, on the north coast, **T** 268-4620290, www.bluewaters.net *Map 1, A3, p280* Rebuilt after the 1997 hurricane, the hotel is now one of the most upmarket on the island, with lush tropical gardens and huge mature trees. The 77 large colonial-style rooms, suites and villas are dressed with chintz

★ **Beach hotels**

Best

fabrics and solid furniture and have patios or balconies, looking out onto a very pretty bay. Rates include breakfast and afternoon tea or you can opt for half board or all inclusive. There is a pool and watersports, a gym and tennis.

LL Carlisle Bay, Old Rd, **T** 268-4840002, www.carlisle-bay.com
Map 1, F3, p280 The sister hotel of *One Aldwych* in London is the newest luxury hotel to hit the Antigua scene with great fanfare. Converted from a previous hotel on the site, the blocks of rooms are modern and functional, but the entrance is grand and stylish with a pavilion and pond before you get to reception and the massive lounge area. Huge beach suites, ocean suites and three-bedroom Carlisle suites have been designed with dark wood furniture, pale cream, white and grey furnishings and clean minimalist lines. Every luxury includes offices in the rooms with wireless internet access, well-stocked minibars, a separate cinema and a library with computers. For exercise there is a Peter Burwash tennis centre with nine courts, pool, a spa and gym. There are two restaurants, Asian or more West Indian. The beach is lovely and calm in a very protected, pretty bay with a view of Montserrat.

LL Curtain Bluff, Old Rd, **T** 268-4628400, www.curtainbluff.com
Closed Jun-Oct. Map 1, F3, p280 A high-class, all-inclusive resort, with huge, opulent suites and apartments all at ground level on a bluff overlooking the sea with a view of Montserrat. Everything is

included here: scuba diving, tennis with pro, squash, deep-sea fishing, snorkelling boat trips. It is rather like a country club with mostly repeat visitors, no room keys, low staff turnover and good service and three meals a day, afternoon tea, canapés before dinner and an extensive wine list: ask to see the cellar where there are 10,000 bottles, the owner's pride and joy. No children under 12 in February but plenty of kids' activities at other times.

LL-AL Admiral's Inn, English Harbour, **T** 268-4601027, www.admiralsantigua.com *Closed September. Map 1, F5, p280*
This handsome Georgian brick building dating from 1788 was once a store room for pitch, turpentine and lead, while upstairs were the offices for the engineers for the Royal Naval Dockyard. It still retains the hand-hewn beams, wrought-iron chandeliers and a bar which is an old work bench scarred by the names of ships that once docked there. Nautical in feel, it is rather like an English port pub, where you can play darts but live music on a Saturday evening in season is steel pan or a traditional string and flute band. With its very British charm the hotel resembles a refined manor house and has 13 rooms of varying sizes in the main house and annex with four-poster or twin beds and exposed beams. Good food in the restaurant is served in a lovely setting overlooking the garden, yachts and harbour. The *Joiner's Loft* is an adjacent two-bedroom apartment. Transport to the beach is provided with complimentary sunfish and snorkelling equipment.

LL-AL Galleon Beach, English Harbour, **T** 268-4601024, www.galleonbeach.com *Map 1, F5, p280* On the beach at Freemans Bay, one-, two- or three-bedroom comfortable, fully equipped and tasteful cottages and villas in different styles with additional sofa beds and verandas are set in spacious grounds with glorious views of the old dockyard at English Harbour and the many yachts at anchor. There is tennis, sunfish, windsurfing, a beach bar and restaurant and ferry to Nelson's Dockyard.

LL-AL Siboney Beach Club, Dickenson Bay, **T** 268-4620806, www.siboneybeachclub.com *Map 1, A2, p280* Proprietor Tony Johnson has made this one of the nicest small, independent places to stay. Twelve comfortable suites in a three-storey block sit in dense tropical gardens on the beach. Decor and view vary but each has a bedroom, separate sitting/dining room with sofa bed, tiny kitchenette tucked away in a cupboard for making snacks, bathroom and balcony with chairs, a/c, fan, CD player, phone. *Coconut Cove,* under separate management, is the best independent restaurant in this area with beachfront dining, lots of seafood and daily specials, happy hour 1530-1900.

L-AL per person Coco's Antigua, Jolly Harbour, **T** 268-4602626, www.cocoshotel.com *Map 1, D1, p280* In a lovely location built on a bluff, there are 14 rooms in romantic chattel-style wooden cottages with gingerbread fretwork, fan, fridge and a view of Jolly Beach and Five Islands from gorgeous balconies with a pleasant breeze. Restaurant, pool, all-inclusive rate.

L-A Country Inn, Monk's Hill Rd, Cobb's Cross, **T/F** 268-4601469, www.countryinnantigua.com *Map 1, E5, p280* Self-catering cottages in traditional gingerbread style on the hillside over-looking Falmouth Harbour: breezy, fabulous view, balconies, hammocks, open-plan accommodation and very colourful. There is a small pool on the hill top and you have to be good at climbing to stay here. Access is up a poor road and steep hill, 4WD essential. Manager Danny will take you hiking or partying.

AL-C Ocean Inn, English Harbour, **T** 268-4601263, www.theoceaninn.com *Map 1, F5, p280* On a hillside overlooking English Harbour, with a spectacular and breezy view of the yachts and old buildings and a small pool. A rather haphazard appearance of rooms having been built below the main house when the owner felt like it. Rooms and bathrooms are small and basic, but they have a TV, a/c, fridge, carpet or tiles, some of the cheaper rooms in the main house share a bathroom. Breakfast is included, other meals on request.

C Cappuccino Lounge, Nelson's Alley off Newgate St, St John's, T 268-5626806, www.caplounge.com *Map 2, B1, p281* Beverley Latibeaudiere opened this guest house in 2004, with renovated rooms upstairs on the first floor: simple, small rooms have very little furniture to clutter them up, a double bed and small bathroom, new linen and are clean, nicely painted and convenient for town and cricket. Breakfast available and packages with beach shuttle, picnic lunch and evening meal at a restaurant elsewhere can be arranged. Downstairs is a restaurant and bar (*open until 0200, happy hour 1630-1830*), serving local food such as curry goat with different daily specials. Nothing over EC$12. TV in bar. Try a speciality coffee, West Indian style.

C Joe Mike's Hotel, in Corn Alley and Nevis St, St John's, T 268-4621142, joemikes@candw.ag *Map 2, D2, p281* Special rates can be negotiated but not by phone. Rooms are OK but there are no balconies, and weak a/c. Downstairs are a fast food restaurant and bar, casino, ice cream parlour, cocktail lounge, beauty salon and mini-mart.

C Murphy's Apartments, All Saints Rd, St John's, T 268-4611183. *Map 2, G2, p281* Run by Elaine Murphy, the apartments have been modernized with every amenity and a lovely garden. Breakfast costs US$5. Longer-term lets are possible.

D-E The Sleep Inn, just outside the gates of Nelson's Dockyard, T 268-5623082. *Map 1, F5, p280* There are 14 rooms in this very simple but tidy inn, with private bath, ceiling fans, shared kitchen, meals on request; very local and good value.

Sleeping

Barbuda

Accommodation is either expensive and exclusive or basic, with little in between. Take mosquito repellent and earplugs if you are in the centre of Codrington at weekends. Several private homes offer accommodation, although these change if a long-term rental is taken. See www.barbudaful.net for further options.

LL K-Club, in the south, just north of Coco Point, **T** 268-4600300, www.kclubbarbuda.com *Open mid-Nov to end-Aug, no under 12s. Map 3, F8, p281* On a fabulous beach of white, powdery sand stretching for miles, untouched and unspoilt. Italian designed in an open plantation-house style, with 45 rooms, everywhere is painted turquoise and white which gets a bit overpowering. It has its own nine-hole golf course, watersports and a pool. Islanders and non-residents are welcomed, and the food is excellent.

LL The Beach House, Palmetto Point, **T** 268-7254042, www.thebeachhousebarbuda.com *Map 3, F6, p281* Newly renovated and redesigned, very light and white, this is the ultimate in luxury on a pink sand beach, where each of the 21 suites is assigned two personal butlers who can organize anything for you. Prices include air fare to and from Antigua and breakfast. All meals can be taken anywhere, any time, on the beach, in the restaurant, in your room, wherever you want. Bicycles, horse riding and massages can be arranged.

A-B The Island Chalet, in the heart of Codrington, Mrs Myra Askie, **T** 268-7730066. *Map 3, D6, p281* Three rooms on the first floor each with a small double bed and a rollaway, so they can sleep three at a pinch, but it gets a bit hot and cramped. Shared kitchen and living room facilities are of a good standard. There is a grocery across the square and the price comes down at weekends when noise levels rise at night.

C Carriage Guest House, Codrington, lynnnedd@tiscali.co.uk
Map 3, D6, p281 Two double bedrooms, two bathrooms, kitchen and open-plan living room, all with a/c, fans and washing machine.

C Nedd's Guest House, Codrington, T 268-4600059. *Map 3, D6, p281* Run by Mcarthur and Natalie Nedd, who can offer excursions and tours with fishing. They also run a supermarket and have a collection of 100 tortoises. Four double rooms with shower room and balcony, shared sitting room and kitchen.

Montserrat

Hotel tax is 10%, service is usually 10%. There are a couple of hotels but most accommodation is in guest houses or rented rooms and apartments. Villa rental is available with own pools, sea views, gardens and maid service. Rental agencies include:
Kirwan's Secluded Hideaway, Olveston, T 664-4913405, F 664-4912546; **Montserrat Enterprises Ltd**, Old Towne, T 664-4912431, F 664-4914660; **Neville Bradshaw Agencies**, Old Towne, T 664-4915270, F 664-4915069; **Jacquie Ryan Enterprises Ltd**, Olveston, T 664-4912055, F 664-4913257; **Tradewinds Real Estate**, Old Towne, T 664-4912004, www.tradewindsmontserrat.com; **West Indies Real Estate**, Olveston, T 664-4918666, www.wirealest.com.

AL Vue Pointe, Old Towne, T 664-4915210, www.vuepointe.com
Map 4, E1, p282 Traditionally the premier hotel on the island, closed because it was within the exclusion zone, it is now being refurbished by the persevering Osborne family, offering fantastic views of the volcano in the distance and close to a black sand beach. Self-catering cottages are in the garden. Meals are being served poolside rather than in the hexagonal restaurant and include continental breakfast, bar snacks for lunch and full dinner, with a Wednesday night barbecue, long a tradition at the hotel.

★ Hotels with a view

Best

- Galleon Beach, Antigua, p121
- Vue Pointe, Montserrat, p125
- Queen's Garden Resort, Saba, p136
- Le Toiny, St-Barthélemy, p141
- Hermitage Plantation Inn, Nevis, p149

AL-A Grand View, Baker Hill, looking towards Antigua, Nevis and Redonda, **T** 664-4912284, www.mygrandview.com *Map 4, C3, p282* Theresa Silcott runs this island-style hotel which really does have a grand view over the island to the sea. Rooms of different sizes are on two floors with twin beds, private or shared bathroom, or double bed, kitchenette and private bathroom. Extra beds can be accommodated and single rooms are also available; TV, parking. The restaurant and bar are open to all with freshly cooked local and international fare. Live jazz featuring local and regional groups on the last Friday of each month to catch the after work crowd. Downstairs is a local radio station, great for ham radio enthusiasts, and internet access. Breakfast and taxes are included in the rates.

A David and Maureen Hodd, Olveston, **T** 664-4915248, **F** 664-4915016. *Map 4, D1, p282* David and Maureen rent out an apartment for two people in their quiet home with views of the sea and the mountains. Weekly and monthly rates available with discounts for Caricom residents. The apartment has a TV, phone, washing machine, kitchen, and meals can be arranged.

A-C Montserrat Moments Inn, Manjack Heights, **T** 664-4917707, flogriff@candw.ag *Map 4, B2, p282* A family home with children of school age, renting three downstairs rooms of different sizes with TV, fridge, a/c or fan, shared or private bathroom. Breakfast is included, other meals by reservation, or you can use the shared kitchenette. Email and laundry facilities available. Credit cards accepted. Florence is a very welcoming and helpful hostess and will find you somewhere to stay if she is full.

B Erindell, Gros Michel Drive, Woodlands, **T** 664-4913655, erindell@candw.ag *Next to Sea Wolf Diving. Map 4, D1, p282* Private entrance to the two pleasant rooms alongside the family home, with twin beds, private bathroom, TV, phone, fans, microwave oven and toaster. A full meal service is offered except on Saturday night, with breakfast and lunch for anyone but dinner for guests only. A welcome pack of snacks, fruit and drinks is provided on arrival. Pool outside the rooms, free laundry, discounts for Caricom residents, internet access, no credit cards. One minute to a bus route, a 15-minute walk to Woodlands beach. Snorkelling equipment is available and hiking and diving packages are offered.

B-C Bachee's, Olveston, **T** 664-4917509. *Map 4, D1, p282* Round the corner from *The Attic* and convenient for other restaurants too. Bachee is a retired Cable & Wireless man who built this as a home and guest house. There are two rooms, one of which is en suite, quiet, comfortable and very good value and in lovely gardens with lots of tropical plants.

B-C Gingerbread Hill, St Peter's, **T** 664-4914582, www.volcano-island.com *Map 4, C2, p282* David and Clover Lea run a delightful guest house with incredible views and lovely 3-acre gardens. Several options on offer: rooms in a separate house , including a backpacker's special in a basic room, or you can rent the whole house, or take the charming room adjoining their own house, bathroom, deck, fridge, TV, phone, email; meals on request. A tent and camping equipment is available, also bikes and a rental car. A family atmosphere, the Leas have three sons to enliven your stay.

Sint Maarten/St-Martin

On the Dutch side there is a 5-8% government tax on all hotel bills and a 10-15% service charge; the French side has a 5% tax. There are several large resort hotels not listed here, offering lots of services and activities with all-inclusive packages available, most on the Dutch side but a few on the French side. Hotel prices are high but summer package deals can be good value if you shop around. For low budget accommodation the Dutch half is better than the French. For long-stay visitors, the best way of finding an apartment is to look in the newspaper. A studio will cost about US$400-500 per month in a good residential location. Apartments at Simpson Bay Beach cost US$350-500 per week. There are agencies for short- or long-term lets: **Carimo**, rue du Général de Gaulle, Marigot, **T** 590-(0)590-875758, carimo@powerantilles.com; **IMAGE**, **T** 590-(0)590- 877804, image@powerantilles.com; **IMMO-DOM**, 34 Les Bosquets, Concordia, **T** 590-(0)590-870038, immo.dom@wanadoo.fr; **Immobilière Antillaise**, **T** 590-(0)590-870095, www.immobiliereantillaise.com; **Impact**, **T** 590-(0)590-872061; **Investimmo**, **T** 590-(0)590-877520; **Sprimbarth**, Coin de la Mairie, rue Victor Maurasse, **T** 590-(0)590-875865, sprimbarth@powerantilles.com; **Cap Caraibes**, Place du Village d'Orient, **T** 590-(0)590-520712, www.cap-caraibes.com. Lots of properties in Orient Bay, beachfront studios to hillside villas, from US$700-9,000 a week. **Jennifer's Vacation Villas**, Plaza del Lago, Simpson Bay Yacht Club, **T** 599-5443107, www.jennifersvacationvillas.com.

LL La Samanna, Baie Longue, **T** 590-(0)590-876400, www.lasamanna.com *Closed Sep-Oct. Map 5, B1, p283* One of the most exclusive resorts in the Caribbean, run by Orient Express since 1997, this white, Mediterranean-style hotel overlooks spectacular beaches and is set in 55 acres with lush gardens. It was originally built in the 1970s as a private home and the name is a contraction of the family's three daughters, but it soon became a luxury hotel. 81 rooms, suites and villas with huge bathrooms have all modern conveniences including data ports. On the beach guests are served fruit brochettes, towels and water. The dining and wine list are excellent with a lovely sea view from the restaurant, and there is a fitness centre, luxury spa, pool, watersports and tennis.

LL-AL Grand Case Beach Club, T 590-(0)590-875187, www.gcbc.com *On a headland at the north end of Grand Case beach with Petit Plage on the other side. Map 5, A5, p283* Large, comfortable, light and airy rooms are in 75 studios and suites in several blocks with kitchenettes, a/c, TV. Very casual with lots going on: tennis, non-motorized watersports, dive shop on site, video security appeals to American guests, room service, car rental.

LL-AL Holland House Beach Hotel, Front St, Philipsburg, T 599-5422572, www.hhbh.com *Map 6, G5, p283* In a tall block downtown but on the beach, convenient for shopping, the casino, public transport, 54 pleasant rooms have kitchenettes, good sized bathrooms and are in good order, painted white. In the lobby there is free internet access beside the open-air bar and restaurant.

LL-A Le Pavillon Beach, Plage de Grand Case, T 590-(0)590-879646, pavillon.beach@wanadoo.fr *Map 5, A5, p283* Modern, elegant hotel on the beach by the lagoon, built in 1991, within walking distance of Grand Case and all the restaurants. Six studios, 17 suites and one honeymoon suite on two floors, breakfast included, kitchenettes, balconies, phones, wheelchair access. Watersports and land sports can be arranged.

LL-A Mary's Boon Beach Plantation, 117 Simpson Bay Rd, T 599-5454235, www.marysboon.com *Map 5, C3, p283* A plantation-style hotel with 24 rooms and studios with kitchenettes, right on the beach between the airport and the sea. Rates are room only plus 20% tax and service, traditional decor, steps up to heavy wooden beds, good bathrooms; avoid the lower lobby rooms which have no view and are dark. Restaurant open for breakfast, lunch and a single sitting at dinner; US$30-40 for three-course set menu with second helpings, excellent food, honour bar.

LL-C White Sands Beach Club, White Sands Rd 34, Beacon Hill, **T** 599-5454370, **F** 599-5452245. *Map 5, C3, p283* A small, private, unpretentious hotel painted pink has 11 rooms with balconies or terrace, kitchenette and sitting area, couples only. Discounts for cash but a US$100 deposit is payable on arrival for breakages and loss of keys. All rooms have an ocean view, although the club is parallel to the airport runway so you can expect aircraft noise.

L-AL The Horny Toad, 2 Viaun Drive, Simpson Bay, **T** 599-5454323, www.thehornytoadguesthouse.com *Map 5, C3, p283* The well-cared-for guest house is between the beach and the airport in a residential area not seriously troubled by aircraft noise, lots of repeat guests, run by Betty Vaughan. Eight different apartments have full kitchens, some with a/c; beachfront apartments have fans and barbecue area. No children under 7.

L-A Pasanggrahan Royal Inn, in Philipsburg, **T** 599-5423588, tini@megatropic.com *Map 6, G6, p283* Formerly the Governor's home, this is the oldest inn on the island and where the Dutch royal family would stay when visiting Sint Maarten. The name comes from the Indonesian word for guest house. The quaint old building surrounded by large trees with a white veranda has a pleasant, casual atmosphere, the royal suite is now a bar, but the 30 rooms in the main house and annex are traditional, with four-poster beds and tiny bathrooms. You can walk through the lobby to reach the beach. There is also a pool and restaurant. No children under 12.

AL Chez Martine, T 590-(0)590-875159, chezmartine@
powerantilles.com *Map 5, A5, p283* This small beach hotel with a
very Creole style has five simple rooms and one suite, each with a
large bed, cane and wicker furniture, a/c and a fridge. Continental
breakfast is included. The restaurant is an open-air veranda built
out over the sand of Grand Case Bay with the waves lapping at the
shore beneath. The food is excellent, bringing many repeat visitors.

AL-B Delfina, 14-16 Tigris Rd, Dutch Lowlands/Cupecoy,
T/F 599-5453300, www.delfinahotel.com *Map 5, C2, p283*
German-run by Boris and Michael, gay friendly. The 12 rooms are
each named after a Hollywood star, in three traditional-style
wooden painted buildings with a/c, fan, fridge. An extended
continental breakfast is included and served upstairs in the
reception building where there is a bar, busy at happy hour. There
is a pool in the gardens, a dog and cats and the beach is in walking
distance. Cell phones are available with prepaid cards for national
and international calls, no fee.

AL-B L'Espérance, 4 Tiger Rd, Cay Hill, T 599-5425355,
www.lesperance hotel.com *Map 5, C4, p283* A pleasant hotel in a
residential area popular with shoppers and local business
travellers, only a five-minute walk to the main street and buses.
There are 22 good value suites with glass doors opening onto a
courtyard garden and pool. The one-bedroom suites have a sitting
room, TV, kitchenette and bathroom, the two-bedroom suites have
a full kitchen but only one bathroom; there is plenty of room to
spread out and internet access in the lobby.

A-B Hévèa, 163 Blvd de Grand Case, T 590-(0)590-875685,
hevea@outremer.com *Map 5, A5, p283* Small colonial-style hotel
in the heart of the restaurant district. Very prettily painted in the
gingerbread style with mosquito nets over the beds, old-fashioned
Caribbean washbasins and antique furnishings, eight rooms, suites

and studios sleeping two-four people, with kitchenettes and high ceilings to the roof, a/c or fans. Three of the rooms are only rented from December to April. There is a gourmet restaurant on site and the beach is across the street.

B-C Royal Beach, Baie Nettlé, **T** 590-(0)590-291212, **F** 590-(0)590-291204. *Map 5, B3, p283* Don't be put off by hurricane damage to the outside of these two concrete blocks at right angles to the beach: the rooms are spotless and excellent value, and the price includes a great buffet breakfast and taxes. All are painted a cool white and blue or green, with a/c and TV. There is a large pool, a shopping arcade alongside with a grocery, post office, bars and restaurants, internet access; convenient and very popular with the French and Martiniquans.

C-E Marcus, Front St, **T** 599-5422419. *Map 6, F3, p283* Right in the centre of town and convenient for the shops and casinos as well as the beach and restaurants, the seven rooms are always full, mainly with Caribbean visitors coming for the shopping, so book well in advance.

Anguilla

A 10% tax and 10-15% service charge will be added to the bill, which makes even the cheaper end of the market quite expensive. Anguilla has the reputation of catering for upmarket, independent travellers. This is reflected in the number of relatively small, chic and expensive hotels and beach clubs. Bargains can be found in the summer months, with discounts of over 50%. Travellers on a lower budget or those wanting to avoid hotels can find accommodation in one of about 10 guest houses. There are also many rental villas and apartments not listed here. The Anguilla Department of Tourism has a list of all types of accommodation.

LL Altamer, Shoal Bay West, **T** 264-4984000, www.altamer.com
Map 7, D1, p284 The height of luxury where you can be pampered
in total privacy in three four-storey villas with pools on a 7-acre
property beside the *Altamer* gourmet restaurant. Weekly rates start
from US$25,000. The five- to six-bedroom villas include fabulous
master bedrooms, open and light in futuristic style with white
concrete and glass, equipped with every high-tech feature
imaginable including elevator, home theatre, fitness centre, office.
Impeccable service with staff of 10: chefs for in-villa dining, butlers,
housekeeping and gardeners. Conference centre alongside.

LL CuisinArt Resort & Spa, Rendezvous Bay, **T** 264-4982000,
www.cuisinartresort.com *Closed Sep-Oct. Map 7, C2, p284*
An imposing spa resort on the beach and in the garden with lots of
health treatments and 'wellness' programme. Food is very
important here and they grow much of their own fruit and
vegetables using hydroponic technology for their three restaurants
and give cooking lessons. There are 93 luxury rooms, of which 60
are suites, all with huge marble bathrooms, blue and yellow colour
scheme, walk-in wardrobes, patio with sunbeds, doors sturdy
enough to withstand 200 mph winds, children's playground.
Popular with guests who like to feel cosseted and eat well.

LL Malliouhana Hotel & Spa, Mead's Bay, **T** 264-4976111,
www.malliouhana.com *Closed Sep and Oct. Map 7, C1, p284*
A well-established hotel on the beach offering every luxury and
attentive service. Vastly expensive but doesn't accept credit cards.
The 55 opulent rooms in cream and white have huge marble
bathrooms with separate tub and shower with two heads. There is
an award-winning restaurant (lots of steps) and a more casual
bistro on the beach. Spa with treatment rooms are rented by the
half day. Most of the watersports are complimentary and there is
tennis and two pools. Children are welcome and there is a
playground and pool by the beach.

LL-L Carimar Beach Club, Mead's Bay, **T** 264-4976881, www.carimar.com *Closed Sep to mid-Oct. Map 7, C2, p284* Colourful bougainvillea climbs over the arches of the patios and verandas and pretty gardens lead to the beach. The 24 comfortable one-three bedroom apartments on two floors in two Spanish-style blocks at right angles to the sand are each privately owned so decor varies, as do the books left for you to read. Full kitchens, balcony or patio, fans, tennis, no pool, no restaurant but several within walking distance, grocery store nearby. A quiet and relaxing place to stay. internet access in lobby. Very friendly, helpful staff.

LL-L Paradise Cove, Lower South Hill, **T** 264-4976603, www.paradise.ai *Map 7, C1, p284* A five-minute walk to the beach at Cove Bay, but right by the new golf course. Huge, comfortable studios, suites and penthouses spread out in three three-storey blocks, even the smallest is a generous 700 sq ft. All are tastefully decorated with large kitchen, patio, a/c, TV, fan, in-room internet access, with connecting doors to make family apartments. There are laundry facilities in each block, meeting rooms, a fitness centre, pool, jacuzzi, kids' pool and pool bar, beach shuttle. Café for breakfast and lunch, while dinner can be ordered from outside and brought in, or you can have a private cook; packages available with car hire.

LL-AL Rendezvous Bay Hotel, Rendezvous Bay, **T** 264-4976549, www.rendezvousbay.com *Closed mid-Sep to mid-Oct. Map 7, C2, p284* This was the first beach hotel on the island on a 60-acre property, owned by the Gumbs family since it opened in 1962. Pleasantly designed with Mexican furniture and every comfort, it is unpretentious, relaxing and friendly with good-value single-storey garden rooms with verandas and a sea view or higher-standard villa rooms on two floors (some with kitchens) on the sand, with more to be built along the lovely 2-mile empty beach, great for walking or jogging. A five-bedroom villa is a bargain at US$575 in summer (plus tax and service). On offer is snorkelling, sunfish sailboats, kayaks, tennis, an art gallery, games room, TV, piano, library, pool, in-room internet access, good open-air restaurant and a fleet of own cars and jeeps for hire.

LL-AL Serenity, Shoal Bay East, **T** 264-4973328, www.serenity.ai *Map 7, A4, p284* Attractive, modern Caribbean-style development set back from the beach. Two-bedroom units, one-bedroom suites with kitchens and four studios with fridge and microwave can be rented. All are very comfortable with dark wooden and cane furniture, but light and airy and good value, particularly in summer. The living/dining area has a sofa bed for extra guests, there is a large marble bathroom with walk-in shower and picture window, with path to beach, room service, maid service. Restaurant on site (*daily 0800-2300*).

AL-B Lloyd's Guesthouse, Crocus Hill, The Valley, **T** 264-4972351, www.lloyds.ai *Map 7, B4, p284* On the highest point at 213 ft, with a good view over The Valley, five minutes' walk to Crocus Bay. Smartly painted in yellow and white, this is the oldest guest house, opened in 1959. Family-run, the 14 small rooms, all with small bathroom gradually being upgraded with good fittings, TV, fan, have an old-fashioned charm. Breakfast is included, other meals on request, family-style dining with other guests, local dishes, drinks served but no bar, pleasant sitting room with selection of books.

AL-B Sea View, Sandy Ground, Road Bay, **T** 264-4972427, www.inns.ai/seaview *Map 7, C2, p284* Has the appearance of a large private house, smartly painted pink and white with a white picket fence outside. The apartments have balconies, one-two bedrooms, ceiling fans, kitchen/dining room and are clean and comfortable in island style. The beach is just across the road, the salt ponds are behind and there is always lots going on in this area.

A-B Syd Ans Apartments, Sandy Ground, **T** 264-4973180, www.inns.ai/sydans *Map 7, C2, p284* Anne Edwards runs this family business of 10 studios or one-bedroom apartments around a courtyard and just across the street from the beach. Some open onto the salt pond to the rear and some onto the courtyard. Close to the *Pump House* and *Johnno's*, it is convenient for nightlife as well as the yacht anchorage in the harbour.

Saba

Hotels do not usually give you a room key; there is no crime. The four policemen on the island boast that the cells are only used as overspill when the hotels are full! There are no resort hotels yet on Saba and even the most expensive are small and friendly. December to April is the busiest, most expensive season, although divers come throughout the year. July is also busy because of Carnival and students return from foreign universities. All the hotels offer dive packages. There is a 5% room tax, sometimes a 3% turnover tax (TOT) and usually a 10-15% service charge. The tourist office has a list of one- to three-bedroom cottages and apartments for rent from US$50 a night, which can be let on a weekly or monthly basis. All houses and hotels on Saba are painted white with green shutters; everybody conforms.

LL Queen's Garden Resort, Troy Hill, The Bottom, **T** 599-4163494, www.queensaba.com *Map 8, H2, p284* A relatively new hotel with a spectacular view overlooking The Bottom through the mountains to the sea below. Beautiful bedrooms with antique furniture from Europe grace the 12 very expensive luxury suites. Nine have a jacuzzi with a view. In the garden there is an horizon pool. There are discounts for weekly rates and lots of packages available. Slightly down the hill enjoy elegant dining at the *King's Crown* restaurant, either inside or sitting outside under the mango tree and the jasmine looking down on the lights of the village, for French cuisine with Caribbean flair using local fresh ingredients and interesting wines. Poolside barbecues, dinner and dance, Sunday brunches, in season.

L-A Juliana's, Windwardside, **T** 599-4162269, www.julianas-hotel.com *Map 8, G3, p284* Run by Johanna van't Hof and Wim Schutten, the hotel is scattered in several buildings. The smaller standard rooms with a garden view are a bit dark, but have a/c; the larger ones with a sea view have a balcony with hammocks, fridge, some kitchenettes, cable TV. There are also a one-bedroom apartment and two renovated Saban cottages with two bedrooms. A common room has internet access and yoga and dive classes are held here, and there is a book exchange. The pool, *Tropics* café and bar are across the road, with sea view. Monday night special with steel pan, lobster and steak menu at 1800, best in high season, is US$16.95. Friday is movie and burger night, US$10, with a screen hung between two flagpoles.

AL Cranston's Antique Inn, The Bottom, **T** 599-4163203, **F** 599-4163469. *Map 8, H2, p284* This is the oldest hostelry on the island and the most traditional in style. The 130-year-old inn has two floors, five rooms with four-poster beds and a pool. It is usually fully booked by travelling businessmen who need to be near the government offices. Good local food.

AL Cottage Club, Windwardside, **T** 599-4162486, cottageclub@unspoiledqueen.com *Map 8, G4, p284* Owned by the Johnson family who own the supermarket, 10 white cottages with red roofs in local style are set on a hill with wonderful views of Mount Scenery, English Quarter and the sea. All rooms are open to the roof, with one or two beds, kitchen for self-catering, good sized bathroom, TV and phone. The swimming pool is in a lovely private area with rainforest trees all around and a view down to the end of the runway. No restaurant but several in walking distance.

AL-B Scout's Place, Windwardside, **T** 599-4162205, www.sabadivers.com *Map 8, G3, p284* Redeveloped by Barbara and Wolfgang, of Germany, after severe hurricane damage several years previously, but they have kept the traditional style and feel to the place. There are four rooms in the former government guest house, 10 rooms in a newer wing, all with cable TV, in-room internet access for your own laptop, US$0.50 per minute, fan and fridge. *Scout's Place* is simple and relaxed, with beautiful views, a pool and boutique. Dive packages available (dive shop in Fort Bay). The restaurant and bar (*happy hour 1700-1800*) serve breakfast, lunch, dinner and snacks, with specials every night. Eat out on the terrace for the ocean view, or indoors to escape the weather.

A-B Ecolodge Rendez-Vous, **T** 599-4163348, www.ecolodge-saba.com *A 5-min hike from the nearest road or a 20-min climb up steps from Windwardside on the way to Mount Scenery, but a quad bike will carry your bags (Eco the donkey became too stubborn).* *Map 8, G3, p284* Out in the middle of nowhere, 11 Saba-style simple rural cabins sleeping two to four (two downstairs, two in the loft), are individually decorated according to each one's name, and have solar shower bags, composting toilets, balcony and hammock. There is a sweat lodge (sauna), like a leather patchwork turtle, cold tub and hot tub. The excellent restaurant uses home-grown fruit, vegetables and herbs. Family-run by artist Heleen Cornet, conservationist Tom van't Hof, their son, Bernt, who is a chef, his partner Angelique and his cousin JJ.

A-C El Momo Cottages, T/F 599-4162265, www.elmomo.com *Halfway up Jimmy's Hill, 5 mins from Windwardside. Map 8, G4, p284* There are 60 steps up to the pool area, many more up to the wooden cottages built in rough Saban style in a beautiful garden and 130 to the top one with the best view and the most privacy, so be prepared. The rooms vary, private or shared bathrooms, with or without kitchenette, solar heated shower bags, simple but clean.

The business is run by Oliver and Angelika Hartleib who have young children. Great breakfast for US$6.50 with home-made bread and yoghurt, snacks and drinks available; family-style dinners a couple of times a week, reservations essential.

Sint Eustatius

Expect a 7% government tax, a 15% service charge and sometimes a 5% surcharge on top of quoted rates. The tourist office has a list of home rentals; some are recently renovated traditional cottages with a/c and lots of other modern conveniences.

LL-AL Old Gin House, Lower Town, **T** 599-3182319, www.oldginhouse.com *Map 10, C5, p285* Owned by *Holland House Hotel* on Sint Maarten and upgraded into a luxury place to stay. Built with the old bricks of an 18th-century cotton gin house, this is the most attractive of the hotels with an olde worlde atmosphere, but you need to take precautions against mosquitoes. There are two fancy suites on the waterfront with a sea view and balcony, 14 dark rooms on the other side of the road behind the Gin House overlooking the pool. All have large beds, bathrooms, a/c, TV, phones, internet access in the lobby. The Belgian chef creates fabulous dinners in the restaurant in the old house. Breakfast and lunch are served on the waterfront across the road.

AL-A Golden Era Hotel, Lower Town, **T** 599-3182345, goldera2003@yahoo.com *Map 10, C5, p285* On the waterfront, a modern block at right angles to the sea so only the end rooms have a sea view. There are 20 large rooms, gradually being remodelled and upgraded to get rid of the tired carpet but they have tiny bathrooms. All have a/c, fridge, TV, phone and a desk. *Scubaqua* dive shop is on the premises. Restaurant and bar on the waterfront with waves crashing underneath, food average; car or scooter hire arranged.

AL-B King's Well, between Upper and Lower Town in King's Well, **T/F** 599-3182538. *North end of beach by Smoke Alley. Map 9, E1, p285* The rooms are past their decorative best but are large and comfortable with ceiling fans, some with a/c, fridge and TV. Some rooms overlook the bar, while the more expensive have a spectacular sea view. One has a water-bed. The hotel is casual and popular with divers and sailors. The restaurant serves good steak, lobster, Jaeger- and Wienerschnitzels, cocktails, open kitchen not particularly clean but friendly atmosphere. Owners Win and Laura like to chat and play cards with guests, reservations requested.

C Country Inn, Concordia, **T** 599-3182484. *Map 9, D2, p285* A bit remote but excellent value, this is a family home with guest rooms attached. Some of the tiled rooms are larger than others but all have a cosy bedroom, a living area with fridge and a good sized bathroom, a/c, TV and open onto a deck with a good breeze from the Atlantic. Some have two double beds and sleep four, with US$10 charged for extra persons. Breakfast US$5, other meals on request. The owner, Mrs Iris Pompier (wife of a policeman), is an excellent cook, caters for government functions, specializing in local delicacies. Price includes tax, but no credit cards accepted.

St-Barthélemy

Some of the Caribbean's most luxurious and expensive hotels can be found on this island, while cheap guest houses are few and far between, but there are no large resorts and no all-inclusive hotels to dominate the beaches. There are many stylish, comfortable villas on the beach or up in the hills with glorious views and sea breezes, and many people choose to take advantage of the well-stocked supermarkets with their French delicacies and cheap wine and cater for themselves. With that in mind, quite a few hotel rooms have kitchenettes. There is no occupancy tax. Significant reductions are available in summer and packages including car hire can be good value. For apartments and villas, in the USA contact **French Caribbean International**, T 800-3222223, www.frenchcaribbean.com. On St-Barth contact **Sibarth Villa Rentals**, Gustavia, T 590-(0)590-298890, www.sibarth.com; **New Agency**, Quai de la République, Gustavia, T 590-(0)590-278114, F 590-(0)590-278767; **Claudine Mora Immobilier (CMI)**, T 590-(0)590-278088, F 590-(0)590-278085; **Ici et Là**, Quai de la République, T 590-(0)590-277878, F 590-(0)590-277828; **St Barth Properties**, rue du Centenaire, Gustavia, T 590-(0)590-297505, www.stbarth.com.

LL **La Banane**, Lorient, T 590-(0)590-520300, www.labanane.com *A few hundred metres from Lorient Beach. Map 11, D3, p286* Pastel-painted bungalows with square modern lines, nine rooms all named after tropical fruits, a/c, fan, phone, TV, DVD, two pools, lots of bananas, fine dining, breakfast, library, boat and car available. Airport transfers and service included in rate.

LL **Le Toiny**, Anse de Toiny, T 590-(0)590-278888, www.letoiny.com *Closed Sep-Oct. Map 11, D5, p286* Out of the way but one of the most high-class hotels on the island. The 15 modern villa suites decorated in white with blue, red or green trimmings have huge four-poster beds, a/c, high-tech entertainment as well as spacious bathrooms with walk-in shower and more personal care goodies than you could imagine, kitchenette with fridge and enormous mini-bar more like a shop, and large plunge pools with ocean view. The hotel has 24-hour room service and every luxury you could possibly desire but at a price. It also has the best restaurant on the island, *Le Gaïac*, world-renowned for refined and elegant dining with a huge menu and wine list and windows open to the pool looking down to the rugged Atlantic coast. The set menu for dinner is €110, while entrées cost between €30-40. Attentive service and faultless attention to detail. Also a great place to come for Sunday brunch.

LL Le Tom Beach Hotel, St-Jean, **T** 590-(0)590-275313, www.tombeach.com *Map 11, D2, p286* Twelve rooms in a small property between the road and the beach but only the most expensive and largest two have a sea view, the rest face in to the patio garden. Luxury four-poster beds, a/c, fans, TV, DVD, video, private terraces, hammocks, multilingual staff. The colour scheme is bright and cheerful or an assault on the senses, depending on your state of mind, with scarlet, blue, green and yellow in the hotel and violet and purple added in the restaurant, part of which is on the sand. The rooms are more muted, which is a relief. Moroccan design around the L-shaped pool with huge cushioned areas for lounging.

LL-AL Le Manoir de Marie, Route de Salines, Lorient, **T** 590-(0)590-277927, www.lemanoirstbarth.com *Map 11, D3, p286* Delightfully romantic yet family friendly just 50 m from the beach with well-stocked supermarkets two minutes away. The main house dates from 1610 and started its life in Normandy before being dismantled and shipped to St-Barth in 1984. Cottages in the garden have been built in the same style. Owner Marie-Dominique Delemazure has put her stamp on the interior design, with French antique furniture, pretty drapes and cushions, daybeds and flowers. Each room is different: some for couples, some sleep up to five, some have kitchenettes and dining areas, some have outdoor bathrooms. Good value packages are available with car hire. Breakfast available but no restaurant.

LL-AL Le Tropical, St-Jean, **T** 590-(0)590-276487, www.tropicalhotel.net *Closed 1 Jun-15 Jul. Map 11, D2, p286* Creole gingerbread style with romantic lacy bedspreads and flowing mosquito nets, set in a lush garden with lots of flowering plants and palm trees. The 20 sea-view and garden-view rooms have a/c, fan, TV, phone, terrace. Have your breakfast on the veranda overlooking the beach or in your room. The pool has a panoramic sea view. No restaurant but it is only a short walk to the beach and restaurants. Excursions arranged.

AL-B Sunset, Gustavia, **T** 590-(0)590-277721, www.st-barths.com/sunset-hotel *Map 12, B8, p286* Upstairs 10 two-star rooms on the waterfront overlooking the ferries. Painted a cheerful yellow and white on the balcony. Newly decorated and a good option for a town centre hotel.

A-B Le Nid d'Aigle, Anse des Cayes, **T** 590-(0)590-277520, www.saint-barths.com *Map 11, C2, p286* Up on the hill with a view over the town and the sea. Three rooms in Gigi's villa with a/c, phone, airport transfers, pets allowed, pool with a view.

C La Presqu'île, Gustavia, **T** 590-(0)590-276460, estflorvillegreaux@wanadoo.fr *Map 12, B7, p286* On the waterfront, 10 rooms overlook the harbour and the boats, all upstairs with a balcony, not large, not fancy, but comfortable, clean and adequate, light and airy. Large lounge and bar area with a view.

St Kitts

There is a 9% occupancy tax and 10% service charge. A wide variety of accommodation ranges from first-class plantation inns and beach hotels to rented cottages, but it is advisable to book in advance. Reductions are available in summer. Breaking with tradition and out of character with the rest of the hotels, a monstrous new five-star *St Kitts Marriott Royal Beach* has been built on Frigate Bay, with 640 rooms, the largest casino in the Caribbean, a golf course alongside, amphitheatre, state-of-the-art gym and spa, restaurants, etc. The *St Kitts/Nevis Hotel Association* can be reached at PO Box 438, Basseterre, St Kitts, **T** 869-4655304, **F** 869-4657746.

LL Golden Lemon, Dieppe Bay, **T** 869-4657260, www.goldenlemon.com *About 15 miles from Basseterre. No children under 18.* *Map 13, B1, p287* On the beach with a view of Saba and Stati, opened in 1963 and still run by the distinguished elderly gentlemen, owner Arthur Leaman and manager Martin Kreiner. There are 34 rooms in a charming old plantation house dating from 1610, with wooden floors, high beds reached by step ladder, or in the one- to two-bedroom new, spacious cottages with pools. It is peaceful and understated, with antique furniture and a modern elegance. No cottage overlooks another, each shaded by trees and gardens. The black sand beach has lots of birds and fishermen, also cows, goats donkeys and dogs, good snorkelling on the reef. The excellent restaurant has a lovely atmosphere with open-air seating on the covered terrace and tropical gardens between the restaurant and the sea. Everything is lemon yellow and white with many ornamental lemons donated by appreciative guests. Casual during the day, at night by candlelight it becomes elegant and romantic. The hosts chat with their guests over drinks and canapés before dinner and service is attentive and friendly. Delicious food, international in style using local ingredients.

LL Ottley's Plantation Inn, Cayon, **T** 869-4657234, www.ottleys.com *Map 13, C2, p287* At 520 ft above sea level in 35 acres with a view to the Atlantic, the rooms are in the 1832 great house or in luxury modern cottages designed to blend in with the plantation house in the beautiful tropical gardens. Sweeping lawns slope down from the house to the cottages and restaurant. The lights on palm trees to guide you down are also popular with huge toads, which sit in the spotlight to catch insects. The cottages are spacious, elegantly furnished, with large bathrooms, a/c, fans, plunge pools. The full size pool is in the ruins of a sugar factory. Ottley's is run by a US family who are very hospitable and knowledgeable. There are nice walks in the area or you can take the beach shuttle. A popular spa for massages is in a little chattel house in the trees. The excellent *Royal Palm* restaurant caters for all diets and provides elegant dining in a cool, natural environment built into the side of old sugar mill buildings.

LL **Rawlins Plantation, T** 869-4656221, Rawplant@caribsurf.com *16 miles from Basseterre in the northwest of the island. Map 13, B1, p287* At 350 ft above sea level looking out over the sugar plantation, the hotel is tranquil and delightful, in British colonial style, and offers grass court tennis, swimming pool, croquet, great walking opportunities, 10 rooms in cottages in the garden of the main house built on the remains of the boiling house, and a honeymoon suite in the sugar mill, decorated with bright cotton fabrics and wooden floors, no TV or minibar. Breakfast and dinner are included in the rates; no credit cards accepted. Mid-morning coffee or afternoon tea on the terrace looking over the sugar estates. The excellent food is under the control of Claire Rawson, a Kittitian chef, who sources her ingredients from the kitchen garden or locally and offers a mix of cordon bleu and local cuisine. The restaurant and bar are in the library, where hotel guests and visitors receive a set menu which changes daily.

LL-L **Ocean Terrace Inn (OTI),** Wigley Avenue, Basseterre, **T** 869-4652754, www.oceanterraceinn.net *Map 13, D2, p287* Nondescript modern architecture, apartments, suites and rooms, a/c, TV, fan, three pools, hot tub, fitness centre, business centre, beach shuttle. *Pro-Divers* and *Fisherman's Wharf* across the road on the sea shore and extending out into the sea so you feel you are right on top of the water. The restaurant is decorated with lots of sailing paraphernalia, has friendly staff and is popular locally for special occasions as well as with guests staying at the OTI. Meals include tasty fresh fish, barbecued chicken and help yourself to vegetables for US$25-35; conch chowder recommended.

LL-A Frigate Bay Resort, Frigate Bay, **T** 869-4658935, www.frigatebay.com *Map 13, E3, p287* It is just a five-minute walk round the hillside to the beach from the 64 rooms, studios and suites, all painted a colourful yellow, white and blue with pool or hillside views, a/c, fan, TV, fridge (studios have kitchens). A pleasant medium-sized hotel, with a casual restaurant by the pool and friendly management.

LL-A Timothy Beach Resort, Frigate Bay, **T** 869-4658597, www.timothybeachresort.com *Map 13, E3, p287* The only hotel in this area actually on the Caribbean. Three-star, good value, connecting rooms and studios with kitchens, versatile arrangements to make apartments or a town house to sleep 2-10, with a mountain or sea view. Internet access, pool, steps down to the sea. The *Sunset Café*, **T** 869-4657085, *(daily 0700-2300)* serves local seafood, burgers and a range of other local and international dishes right beside the sea in the open air or under cover. Good quality and good value, priced in EC$.

LL-B Angelus, Frigate Bay, **T** 869-4666224, www.angelusstkitts.com *Map 13, D3, p287* Next to the Marriott and the golf course, the hotel's land stretches down to the sea where there's a beach bar. Three-storey blocks of one- to two-bedroom suites have sea or golf course views, high ceilings, kitchenettes, washing machines. Still building in 2004 so good value introductory rates are offered. Restaurant and bar.

A-B The Mule House, Brighton Plantation, **T** 869-4668086, www.holiday-rentals.co.uk/mulehouse *Map 13, C2, p287* Brighton is the oldest plantation on the island and the Mule House has been built on the site of the former mule barn in the plantation yard alongside the ruins of the house which burned down a few years ago. Sue (English) and Ray (returned Kittitian) Wharton have built a sympathetic home here with four self-catering apartments in the house, each with their own entrance, kitchen, lounge/diner, CD player, huge shower room and two bedrooms with mosquito nets, books and a balcony with sea view. Fruit and flowers from the beautiful garden, together with rum, are offered as a welcome pack and they meet you at the airport and help with excursions.

B Gateway Inn, Frigate Bay, **T** 869-4657155, gateway@caribsurf.com *On the Frigate Bay Rd opposite the Sands complex where there are 2 restaurants and night-time entertainment. Map 13, D3, p287* Built in a horseshoe shape and surrounded by lawns, the 10 self-catering apartments, all on the ground floor with their own entrance, are comfortable and in a great neighbourhood, but not luxurious with a/c, phone, TV and laundry. Just 10 minutes from the beach or golf course and one of the cheaper options in this area.

C Rock Haven Bed & Breakfast, Frigate Bay, **T/F** 869-4655503. *Map 13, E3, p287* Two suites are available at this bed and breakfast, with views of both coasts. One is an attractively decorated, roomy bed-sitting room with its own patio surrounded by the garden. It has twin beds, fully-equipped kitchen, spacious bathroom, ceiling fan, TV and phone. The other suite upstairs is spacious and airy with mahogany louvred windows looking onto the garden.

C-D Inner Circle Guest House, in the village of St Paul's, **T** 869-4665857. *14 miles from Basseterre. Map 13, B1, p287* Newly built two-storey guest house in the middle of village life, on a bus route to get around the island. If you are interested in local culture rather than non-stop beach activities, then this is a perfect place to stay. It is also a popular night spot so expect action and noise.

Nevis

Accommodation on Nevis tends to be upmarket, in reconstructions of old plantation Great Houses, tastefully decorated in an English style (collectively called *The Inns of Nevis*). They are small and intimate in contrast to the 218-room *Four Seasons Resort Nevis* which dominates Pinney's Beach with its luxury spa and golf course.

LL Montpelier Plantation Inn and Beach Club,
T 869-4693462, www.montpeliernevis.com *Map 15, F3, p288* In 2002 the Hoffman family took over and redecorated this beautiful old property on 30 acres, 750 ft above sea level, a favourite with British tourists. Luxury touches include a welcome with cold towels and rum punch, being taken straight to your room, registering later. The long-serving staff are delightful, friendly and helpful. There is a pool, tennis, lovely gardens, beach shuttle, a library and 17 white rooms with cool green or blue flourishes and fresh fruit daily; child reductions. The *Terrace Restaurant* offers fine dining. Lots of tropical fruits are grown on the estate, as well as organic herbs and vegetables used in the kitchen. After drinks in the Great Room, a sitting room cum library off the bar, you move to the outdoor terrace for dinner from where you can see the lights of St Kitts. The menu is a limited choice, but varied. In *The Mill*, no more than 12 guests dine by candlelight with a gourmet *prix fixe* dinner.

LL Nisbet Plantation Beach Club, St James, on ½-mile beach close to airport, **T** 869-4699325, www.nisbetplantation.com *Map 15, A4, p288* The only plantation inn on the beach; 38 comfortable rooms in hexagonal cottages/suites in the gardens of the 1776 Great House, spread out down the hill to the sea. All have a/c and fans. There is tennis, a pool, croquet and a beach bar for lunch. The restaurant, bar and TV lounge are in the traditional plantation-style Great House. Huge breakfasts, delicious afternoon tea and excellent dinner are included in the rates, lots of repeat guests.

Sleeping

LL-L Hermitage Plantation Inn, St John's Parish,
T 869-4693477, www.hermitagenevis.com *Map 15, F3, p288*
Richard and Maureen Lupinacci have created a very friendly
atmosphere in their collection of beautiful individual wooden
cottages, some rather small, all with four-poster beds. The *Planter's
House* dating from 1680-1740 is believed to be the oldest wooden
house in the Lesser Antilles. There is tennis, a pool and stables for
horse riding and carriage tours on site, all in a stunning rural
setting with a view down to the sea. Romance/equestrian/
adventure/diving packages are offered. Lunch is on the terrace,
dinner is indoors. The lamb and pork are home grown, as are the
fruit and vegetables, and local fishermen bring fresh fish and
seafood. Try too Maggie Lupinacci's *Hermitage Beach Club*, just
north of the *Four Seasons Hotel* on Pinney's Beach which offers light
lunches and more substantial dinners. A great place for the day
with beach chairs on the sand, sunset cocktails and happy hours on
Fridays. Occasional live music, dress code smart casual.

LL-L Old Manor, **T** 869-4693445, www.oldmanornevis.com
Map 15, F4, p288 In a restored 1690 sugar plantation, which has 12
spacious rooms and suites incorporating the stone walls of the old
mill buildings, with wooden walls, shutters, old furnishings, and
prints of old maps. At 800 ft above sea level, it is delightfully
breezy and cool, no a/c needed. There is a good restaurant with a
view to Montserrat, tropical gardens, beach shuttle and pool.

LL-AL Golden Rock Plantation Inn, St George's Parish,
T 869-4693346, www.golden-rock.com *Map 15, E5, p288* Seven
cottages, 14 simple but comfortable rooms cluster around an 18th-
century plantation house, all with antique furniture and four-
poster beds, and there is a two-storey suite in an old windmill.
There is plenty of breeze up on the hill, and an ocean view to
Montserrat. The sugar mill cistern is now a pool; tennis, beach
shuttle, eco-tours and excellent hiking excursions are available.

Enjoy afternoon tea and watch the monkeys. The *Golden Rock Beach Bar* on Pinney's Beach is open for lunch and lobster sandwiches.

LL-AL Oualie Beach Hotel, **T** 869-4699735, www.oualiebeach.com *Map 15, B2, p288* Comfortable, 32 well-equipped rooms and studios in cottages with a view of the bay, or deluxe rooms on the beach, safe for children. The relaxed bar and restaurant are on the sand under tamarind trees: Caribbean buffet on Saturday with live music and masquerade dance, surf-and-turf beach barbecue on Tuesday with rhythm and blues, and steel pan on Sunday. Mountain bikes, diving, kayaking are available.

L-AL Banyan Tree Bed & Breakfast, **T** 800-6396109, www.banyantreebandb.com *Map 15, F3, p288* Two rooms in the guest house and a one-bedroom suite with kitchenette in the Bamboo House, 700 ft above sea level near Morning Star village on a 6-acre farm growing flowers, spices and raising Barbados black-belly sheep, fruit trees and a 300-year-old banyan tree.

L-B Philsha's, Pinney's Rd, **T** 869-4695253, www.geocities.com /philshas *A few minutes from Charlestown.* *Map 15, E1, p288* Family-run, close to the beach, a modern building, white with turquoise trimmings. Clean, new single and double rooms, a/c, with TV, laundry facilities and phone, are large with tiled floors.

B-D Sea Spawn Guesthouse, outskirts of Charlestown, **T** 869-4695239. *Map 15, E1, p288* This guest house of 18 newly renovated rooms with TV and phones is in a modern, cream and blue building with balconies, an ideal location for beach and town.

C JP's, in town near pier and market, **T** 869-4690287, jpwalters@caribsurf.com *Map 15, E1, p288* Popular with yachties wanting *terra firma* for a night or two. Simple rooms with a/c, fans, fridge and a lounge with TV, restaurant on site.

Eating and drinking

Restaurants range from gourmet to cafés or street stalls but they will all make the most of local ingredients. If you are economizing, find a local place and choose the daily special, which will give you a chance to try the typical food of the island, usually in generous portions. Plenty of restaurants serve pizza and pasta, popular with families.

Meal times vary, but as a general rule breakfast is from around 0800, and a meal of saltfish and its accompaniments can be taken any time in the morning or for an early lunch. Lunch starts from 1200 and is usually fairly substantial even if picked up as a takeaway. A filling snack is the *roti*, a very popular chapatti wrap, filled with spicy or curried meat, fish or vegetables. Originally from Trinidad, it has spread up the island chain. Restaurants usually start to serve dinner from 1800 or 1900 and closing times are extremely flexible. A restaurant with a bar will open early for happy hour and stay open late, although the kitchen may close from 2200 or 2300. On a quiet island like Saba, however, many restaurants close by 2130.

Eating codes

Price

▦▦▦	US$20 and over
▦▦	US$10-20
▦	US$10 and under

Prices refer to the cost of a main course. Service is usually 10%.

As you might expect of islands, there is a wide variety of fresh seafood on offer. Fish of all sorts, lobster and conch are commonly available and usually better quality than local meat. Beef and lamb are often imported from the USA or Argentina, but goat, pork and chicken are produced locally. There is no dairy industry to speak of, so cheeses are also usually imported. There is, however, a riot of tropical fruit and vegetables. The best bananas in the world are grown in the Caribbean on small farms using the minimum of chemicals, if not organic. They are cheap and incredibly sweet and unlike anything you can buy at home. Many of the wonderful tropical fruits you will come across in juices or in ice cream. Don't miss the rich flavours of the soursop, the guava or the sapodilla. Mangoes in season drip off the trees and those that don't end up on your breakfast plate can be found squashed in abundance all over the roads. Caribbean oranges are often green when ripe, as there is no cold season to bring out the orange colour, and are meant for juicing not peeling. Portugals are like tangerines and easy to peel. Avocados are nearly always sold unripe: wait several days before attempting to eat them. Avocados have been around since the days of the Arawaks, who also cultivated cassava and cocoa, but many vegetables have their origins in the slave trade. The breadfruit, a common staple rich in carbohydrates and vitamins A, B and C, was brought from the South Seas in 1793 by Captain Bligh, perhaps more famous for the mutiny on the *Bounty*. The slaves were needed for work in the sugar plantations and sugar cane is still grown on St Kitts today, often ending up as rum.

Antigua

In addition to a wide selection of imported delicacies served in the larger hotels, local specialities, found in smaller restaurants in St John's, often very reasonable, should never be missed: **saltfish** (traditionally eaten at breakfast in a tomato and onion sauce), **pepper-pot** with **fungi** or **foungee** (a kind of cornmeal dumpling), **goat water** (hot goat stew), **shellfish** (the local name for trunk fish), **conch stew** and the local staple, chicken and rice. **Johnny cake** is rather like a savoury doughnut, but you will find variations on the theme on other islands. **Ducana** is made from grated sweet potato and coconut, mixed with pumpkin, sugar and spices and boiled in a banana leaf. Tropical fruits and vegetables found on other Caribbean islands are also found here: breadfruit, cristophene, dasheen, eddo, mango, guava and pawpaw (papaya). Oranges are green, while the native pineapple is called the Antigua black. Locally made **Sunshine ice cream**, American-style, is available in most supermarkets. Imported wines and spirits are reasonably priced but local drinks (fruit and sugar cane juice, coconut milk, and Antiguan rum punches and swizzles, ice cold) must be experienced. The local **Cavalier rum** is a light golden colour, usually used for mixes. Beer can be bought at good prices from most supermarkets and the Wadadli Brewery on Crabbs peninsula. There are no licensing restrictions. Tap water is safe all over the island but bottled water is available if you are unsure or prefer it. A 7% tax on all meals and drinks is added to your bill and usually 10% service.

Be aware that there is **ciguatera** in the waters around Antigua and across to Florida which accumulates in fish high up the food chain such as barracuda, king fish and even large snapper. If you start to feel unwell after eating such fish, take yourself straight to the hospital. Ciguatera will give you a very bad dose of food poisoning which can result in death. Fish caught further south are safe, so if in doubt, ask where it is from.

¥¥¥ **Alberto's**, Willoughby Bay, English Harbour, **T** 268-4603007. *Open Nov-May, Tue-Sun dinner only. Map 1, F5, p280* Choice dining spot frequented by ex-pat 'locals' plus celebrities like Eric Clapton, who has a house near here. Italian-run in an open-air tropical setting under a gazebo; fresh seafood and pasta always available. Expect to pay over US$55; reservations essential.

¥¥¥ **Chez Pascal**, Galley Bay Hill, Galley Bay, **T** 268-4623232. *Daily lunch and dinner. Map 1, B1, p280* With a wonderful view overlooking Galley Bay, you can eat indoors in the cool or on the patio by the pool and enjoy authentic French food from French chef Pascal Milliat, with an extensive French wine list. Considered one of the best restaurants on the island and the place to come for a special meal or for a celebration. Accommodation available.

¥¥¥ **Le Bistro**, Hodges Bay, **T** 268-4623881, www.joinusinparadise .com/lebistro *Tue-Sun dinner only. Map 1, A4, p280* Excellent French food prepared by head chef, Patrick Gauducheau, in another leading Antiguan restaurant, featured in international magazines and TV programmes. The varied menu includes vegetarian options, delicious paté, melt-in-the-mouth pastries. Reservations required.

¥¥¥-¥¥ **Harmony Hall**, Brown's Bay, **T** 268-4604120, www.harmonyhall.com *Daily from 1000 for lunch, drinks, snacks, dinner Fri-Sat, closed mid-May to early Nov. Map 1, D7, p280* A former sugar estate Great House and mill dating back to 1843 is now principally a restaurant and art gallery with accommodation. The restaurant on the patio overlooking Nonsuch Bay and Green Island serves excellent Italian cuisine; reservations essential. Bar in the mill. There are six rooms in two villas in the existing 9-acre grounds and more are to be built in an adjacent 2.6 acres at the end of Browns Bay. There is a pool and you can walk down to the beach. Boat trips to Green Island are complimentary for guests and there is a dock for visiting yachts. Car hire recommended.

▶ Rum with a punch

There is nothing better at the end of a busy day than finding a pleasant spot overlooking the sea with a rum in your hand to watch the sunset and look out for the green flash. The theory is that the more rum you drink, the more likely you are to see this flash of green on the horizon as the sun goes down.

There are hundreds of different rums in the Caribbean, each island producing the best, of course. The main producers are Jamaica, Cuba, Barbados, Guyana, Martinique and the Dominican Republic, but other islands such as St Kitts also produce excellent brands, while even Anguilla has a blending and bottling business. Generally, the younger, light rums are used in cocktails and aged, dark rums are drunk on the rocks or treated as you might a single malt whisky.

Many Caribbean hotels offer you a welcome cocktail when you stagger out of the taxi, jet-lagged from your transatlantic flight.

This is often an over-sweet, watered-down punch, with a poor quality rum and sickly fruit juice. You are more likely to find something palatable in the bar, but it always depends on which blend of juice the barman favours.

The standard recipe for a rum punch is: 'one of sour, two of sweet, three of strong and four of weak'.

If you measure that in fluid ounces, it comes out as:
1 oz lime juice
2 oz syrup (equal amounts of sugar and water, boiled for a few minutes)
3 oz rum
4 oz water, fruit juices, ginger ale, or whatever takes your fancy.

You could add ice and a dash of Angostura Bitters from Trinidad, use nutmeg syrup from Grenada or Falernum from Barbados instead of sugar syrup, and garnish it with a slice of lime.

Delicious.

ŦŦŦ-ŦŦ **Home**, Lower Gambles Terr, St John's, **T** 268-4617651. *Mon-Sat 1800-2300, lunch Sat from 1200. Map 1, B3, p280* A 20-minute walk from tourist area but worth it. Antiguan Carl Thomas and his German wife Rita run this restaurant in a typical West Indian house and garden. A la carte menu and blackboard specials use fresh, local ingredients in dishes such as pork tenderloin with tamarind sauce and exotic desserts. Very elegant but friendly with no stiff formality, excellent service , welcoming to families.

ŦŦŦ-ŦŦ **Julian's Alfresco**, Barrymore Beach Club, Runaway Bay, **T** 268-5621545. *Tue-Sun lunch and dinner. Map 1, A2, p280* Beautifully presented and tasty food with a mixture of West Indian, European, Asian and South American influences, washed down with New World wines, make this a popular dinner venue in lush gardens by the beach, casual and cheerful colours. Reservations are advised in high season.

ŦŦŦ-ŦŦ **The Beach**, Antigua Village, Dickenson Bay, **T** 268-4806940. *Daily breakfast, lunch and dinner. Map 1, A2, p280* East meets West theme, with smoked sushi, Middle Eastern dishes and salads, pastas and seafoods, ribs and burgers, something for everyone in a lively atmosphere overlooking the sea, DJ on a Friday night, credit cards accepted, reservations suggested. Parking at Antigua Village.

ŦŦŦ-Ŧ **Commissioner Grill**, Redcliffe St, St John's, **T** 268-4621883. *Daily 1000-2300. Map 1, C1, p280* A casual restaurant on the street corner in the heart of town, high ceilings and fans cool things down while staff sweat over their pans at the back. Local chef Conroy White prepares West Indian dishes with a breakfast of saltfish and plenty of seafood, lobster, steak, chicken, burgers, ribs and salads and sandwiches. Excellent vegetable plate with mixed vegetables, plantain, black beans and foungee or rice and peas, but if you are vegetarian ask them not to fry the plantain in the same oil they use for fish. Draught beer.

¶¶¶-¶ **The Sticky Wicket**, 20 Pavilion Drive, at the airport, T 268-4817000, www.thestickywicket.com *Daily, lunch and dinner. Map 1, A4, p280* Restaurant and bar overlook the cricket ground with TVs for watching sporting events, convenient if you have a long wait for your plane but expensive with an international menu, steaks and fish. You can get burgers or nachos if you just want a snack. Under the same ownership is **Pavilion**, a very expensive five-star, formal restaurant with wrap-around veranda overlooking the cricket ground, open for dinner only and costing US$100 per head, reservations essential, T 268-4806800.

¶¶¶-¶ **Tree Tops**, Silver St, Coolidge, T 268-4613014. *Mon-Thu 1200-1800, Fri-Sat 1200-2400, Sun 1000-1500. Map 1, A4, p280* Attractive café attached to a garden centre, designed primarily to keep partners happy while gardeners browse and shop. On weekdays they serve health conscious lunches followed by afternoon tea; on Saturday, local dishes of souse, goat water, season rice and rice pudding to eat in or take away. On Friday and Saturday from 1800 there is an evening 'lime' and on Sunday, a buffet brunch with all you can eat for EC$85, children under 12 free.

¶¶ **HQ**, upstairs in the historic Headquarters Building inside English Harbour, T 268-5622562. *Daily, breakfast, lunch and dinner. Map 1, F5, p280* Dining tables are inside and outside on the veranda overlooking Nelson's Dockyard, popular with a lively yachting crowd and there is live music some nights. Their speciality is fish and there is a lobster tank. Dinner reservations suggested.

¶¶-¶ **Catherine's Café**, at the Antigua Slipway in Nelson's Dockyard, English Harbour, T 268-4605050. *Wed-Mon, lunch, drinks and dinner. Map 1, F5, p280* French chef, divine crêpes, quiches and assorted salads. Lovely setting right on the water with a boardwalk where you can sit and watch the yachts.

¶¶-¶ **Mama Lolly's**, in Redcliffe Quay, St John's, **T** 268-5621552, mamalol@candw.ag *Mon-Sat 0830-1700. Map 2, D1, p281* In the heart of the shopping area, Mama serves the best vegetarian lunch, with lasagne, bean stew, tofu, salad bar and choice of cooked dishes plus a salad for a set price, and great mixed fruit and vegetable juices, freshly extracted. There is limited seating; locals often get a takeaway.

¶¶-¶ **Papa Zouk**, Hilda Davis Drive, Gambles, St John's, **T** 268-4646044. *Mon-Sat 1800-2300 in season, otherwise Wed-Sat. Map 1, B3, p280* Unprepossessing and casual place known for its specialities of bouillabaisse, a meal in itself, paella Creole, fresh fish and seafood, although chicken and meat is also available as is vegetarian food on request. Congenial host, Bert Kirchner, chats and goes through the daily specials with you while zouk music is played in the background. A very popular place and always full. Don't forget to visit the bathroom to see the unusual toilet seat.

¶¶-¶ **Turner's Beach Bar**, Johnson's Point, Jolly Harbour, **T** 268-4629133. *Daily 1000 until everyone goes home. Map 1, E1, p280* Beach bar at the end of a long stretch of sand with a covered terrace or umbrellas on the beach. You can get breakfast, lunch, snacks, drinks or dinner: local food, salads, huge *roti*, fish and chips, tender conch; a place to base yourself for the day.

¶ **OJ's Beach Bar & Restaurant**, Crab Hill, Jolly Harbour, **T** 268-4600184. *Daily 1000-2200. Map 1, E1, p280* Excellent setting on the beach with a simple menu but good food and service: fresh seafood, delicious snapper, great lobster salad as well as burgers and sandwiches all at economical prices, no credit cards. Good any day, but on Sunday there is live jazz from 1600.

Barbuda

There are not many restaurants and they tend to close in the evening, so check beforehand. You can ask local people to cook for you but be prepared to fend for yourself sometimes. For home cooking try *Claudia Hopkins*, **T** 268-4600022, or the *Block Boys*, **T** 268-4600012, at weekends.

Ψ Palm Tree, at the edge of Codrington, **T** 268-4600517. *Advance booking required. Map 3, D6, p281* Cerene Deazle runs this restaurant as well as her guest house serving local food on request such as lobster, conch, fish and venison. The local deer are a speciality on Barbuda. Alternatively she will cook you chicken or burgers and fries.

Ψ Eda's Joint, Codrington, **T** 268-4600412. *Wed, Sat, advance booking required. Map 3, D6, p281* Eda Frank cooks traditional Barbudan food and on Wednesday and Saturday come here for pepperpot, ducana and saltfish and seasoned rice. On request, and in season, she will also cook venison and land crabs.

Montserrat

Several places do takeaway meals and there are lots of 'snackettes' where you can pick up a decent local lunch on the side of the road. Bakeries are also good places to get a snack. Some places only open if you make a reservation in advance, so it is best to check. Restaurant opening times are from 0730-1000, 1130-1400 and 1900-2200, although not all are open for breakfast and several only open in the evenings if there is demand. A large frog called **mountain chicken**, indigenous here and in Dominica, is the local delicacy. **Goat water** stew is another local dish commonly found on the menu. Most other foods, like steak and fish, are imported.

¶¶¶-¶¶ **Gourmet Gardens**, Olveston, **T** 664-4917859. *Thu-Tue 1100-1400, 1800-2000. Map 4, D1, p282* Approached up an alley-way and set in lovely gardens, the restaurant is in a plantation-style outhouse with thick stone walls and a veranda. Dinner is by appointment only, so call ahead. Good food and good wines. Dutch run, so more European dishes than Caribbean on the menu.

¶¶¶-¶¶ **The Windsor Restaurant**, Cudjoe Head, **T** 664-4912900. *Daily, breakfast from 0800, lunch from 1200, tea 1600, dinner 1930 by reservation only. Map 4, C2, p282* A new building on three floors, with rental apartments downstairs, restaurant on the middle floor and boutiques to come on the top floor. Quite smart, a/c, with good views, the restaurant aims for the top, serving Caribbean and international cuisine, and is proving popular. EC$25-30 for lunch; expect to pay double at dinner. Small stage for occasional music.

¶¶¶-¶¶ **Ziggy's Restaurant**, Mahogany Loop, Woodlands **T** 664-4918282, the second turning on the right from the main road. *Dinner only, by reservation only. Map 4, D1, p282* The island's leading restaurant for many years, with good international cuisine, is right on top of the hill overlooking Salem. You dine under canvas in the cool of the gardens; the area is like parkland. Ziggy has been serving great food since the early 1990s: try the lobster quadrille, jerk pork or chocolate sludge. She has an excellent wine list with Chilean and Australian reds. Dinner with wine will cost around EC$100. ● *A good wine store has opened next to Ziggy's.*

¶ **Tina's Restaurant**, Brades Main Rd, **T** 664-4913538. *Lunch and dinner. Map 4, B2, p282* Like many restaurants, this is a new wooden building in plantation style with a veranda. Very popular with locals, it is a good meeting place serving local food, chicken, fish and vegetables, prices from US$16.50-24 for a meal. Its wine list is improving, bringing in the ex-pat market. Set back off the main road it has the best car park on Montserrat.

¶¶-¶ **Jumping Jack's Bar**, Olveston, **T** 664-4915645. *Wed-Sat, lunch and dinner. Map 4, D1, p282* Danny and Margaret have moved back on to the beach after a few years serving from their home. Originally a dive shop, the building is now a restaurant and pavilion for the tennis players, as it overlooks the tennis courts and is the cheapest place to get a simple but adequate meal. The fish is recommended here, all caught by Danny and very fresh.

¶ **Bitter End Beach Bar**, Little Bay, **T** 664-4913146. *0600-late. Map 4, A2, p282* Seafood and snacks on the beach, lunch from US$5.50-9.50, dinner from US$7.50. Moose always seems to be open. Look out for his lobster-special nights. Occasionally presents live bands from Antigua and the wider Caribbean.

¶¶-¶ **JJ's Cuisine**, Main Rd, St John's, **T** 664-4919024. *Breakfast, lunch and dinner. Map 4, B3, p282* A roadside timber restaurant just round the corner from *Tropical Mansions*, so guests come here to eat. The international food is excellent and popular with locals for lunch; call ahead for evening reservations. It is perhaps a little small so not so good for large parties.

¶ **La Colage Bar & Restaurant**, Sweeney's, **T** 664-4914136. *Map 4, B3, p282* Creole cuisine, lunch from US$5.50, dinner from US$7.50, very good value. People come here after work for something quick and a couple of drinks. There is a veranda and a pagoda in the garden, popular with lovers. Local fishermen supply the restaurants and sell the surplus in a fish shop alongside.

¶ **Morgan's Spotlight Bar & Restaurant**, Sweeney's, **T** 664-4915419. *Lunch. Map 4, B3, p282* Adjacent to the hospital and long established in an old-rum-shop style building, with the restaurant at the back of the bar serving large portions of local food. It is traditional to come here for Friday lunchtime to eat goat water – people travel miles for it.

Sint Maarten/St-Martin

Meals cost from around US$6 for a simple pasta dish or fresh tuna burger, but a restaurant meal will start at about US$12. On the **Dutch side**, there is a cluster of reasonable eating places around the **Maho Beach Resort and Casino** which are lively at night. If you pick one overlooking the street you will be entertained at times by dancers from the casino show, who come out onto the street and plaza to do a routine. **Simpson Bay** is another area for a wide variety of restaurants, all around the bridge and the yacht club. In **Philipsburg**, for the budget-minded try Back Street, where you mostly find Chinese and *roti* places. The traditional Sint Maarten liqueur is **guavaberry**. Unrelated to guavas (botanical name *Eugenia floribunda*), it is made from rum and the local berries. The berries, found on the hills, ripen just before Christmas and are used in cocktails.

On the **French side**, check the dollar/euro exchange rate as not all restaurants use the same rate; ask for your bill to be made out in whichever currency is the stronger to avoid overcharging. For travellers on a small budget try the snackbars and cafés on rue de Hollande, **Marigot**. Many bars on the waterfront serve barbecue lunch and dinner. There are also lots of restaurants overlooking the boats at **Marina Port Royale**, many with open-air dining. **Grand Case** reputedly has more restaurants than inhabitants. Most are open only for dinner and are on the street next to the beach, but these are generally more expensive than those on the other side of the boulevard and not recommended on a windy night. From the small snackbars, *lolos*, near the little pier come savoury smells of barbecue fish, chicken, ribs and lobster as well as other local snacks which are good value at less than US$12 for full meals, or US$4 for just ribs. Lunch is usually from 1200-1500 and dinner from 1800-2200, although times vary and a restaurant with a bar will stay open after the kitchen has closed. At weekends there is usually live music in one of the bars/restaurants along the beach.

Sint Maarten

Antoine, 119 Front St, Philipsburg, T 599-5422964.
1130-2200. Map 6, F4, p283 Supposedly French and Italian cuisine, but more of an international mix using local fish and seafood, although you can eat frogs' legs if you want. Great for lunch on the beach or dinner on the deck overlooking the sand.

Da Livio, 189 Front St, Philipsburg, T 599-5422690,
dalivio@megatropic.com *Lunch Mon-Fri 1200-1400, dinner Mon-Sat 1800-2200. Map 6, G1, p283* In this high-class Italian restaurant on the waterfront, run by Livio Bergamasco and his British wife, excellent seafood and pasta is served by some of the best waiters. It is not cheap at around US$60 per person for a full meal but they do have a selection of ports and brandies going back to 1954.

L'Escargot, 96 Front St, Philipsburg, T 599-5422483,
www.lescargotrestaurant.com *Dinner only. Map 6, F1, p283* For US$50 per person, in this Americanized French restaurant you will find eight different recipes for snails, 50 bottles of hot sauce, and the owners do cabaret on Friday night; book two days in advance.

Old Captain, Front St 121, Philipsburg, T 599-5426988,
www.old-captain.com *Mon-Sat 1100-2400, Sun 1100-1800. Map 6, F4, p283* Chinese and Japanese cuisine for US$30-40 per person, great sushi also vegetarian options, 10% discount for takeaway. Waterfront restaurant, where you can sit at the bar, on the porch, on the deck, in the dining room or on the beach. Valet parking.

Temptation, Atlantic Casino, Cupecoy, T 599-5452254.
Dinner only, 1830-2230. Map 5, C2, p283 A sophisticated restaurant run by an award-winning chef, Dino. His excellent food is accompanied by great wines and superb service. Traditional staples such as filet mignon or a surf 'n' turf of grilled shrimp and

tenderloin are beautifully presented and accompanied by a variety of vegetables. Leave room for desserts: champagne and fig sorbet, or a deliciously light ricotta cheesecake. The entrance has water running in sheets down the windows and is cool and inviting.

¶¶ **The Boathouse**, Simpson Bay, **T** 599-5445409. *Daily lunch and dinner, closed Sun in low season. Map 5, C3, p283* A great place for fresh fish with excellent catch of the day, lunch specials, very good wraps and burgers. The main menu offers coconut shrimp, filet mignon, scallops and there is also a children's menu. The dining terrace is on the lagoon, with a bright nautical atmosphere and there is a bar with widescreen TV. Service is fast and efficient.

¶¶ **Top Carrot**, Plaza del Lago, Simpson Bay Yacht Club, Simpson Bay, **T** 599-5443381. *Mon-Sat from 0730 until late. Map 5, C3, p283* Great-tasting health food, juice bar, vegetarian and gourmet café, makes you feel good about eating well.

¶¶-¶ **Harbour View**, Front St 89, Philipsburg, **T** 599-5425200. *Mon-Sat 0800-2200. Map 6, F1, p283* Very popular, right by the sea with some tables on the sand, European and local food for breakfast, lunch or dinner. Choose from salads, sandwiches, burgers, fresh fish, very tender conch, ribs and local dishes such as goat curry with potato salad and macaroni cheese as traditional side dishes.

¶¶-¶ **Hot Tomatoes**, 46 Airport Rd, Simpson Bay, **T** 599-5452223, www.hottomatoes.net *Daily from 1500. Map 5, C3, p283* Facing the lagoon and marina, yachtsmen can tie up their dinghies here. It is a good happy-hour spot with tapas and a pizza menu. The main menu has tuna ceviche, Aruban-Creole calamari, Anguillian lobster thermidor and pizza from the island's only wood-burning oven. Live music every night.

¶ **Carl's Bakery**, in the airport, at Cole Bay, **T** 599-5442812, and Philipsburg, **T** 599-5431059. *0700-2000. Map 5, airport C3, Cole Bay C5, Philipsburg D5, p283* Wonderful pastries and snacks, excellent bread and cakes. Their main outlet is at the hotel, *Carl's Unique Inn*, www.carlsinn.com.

¶ **Kan Kantrie**, Front St 5, Philipsburg, **T** 599-5428702. *1000-2100. Map 6, G6, p283* Authentic Surinamese and local cuisine, right on the beach, wonderful food for less than US$10.

¶ **Sint Rose Café**, Sint Rose Arcade, Front St, Philipsburg, **T** 599-5541579, info@sintrose.com *Daily 0800-1800, closed Sun in low season. Map 6, G6, p283* An outdoor bar with tables on the plaza , a perfect place to stop before or after shopping for breakfast, light lunches, salads, paninis, drinks and ice creams.

St-Martin

¶¶¶ **Fish Pot**, 82 Blvd de Grand Case, Grand Case, **T** 590-(0)590-875088, fish-pot@wanadoo.fr *1130-1500 in high season, dinner 1800-2230. Map 5, A5, p283* A romantic location overlooking the sea; ask for a table away from the lobster tank if you don't want to see the chef arguing with the occupants. Excellent seafood and formal service at a price, starters from €8, main courses from €22, desserts from €7 and wine from €25.

¶¶¶ **L'Alabama**, 93 Blvd de Grand Case, Grand Case, **T** 590-(0)590-878166. *Dinner only. Map 5, A5, p283* In one of the top restaurants on the island, elegantly decorated with classic art work, welcoming owners Pascal and Kristin serve traditional French food with local touches in a garden away from any traffic noise; US$30-50 per person. If you like *foie gras* you can have it stuffed with mango, apricot or fig, or try a starter of scallops with sesame on sweet potato mousse with honey, rum and a hint of curry.

¶¶¶ **L'Auberge Gourmande**, Blvd de Grand Case, Grand Case,
T 590-(0)590-877337. *Dinner only. Map 5, A5, p283* In a 19th-
century house, a good example of French Antillean architecture,
owned by Martine and Daniel Passeri, local wine merchants, with a
cellar of 1,300,000 bottles. The French food is delicious and the
service, excellent. Many ingredients come from France but the fish is
local. Start with baked goat's cheese and Roquefort salad or scallops
with olive tapenade and finish with the three-chocolate dessert.

¶¶¶ **Le Cottage**, Grand Case, **T** 590-(0)590-290330 (or
T599-5478820 from the Dutch side). *Dinner only. Map 5, A5, p283*
Run by Bruno and Stephane this is a high quality restaurant,
somewhere to come for a special meal. A treat for lobster lovers,
who can opt for the lobster four-course dinner: the lobster ravioli is
especially good. However, there are other excellent dishes with a
more local flavour, such as shrimp with mashed sweet potato and
spinach. All their seafood is delicious.

¶¶¶-¶¶ **La Cigale**, Baie Nettlé, **T** 590-(0)590-879023. *By Laguna
Beach Hotel. Lunch and dinner. Map 5, B3, p283* A friendly,
family-run restaurant on the beach. where you feel as though you
are eating in someone's home rather than in an upscale French
restaurant. Very good food: try the Cigale appetizer plate to start
and end with the home-made, rum-based digestif.

¶¶¶-¶¶ **Rainbow**, 176 Blvd de Grand Case, Grand Case,
T 590-(0)590-875580, www.rainbow-café.com *Map 5, A5, p283*
Traditional French cuisine but with oriental and Caribbean touches
such as tuna sashimi or crispy roast duck with banana rum sauce.
Good service, on the seafront in simple blue and white decor with
an open-air terrace and bar on the second floor overlooking the
bay. Take your dessert and coffee out onto the deck. One of the
best restaurants on the island with an extensive wine list.

♦♦ **Bikini Beach**, Baie Orientale, **T** 590-(0)590-874325, www.bikinibeach.net *Breakfast, lunch and early dinner. Map 5, A6, p283* A variety of culinary influences in a great location right on the beach, helped along with Brazilian music some nights. Spanish tapas, paella and sangria, as well as Angus beef and seafood. Try the baked garlic mussels or spicy Thai noodles with shrimp. Generous portions but don't expect speedy service.

♦♦ **Claude Mini-Club**, Marigot, **T** 590-(0)590-875069. *Lunch and dinner, closed Sun evening, closed Aug and Sep. Map 5, B4, p283* Seafront restaurant with a bar and dining arbour. The cuisine is typically French and Creole, with lots of fish and seafood, great crab. Caribbean buffet including lobster Wednesday and Saturday with all-you-can-eat and drinks for US$40, also a children's menu.

♦♦ **Le Ti Coin Créole**, 2 rue Mezzanille, Blvd Grand Case, Grand Case, **T** 590-(0)590-879209. *Map 5, A5, p283* A traditional gingerbread house is the setting for this reasonably priced restaurant serving French-island cuisine. Seafood is a speciality, with lobster bisque, tender conch, roasted or grilled snapper and shrimp, but you can also have curry goat.

♦♦ **Paradise View**, Hope Hill, Baie Orientale, **T** 590-(0)590-294537, paradiseview4@yahoo.com *Sun-Fri 0900-1800. Map 5, B5, p283* Up on the hill, with a tremendous panoramic view over Orient Bay, breezy, coach-stop, gift stalls outside. Run by Claudette Davis, who has written a cookbook of local recipes. Burgers, sandwiches, soups and salads under US$10, main courses, conch and dumplings US$15.

♦♦ **The Bridge**, Sandy Ground, Marigot, **T** 590-(0)590-29635. *Wed-Mon 1830-2230, closed Sep. Map 5, B4, p283* This grill, café and bar overlooking the lagoon (at night you can see huge fish feeding on shrimp and small fish) serves good local and Creole food, seafood, goat curry and delicious coconut tart. Starters US$6-11, main courses US$11-20 (more for lobster). On Friday they put on a Grand Buffet Creole, costing US$30, with a live band.

♥ **Zee Best**, Marina Port Royale, rue de la Liberté, Marigot, **T** 0590-(0)590-872751. *0800-1800. Map 5, B4, p283* This café on the waterfront in the marina is a great place to start the day with a breakfast of croissants and brioche. They serve wonderful pastries, melt-in-the-mouth chocolate almond or cinnamon sugar, and it has a real Parisian sidewalk feel if it weren't for the tropical heat – it also makes a good rest stop from shopping for a quick lunch of omelettes, quiche, crêpes and strong coffee. There is another branch near Saratoga in Simpson Bay, the Dutch one run by husband, Danny, and the French one run by wife, Tamela.

Anguilla

There are many excellent places to eat on the island from elegant restaurants to beach barbecues. Many places offer 'early-bird' specials, so you can eat more cheaply if you eat early. Beach bars and casual waterfront places provide a good lunch, for example **Uncle Ernie's**, Shoal Bay. The tourist guide *What We Do In Anguilla* has listings. Most of the restaurants are small and reservations are needed, particularly in high season. '**Relish**' is the local word for meat, not the accompaniment to it. Fresh fish is brought to the **fish market** (The Fishery) on George Hill (*Mon-Sat, 1730-1900, T 264-4973170 to check what time the boats are coming in*). You might be approached on the beach by men selling live lobsters, which are on practically every menu on the island.

There is a smooth Anguillian **rum**, a blend from other islands matured in oak barrels, designed to be drunk on the rocks rather than in a punch. Visit the rum-tasting room at **PYRAT Rums'** factory on Sandy Ground Rd, **T** 264-4975003 (*Mon-Fri 0800-1700*).

¥¥¥ **Altamer**, Shoal Bay West, **T** 264-4984040, www.altamer.com/restaurant *Breakfast, lunch and dinner, closed Wed, closed Aug-Oct. Map 7, D1, p284* On the beach and presided over by executive chef Maurice Leduc in a stainless steel kitchen behind glass and probably the best restaurant on the island, with fabulous food. There is a special sampler menu. Expect to pay around US$100 per person with wine. Nightly entertainment in season.

¥¥¥ **Blanchard's**, Mead's Bay, **T** 264-4976100, blanchards@anguillanet.com *Dinner only, closed Sep to mid-Oct. Map 7, C1, p284* In a delightful situation on the beach, with sea-blue shutters, fine dining with Asian influences and an elegant wine list. Bob and Melinda Blanchardserve the usual seafood in interesting sauces with local ingredients, and a Caribbean sampler of baked *mahi mahi* with coconut, lime and ginger, roast lobster, jerk chicken and grilled cinnamon-rum bananas for US$52. Vegetarian dinners on request.

¥¥¥-¥¥ **Deon's Overlook**, Back St, South Hill, **T** 264-4974488. *Lunch, dinner and cocktails. Usually closed in summer. Map 7, C2, p284* A tremendous view over Sandy Ground from the top of cliff and great food island-style served up by chef Deon Thomas, who has done the rounds of hotel-restaurants before opening his own, very popular place. His trade mark is the garlic-crusted snapper, but there is usually pasta, steak, braised goat, Jamaican jerk chicken or crayfish with coconut run down. Happy hour, 1700-1900. Hand-hewn tables and chairs and colourful artwork. In the summer, Deon moves to his other restaurant in Martha's Vineyard.

¥¥¥-¥¥ **Flavours**, Back St, South Hill, **T** 264-4970629. *Mon-Sat, lunch and dinner (1830-2200), closed mid-Aug to end-Oct. Map 7, C2, p284* With a view over Road Bay, run by Anguillian chef Rexie Fleming. Caribbean ingredients with international flavours such as roasted rack of goat in red wine sauce, as well as staples like fried plantain and breadfruit chips; main courses US$13-17.

¶¶¶-¶¶ **Hibernia**, Island Harbour, **T** 264-4974290, www.hiberniarestaurant.com *Lunch and dinner, closed Jul to mid-Oct.* *Map 7, A5, p284* Run by French and Irish couple, international menu with influences from their travelling experiences gathered when the restaurant is closed annually. Only 11 tables, in open-air West Indian house on the beach. Large wine cellar with wines imported directly from France.

¶¶¶-¶¶ **Jacquie's Ripples**, Sandy Ground, **T** 264-4973380. *Daily 1200-2400.* *Map 7, C2, p284* A varied menu including vegetarian options from this award-winning chef: anything from shepherd's pie to coconut soup using coconuts from the back garden – try his lobster fritters. Early bird specials on Saturday 1700-1900 and happy hour every night 1700-1900. Friendly, fun, the bar stays full.

¶¶¶-¶¶ **Tasty's**, South Hill, **T** 264-4972737, chefcarty@ anguillanet.com *Fri-Wed 0800-2200, closed Sep-Oct.* *Map 7, C2, p284* One of the best independent restaurants on the island, owned by Dale Carty, chef, aided by his cousin, Patrick, sous-chef. Mainly seafood but also chicken, meat and vegetarian options; a varied menu includes local goat curry; main dishes around US$15-25 for dinner, cheaper for lunch. Try fried fish and johnny cakes for breakfast and great salads for lunch. Dining is indoors or on the porch with Susan Croft murals there and in the bar.

¶¶¶-¶¶ **Trattoria Tramonto & Oasis Beach Bar**, West Pond Rd, Shoal Bay West, next to Blue Waters, **T** 264-4978819. *Tue-Sun lunch casual 1200-1500, sunset champagne cocktails 1700-1800, dinner 1900-2130, closed Sep-Oct.* *Map 7, D1, p284* Northern Italian chef, serious Italian cuisine and the best on the island. There are only 10 tables in this modern white building with blue shutters raised to allow an open-air feel, so reservations are essential for dinner. Beach chairs are provided for guests and the bar is open all afternoon: a great place to spend the day.

★ **Cheap eats**

B e s t

- OJ's Beach Bar & Restaurant, Jolly Harbour, Antigua, p159
- E's Oven, South Hill, Anguilla, p172
- Rainforest Restaurant, Ecolodge, Saba, p174
- Chez Andy – The Hideaway, St-Jean, St-Barth, p178
- Gallipot, on the beach north of Oualie, Nevis, p183

♙-♙ E's Oven, South Hill, **T** 264-4988288. *Wed-Mon 1200-2400, closed mid-Sep to mid-Oct. Map 7, C2, p284* Look for the brightly painted red and yellow building on the main road. 'E' was the owner's late mother, who used to bake in the stone oven which stood where the bar now is. Mostly local flavours with an eclectic menu ranging from blue fish in basil cream sauce to sandwiches, owned by award-winning chef, Vernon Hughes.

♙-♙ Fat Cat, Main Rd, George Hill, **T** 264-4972307, www.news.ai/ref/fatcat.html *Mon-Sat 1000-1800. Map 7, C3, p284* Gourmet meals to go from the freezer, picnics, pies and cakes.

♙-♙ Gee Wee's Bakery & Catering, on West End, between Shell station and *La Sirena Hotel*, **T** 264-4976462. *Mon-Sat 0900-1800. Map 7, C1, p284* Breads, cakes, pastries, sandwiches, Jamaican jerk chicken and pork, parties catered for, eat in, takeaway or delivery.

♙-♙ Roy's Place, beachfront, Crocus Bay, **T** 264-4972470. *Tue-Sun 1200-1400, 1800-2100, happy hour 1700-1900. Map 7, B3, p284* Draught beer, fresh seafood, popular fish and chips, Sunday brunch of roast beef and Yorkshire pudding. Roy and Mandy run their bar pub-style with the restaurant on the beach. Happy hour on Friday is an institution, with entrées going cheap as well as drinks but get there early as tables fill up by 1800. Free Internet access. Roy also has some apartments to let.

Saba

Many restaurants close by 2130, so eat early. Cuisine is fairly international with local fruit and vegetables. Pizzas and burgers are as readily available as catch of the day. If you are self-catering remember that the **supply boat** only comes in once a week, so check when that is so you can get things fresh. Supermarkets are small and carry a limited stock of a wide variety of items.

♥♥♥ **Gate House**, Hell's Gate, **T** 599-4162416, www.sabagatehouse.com *Breakfast, lunch, dinner. Map 8, F4, p284* Food is taken very seriously here. The French hosts have lived in the USA, so the menu is a fusion of French and international with Saban touches, using lobster, lamb, pork and seafood. Assistance is given in choosing a wine suited to your food from the excellent list. Dining is indoors in an old Saban house on a hillside and accommodation is available, with rooms in the main house, a villa and a cottage, **AL**. Breakfast included with lots of fruit and home-made jam.

♥♥-♥ **Brigadoon**, Windwardside, **T** 599-4162380. *Daily 1800-2100. Map 8, G4, p284* In an old Saban house close to the centre of the village enjoying a good reputation with the locals. Dinner costs from US$10, lunch for groups by reservation only. International, Creole and Caribbean food, fresh seafood, lobster tank.

♥♥-♥ **Lollipop**, The Bottom, **T** 599-4163330. *Breakfast, lunch or dinner. Map 8, H2, p284* A small restaurant on the mountainside overlooking The Bottom on the way to St John's. Free taxi pick-up (waiter is also the driver), excellent three-course meal for about US$20, fresh lobster, conch melts in the mouth, local cuisine including goat and land crab. A good place to have lunch: you can walk it off afterwards on the trails.

♈-♈ Rainforest Restaurant, at *Ecolodge Rendez-Vous*, Windwardside, **T** 599-4163348, www.ecolodge-saba.com *Breakfast, lunch and dinner.* *Map 8, G3, p284* Situated along the Crispeen Trail just past the junction and rest halt for the Mt Scenery Trail. Work up an appetite climbing the steps from the Trail Shop in Windwardside, or drive along to the end of the Mountain Road and walk five minutes down from there. Wonderful fresh juices, guava from the garden, salads, sandwiches, fish, shrimp in red curry/ coconut for lunch. The dinner menu has more entrées with barbecue ribs and steak. Lots of home grown fruit, vegetables and herbs, fresh and very tasty. Accommodation available, see p138.

♈-♈ Saba's Treasure, Windwardside, **T** 599-4162819, sabastreasure@hotmail.com *Mon-Sat 1000-2200.* *Map 8, G4, p284* Pub atmosphere with historical theme, maps and old pictures on the walls, high pews, dark wood tables bound with fishing ropes. Popular thick-crust pizzas baked in stone oven, US$7-11 depending on the size with extra toppings. Medical students come here to be filled up. Short menu of steak, shrimp, chicken and catch of the day, served with rice, fries or baked potato, followed by Saba lime pie or Saba spice walnut cake. Three rooms are available upstairs, sharing a living and dining room, kitchen and bathroom, or you can rent the whole place, separate entrance.

♈-♈ Y2K Café, Lambee's Place, Windwardside, **T** 599-4162538. *Mon-Sat 1100-1430, 1830-2030.* *Map 8, G3, p284* Excellent casual restaurant, eat on the patio or under cover, a few steps away from the foot of the Mt Scenery Trail. Extensive menu with salads, sandwiches and burgers. Try the 'Divers-up/Hikers-down' with mushrooms, onions, peppers, bacon, Swiss cheese and blue-cheese dressing. Main-course prices range from US$11-15 and pasta from US$7.50-15.50. Friday is a special burger and salad day when you can choose your own toppings, burger platters from 1500-2030 with Heineken at US$1.

Sint Eustatius

There are few restaurants but you can eat in the hotels and bars as well as those places listed below. For **fresh fish**, go to the fish processing plant (Statia Fish Handling) at Lower Town opposite short pier (*Mon-Fri, usually 0800-1300, depending on the catch*), they will clean the fish for you. Otherwise approach the local fishermen. Grocers sell frozen fish. Lobster is available fresh from November to March. **Bread** is baked daily and best bought at 'fresh bread time', which varies according to who makes it. Bake sales are announced by the town crier. Open-air takeaway local dishes are on offer some Fridays and Saturdays from 1100, usually at **Charlie's Place**, just below Mazinga Gift Shop and Africa Crossroads Park opposite the museum. Hotels serve purified water. Bottled water is sold at groceries. Tap water is usually rainwater and not for drinking.

¶¶-¶ **Blue Bead Bar and Restaurant**, by the dock, **T** 599-3182873. *1000-2200, bar until 2300. Closed Mon-Tue in May. Map 10, F6, p285* One of the prettiest places to eat, especially at night looking out to the lights of boats. Understandably popular with a very good menu based on fish and seafood with interesting twists, also meat and pizzas; friendly service.

¶¶-¶ **Ocean View Terrace**, just by tourist office and Governor's House, **T** 599-3182733. *Wed-Mon lunch and dinner. Map 10, C6, p285* An ideal place to watch the sunset. Seafood and shrimp Creole, daily specials are reasonably priced, occasional live music, happy hour and barbecue on Friday. A good place to meet locals, although service could be friendlier. Reduced hours in low season.

¶¶-¶ **Sonny's Place**, next to *Mazinga Gift Shop*, **T** 599-3182609. *Lunch and dinner. Map 10, C7, p285* Popular hang-out for locals and terminal employees, pool and football tables, and good music. Sonny serves good Creole and Chinese food at reasonable prices.

St-Barthélemy

St-Barth is a gourmet delight. Some people visit the island simply to eat great French Creole food three times a day but it can be expensive as nearly everything is imported from France or from the French Antilles. Expect to pay a minimum of US$25 for dinner; you'll more likely end up paying US$75-100 with drinks and three courses. There are around 70 restaurants on this small island, many of them excellent, mostly French but some Creole, Italian and even Indonesian, with a few vegetarian options and lots of seafood. Some of the best restaurants are in the top hotels, such as *Le Gaïac* in Le Toiny see p141. Many restaurants only open for dinner, from 1800-2300; others open for lunch as well, a leisurely affair between 1200-1600. See *Ti Gourmet Saint-Barth*, a free booklet, for listings, the *Ti Creux* section lists snacks and takeaways. There are excellent supermarkets in Gustavia, at the airport, and in St-Jean and Lorient. This is a duty-free island, so wine and spirits are very cheap. Many supermarkets close at lunchtime and Sunday afternoons.

♥♥♥-♥♥ **Le Gommier**, opposite salt pond, La Grande Saline, **T** 0590-(0)590-275057. *Lunch and dinner.* Map 11, E3, p286 It can be a bit smelly at the edge of the pond, but the restaurant is in a delightful spot, housed in an airy, wooden building, open-sided with shutters propped to catch the breeze. Stylish, excellent food, a mix of local and European dishes, includes curry goat, coconut chicken, stuffed crab, lobster and salads at lunch and more elegant options in the evening with a *prix fixe* menu as well and live music.

♥♥♥-♥♥ **L'Esprit Salines**, opposite salt pond, La Grande Saline, **T** 0590-(0)590-524610, lesprit3@wanadoo.fr *Lunch and dinner, closed Tue dinner-Wed lunch and low season.* Map 11, E3, p286 In direct competition with *Le Gommier*, also offering upmarket French Caribbean cuisine. Started by chefs formerly at *Maya's* in Public, it has attracted an enthusiastic clientele. Quite casual with a garden dining room and bar, it's a great place for a leisurely lunch after a morning on the beach nearby. Finish with a home-made digestif of lemon-grass rum; the lemon grass is grown on the property.

Ⅲ-Ⅰ Dō Brazil, Shell Beach, Gustavia, **T** 590-(0)590-290666, www.dobrazil.com *Lunch and dinner. Map 12, F6, p286* Created by Boubou and Yannick Noah, the tennis player, this is a lively restaurant and snack bar on the beach. Upstairs there is a Brazilian-themed dining room for evening meals (however the chef is keen on Thai food); downstairs the beach bar serves snacks, sandwiches and fresh fruit cocktails. Caiparinhas a must-try. The bed on the beach is a nice touch, but has seen too much weather.

Ⅲ-Ⅲ K'fe Massai, Centre l'Oasis, Lorient, **T** 0590-(0)590-297678. *Thu-Tue, dinner only. Map 11, D3, p286* African-inspired funky decor but the food is mostly French with exotic touches, and an excellent value three-course *prix fixe* dinner for €30. The manager was a wine merchant and has added a tapas and wine bar.

Ⅲ-Ⅲ La Mandala, Gustavia, **T** 0590-(0)590-279696. *Dinner only. Map 12, E9, p286* Up on top of a steep hill this Far Eastern restaurant and cocktail bar has the same owners and chef, Kiki Barjettas, as *Dō Brazil*. The decor is designed to take you away from your everyday life to a higher place, watched over by Buddha and other statues. Delicious Thai cooking with French Caribbean ingredients make this one of *the* places to eat and be seen.

Ⅲ-Ⅲ Maya's, Public, **T** 0590-(0)590-277573. *Mon-Sat dinner only. Map 11, D1, p286* Almost an institution, *Maya's* has been serving regular visitors for years at this colourful spot right on the water and providing a training ground for some of the best chefs on the island. Maya is from Martinique (then Guadeloupe) and you can expect the real deal with her French Creole cuisine. The menu changes daily depending on the local ingredients available. The restaurant's popularity means it can get crowded and noisy if a party comes in. **Maya's to go**, Les Galeries du Commerce, St-Jean, **T** 590-(0)590-298370, mayastogo@wanadoo.fr opposite the airport, is great if you are in a villa and want a special meal without having to cook, or a picnic, snacks, pastries – whatever you fancy. There are stools outside under an arbour if you want to eat there.

¶¶¶-¶¶ **Zanzibarth**, Route de Saline, St Jean, **T** 0590-(0)590-275300. *Dinner daily until 2300, brunch Sat, Sun. Map 11, D2, p286* Opened in 2003 with a minimalist design, all white in the restaurant with modern art canvasses on the walls. The food, a mixture of French, Belgian and Italian, is very good. Opt for the French menu rather than the English version, as the translations are unintelligible.

¶¶-¶ **Chez Andy – The Hideaway**, Villa Creole shopping plaza, St-Jean, **T** 590-(0)590-276362, www.hideaway.tv *Tue-Sat 1200-1400, 1900-2030, Sun 1900-2030. Map 11, D2, p286* Andy (British) doesn't take himself too seriously and offers 'corked wine, warm beer, lousy food, view of the car park'. However he serves up some of the best food at good prices and the restaurant is always full and cheerful. Interesting salads, lots of choice of entrées and huge, really thin-crust pizzas. The vanilla rum digestif is a winner.

¶¶-¶ **Cocoloba Beach Bar**, Grand Cul de Sac. *Tue-Sun 1000-2230. Map 11, C5, p286* Open-air seating under the shade of sea grape (*cocoloba*) trees with rustic, brightly painted wooden tables and benches for tasty panini, burgers and salads, standard desserts, and cocktails. Waitresses are rushed off their feet at lunchtime.

¶¶-¶ **Wall House**, on the waterfront near the museum, Gustavia, **T** 590-(0)590-277183, www.wall-house-stbarth.com *1200-1400, 1900-2100. Map 12, B7, p286* French cuisine offering light lunches and gourmet dinners with a harbour view, *plat du jour* at lunch €9, dinner good five-course menu €25, wines to suit all tastes.

Eddy's, Gustavia, **T** 590-(0)590-275417. *Dinner only. Map 12, E8, p286* Tucked down a side street in the town centre, opposite the Anglican Church, a combination of colonial French and Southeast Asian after Eddy's travels to Thailand, with mahogany furniture and palm trees. Try the green papaya salad, grouper in ginger sauce, beef and shrimp on noodles and rhubarb tart. Good for vegetarians too with a vegetable platter and veg with noodles. Eddy is very welcoming and the restaurant is always crowded. No reservations.

St Kitts

There is a wide variety of fresh seafood (red snapper, lobster, kingfish, blue parrot) and local vegetables as well as imported produce. Local dishes to try include **conkey** (usually available during Easter), **ital** which the local rastas make (food seasoned with natural spices, no salt but very delicious) and also black pudding, goat water, saltfish, johnny cakes and souse – all foods which Kittitians love to eat, especially on Saturdays when no one wants to eat at home. Many Plantation Inns on St Kitts and Nevis offer Sunday brunch, a three-course meal and excellent value at around US$25 per person. Most restaurants close on Sunday in Basseterre. There are many places offering snacks, ice creams, great local patties and fruit juices in Basseterre and in the Frigate Bay area. Local bakeries also have a variety of savoury and sweet baked goods and many have dining sections.

The excellent local spirit **CSR** (Cane Spirit Rothschild) is produced in St Kitts by Baron de Rothschild (in a joint venture with Demerara Distillers Ltd of Guyana) and drunk neat, with ice, water, or 'Ting', the local grapefruit soft drink. Tours of the CSR factory are possible.

Marshall's, at *Horizons Villa Resort*, Frigate Bay, **T** 869-4668245. *Map 13, E3, p287* Romantic poolside dining with an ocean view and exquisite food – not to be missed. Visitors come here for fine dining and locals for special occasions.

♦♦♦-♦♦ Waterfalls, Fortlands, **T** 869-4652754. *0700-2200. Map 13, D2, p287* This cool, romantic open-air restaurant, with the sound of running water in the pond surrounded by lush plants, overlooks Basseterre and the coast. Trademark dishes include ginger-scented duck breast or medallion of beef with blue cheese, croutons and roasted garlic. For more seclusion, book the a/c private dining room.

♦♦♦-♦ Turtle Beach Bar and Grill, at the end of the peninsula, **T** 869-4699086, www.turtlebeach1.com *Daily 0945-2300, later at weekends, reduced evening opening out of season. Map 13, F4, p287* A typical wooden beach bar with seating under cover or on the deck. Good food, vegetarian options, friendly, but expensive: US$8 for a Carib beer, check your bill. Dancing is usually from sunset until midnight. There is a live steel band on Sundays in season.

♦♦ New Thriving Chef Chinese Restaurant, Upper Church St, Basseterre, **T** 869-4668518. *Mon-Thu 1000-2200, Fri-Sat 1000-2300. Map 14, E7, p287* A classy new Chinese restaurant with sumptuous oriental decor, Chinese lamps, red carpet, dark oak tables topped with faux marble in a spacious setting. Try the seafood and tofu in a pot or the grilled lobster with satay. Staff speak very little English but know the menu names and have hired a Kittitian to help.

♦♦ Star of India, Victoria Rd, Basseterre, **T** 869-4661537. *0900-2200 closed Sun. Map 14, C7, p287* The chef is from Bombay, so this is the place to come for authentic Indian food with good tandoori and curries. Many locals get takeaway, but there is seating if you prefer although it is very open. It is a favourite haunt of the medical school students, many of whom are of Indian descent.

♦♦-♦ Ballahoo, on the corner of Bank St and Fort St, Basseterre, **T** 869-4654197, www.ballahoo.com *Mon-Sat 0800-2200. Map 14, E7, p287* This is a great central meeting place with a lovely view of

The Circus, serving excellent local food at reasonable prices with a fun, laid-back atmosphere.

¶¶-¶ **Circus Grill**, The Circus, Basseterre, **T** 869-4650143. *Mon-Sat 1130-2200. Map 14, E7, p287* Good well-presented food and friendly staff, a bit more expensive and less laid-back than *Ballahoo* but popular with the office trade as well as visitors.

¶¶-¶ **Island Spice**, underneath *Bobsy's* at the Sugar's Complex, Frigate Bay Rd, **T** 869-4650569. *Mon-Fri 1100-2300, Sat-Sun 1800-2300, closed holiday Mon. Map 13, E3, p287* Award-winning chef Lynn Williams' speciality is the national dish of the Federation – spicy plantains, coconut dumplings, stewed saltfish and seasoned breadfruit – but you can opt for sandwiches and burgers from EC$19, omelettes, salads, pasta or catch of the day in a casual, a/c atmosphere. Daily hot specials such as curry mutton for EC$32.

¶¶-¶ **Rank's Eat Rite Specialities**, corner Johnston Av and Union St, Basseterre, **T** 869-4658190. *Map 13, D3, p287* Very local and gaily painted, for takeaway light meals rather than the family dinner. Good for vegetarians and Rastafarians. Fresh, low-fat meals, veggie/fish burgers, tuna melt, fish meals, local drinks.

¶¶-¶ **Sprat Net**, Old Road Town, by the sea, **T** 869-4656314. *Thu-Sun. Map 13, D1, p287* Run by the Spencer family, this is one of the places to be at weekends, when it gets busy. People come from all over the island for their fresh fish and goat water. Highly recommended for a good atmosphere and reasonably priced food.

¶¶-¶ **Stone Walls**, Princes St, Basseterre, **T** 869-4655248. *Mon-Sat 1700-2300. Map 14, E7, p287* Excellent food, special theme nights, in a pleasant garden surrounded by a stone wall. Lovely atmosphere, very secluded and private.

¶ **Lamby's Weekends**, just outside Basseterre heading east at entrance to Keys village, **T** 869-4656830. *Fri-Sun 1700-2300. Map 13, D3, p287* Delicious traditional local food not found anywhere during the week – specializes in black pudding and souse. A family atmosphere around four tables in the plain white inside and two on a narrow terrace with a great view of the sea. Come with time on your hands and be patient, the food will be worth waiting for.

¶ **Razba's Veggie Pizza Parlour**, on Johnston Av, Basseterre, **T** 869-4656738. *1830 until the last customer leaves. Map 13, D3, p287* For a very local experience, most of the clientele are Rastafarian vegetarians who come for a good 'lime' and are friendly to new faces. Decorated in the Rastafarian red, green and gold, with a mural in red painted by the Guinness company.

Nevis

The best restaurants are in the hotels, see p148, and it is usually necessary to reserve a table. They offer exceptional cuisine as well as barbecues and entertainment on certain nights of the week. There are very few eating places in Charlestown and none of them is expensive. In the off season most restaurants only open in the evenings, and some shut completely.

¶¶¶ **Miss June's**, Jones Bay, **T** 4695330, www.missjunes.com *Open on request when there is enough demand. Map 15, B2, p288* Miss June, originally from Trinidad, serves a Caribbean five-course dinner party in an old West Indian plantation house setting with lush foliage and open-air terraces. Cocktails and hors d'oeuvres are served on the veranda at 1930. Wine, coffee and liqueurs with limitless refills are included in the price of US$65 including tax but not service. Credit cards are accepted and reservations are essential. Acclaimed by many food critics and even Oprah Winfrey gave it the thumbs up.

¶¶-¶¶ Bananas, Cliffdwellers at Tamarind Bay, **T** 869-4691891. *Dinner only Mon-Sat 1800-2200. Map 15, B2, p288* Perched up on the cliff top with spectacular views of St Kitts, you take a cable car up to the bistro. There is a lounge with comfy sofas, Turkish style, where you can wait for your table with a drink or retire after dinner with a coffee and another drink. A different menu nightly offers a mix of Thai, European and Caribbean dishes, salads, ribs and seafood. Main courses US$16-30. Live music on Saturday from 2100 until about 0200 depending on demand.

¶¶-¶ Café des Arts, between the museum and Unella's, on the waterfront, Charlestown, **T** 869-4697098. *Mon-Fri 0800-1600, Sat 1000-1500 Map 15, E1, p288* Open for breakfast and lunch, tables outside under the trees and parasols for salads, sandwiches, quiche. Upstairs and at the back of the house is an art gallery exhibiting and selling work of local artists from St Kitts and Nevis.

¶¶-¶ Cla Cha Del Restaurant and Bar, Cades Bay, **T** 869-4691841. *Lunch and dinner, closed Thu and Sun lunch. Map 15, C1, p288* For excellent local food and large portions, lots of seafood and fish, but try vegetables such as cristophene and sample Pas' great cocktails such as mango colada. Out of the way with a good atmosphere at weekends when there are sometimes parties and music, the restaurant opens out onto the beach.

¶¶-¶ Eddy's, on Main St opposite Memorial Sq and the handicraft cooperative, Charlestown, **T** 869-4695958. *Lunch and dinner. Map 15, E1, p288* A tourist favourite for local food, drinks and music: string bands, bush bands or steel bands Saturday 2000-2300, happy hour Wednesday 1700-2000. Karaoke, dancing till early morning.

¶¶-¶ Gallipot, Tamarind Bay, on the beach north of Oualie, **T** 869-4698230. *Thu-Sat 1200-2200 (kitchen open 1200-1500, 1800-2100), Sun 1200-1730. Map 15, B2, p288* Lovely location, perfect for yachts, providing showers with towels and shampoo if you ask, laundry and cottages as well as food. Family-run, you can spend all day here. Great fresh fish any day but known for Sunday special roast beef lunch, very popular, reservations essential.

🍴-🍴 **Jade Garden**, Newcastle, **T** 869-4699762. *Tue-Sat 1000-2200. Map 15, B3, p288* A casual café and bar set in extensive grounds with an organic vegetable garden producing for the kitchen. Healthy cuisine with an extensive menu catering for everyone, salads, pizza (Veggie Volcano), seafood (Shanghai Shrimp), deli. You can use the pool or the games room.

🍴-🍴 **Le Bistro**, Chapel St, Basseterre, **T** 869-4695110. *Mon-Fri lunch and dinner. Map 15, E1, p288* Owned by chef Matt Lloyd, who used to work at the *Montpelier Inn*, this tiny restaurant in a 1930s, typically West Indian chattel house offers a variety of food, from quiche to curry or coconut chicken. Fresh fish is usually caught by Matt himself. Even if you don't want to eat here, come on Friday for happy hour, 1700-1900, when it fills up with the after-work crowd and the place is buzzing.

🍴-🍴 **Seafood Madness**, Pinney's Rd, Charlestown, **T** 869-4690558. *0730-2100. Map 15, E1, p288* Great for takeaway orders, all sorts of seafood, also chicken and ribs. Reservations are preferred for dinner, when the place is transformed with fairy lights and candles. Very tasty blackened or Creole fish, also conch or steak. Rum cocktails a speciality.

🍴 **Martha's Tea House**, at the Botanical Gardens, **T** 869-4693680. *1000-1700. Map 15, F3, p288* For breakfast, lunch, tea or drinks, serves sandwiches, salads, a ploughman's lunch with cheese and pickled onions, scones with Devonshire cream and tapas. The tea house is inside the Botanical Gardens with panoramic views from the veranda over the island.

Nightlife varies tremendously between islands. Some are quiet most of the time, such as Nevis or Saba, where occasional live music in restaurants is the norm, while others, such as Sint-Maarten, are determined to keep their visitors hopping all night.

Restaurants, bars and clubs all host bands from time to time and are the best places to catch live music. Very popular are soca, reggae, zouk, rock, rap and calypso and DJs are often cult figures. Antigua, St Kitts and Sint Maarten/St-Martin have casinos, where you can gamble all night long.

There is no home-grown movie industry on any of the islands, but they have frequently been used as film locations. English Harbour on Antigua is a favourite for historical dramas, see p41. Some islands have state-of-the art cinemas, showing all the latest releases, while others, such as Montserrat, Saba and Statia rely on video showings.

Several islands hold festivals of the arts which pack a lot into a short period. All the islands celebrate a version of Carnival, but not all at the same time.

Antigua

The largest hotels around the island provide dancing, calypso, steel bands, limbo dancers and moonlight barbecues so their guests need never leave the property. Entertainment comes to them, with live acts rotating between the various hotels. English Harbour area has become the hot spot for tourists, particularly for the yachting fraternity. Most live music happens in bars, or restaurants with bars. There are a couple of clubs frequented by Antiguans in their 20s, where you can dance into the small hours. Try the popular and erotic bump and grind dance style, where the man grasps the girl's hips from behind, pulls her close against him and together they move to the beat. A free newspaper, *It's Happening, You're Welcome*, contains information on forthcoming events. Plays are sometimes put on at the **Cathedral Cultural Centre**.

One of the most successful Antiguan artists in recent years is **Onyan** (Toriano Edwards), who has been crowned the Calypso Monarch several times. Founder of **Burning Flames**, Antigua's leading zouk/soca band, he has recently teamed up with **Art Ski**, who played with **Wadadli Experience**, Antigua's number one reggae band. Together, as **Onyan Art**, they have recorded two albums, a blend of rock, soca, calypso and reggae. The latest, *Hurricane is Coming*, released in 2004, also features Mykal Kumasi Jones from Wadadli Experience adding DJ vocals. Another Antiguan band heavily involved in Carnival, having won the Road March title, is **High Intensity** whose most recent album is *Rydin da Tydes*.

Bars and clubs

Abracadabra, just outside Nelson's Dockyard, English Harbour, **T** 268-4602701. *Bar 1800, dinner 1900-2230, closed Sep-Oct. Map 1, F5, p280* A restaurant and video bar with a deck under the palm trees which is nearly always lively with dancing late into the night. Live music some nights. Casual, no strict dress code.

▶ Music

Calypso was originally developed in Trinidad. Calypsonians (or kaisonians, as the more historically minded call them) are the commentators, champions and sometimes conscience of the people. This unique musical form, a mixture of African, French and, eventually British, Spanish and even East Indian influences, dates back to Trinidad's first 'shantwell', Gros Jean, late in the 18th century. Since then it has evolved into a popular, potent force, with men, women and children battling for the Calypso Monarch's crown during Carnival. The season's calypso songs blast from radio stations and sound systems all over the islands and visitors should ask locals to interpret the sometimes witty and often scurrilous lyrics, for they are a fascinating introduction to the state of the nation. In 2004, Antigua reunited all the Calypso Monarchs of the last 47 years during its Carnival and each of them sang the song which won him the title.

Pan music has a shorter history, developing in the 20th century from the tamboo-bamboo bands which made creative use of tins, dustbins and pans plus lengths of bamboo for percussion instruments. By the end of the Second World War some ingenious souls discovered that huge oil drums could be converted into expressive instruments, their top surfaces tuned to all ranges and depths (eg the ping pong, or soprano pan, embraces 28 to 32 notes including both the diatonic and chromatic scales). Aside from the varied pans, steel bands also include a rhythm section dominated by the steel, or iron men. Steel bands have been inextricably linked with tourism in recent years and you will find them performing at most of the large hotels one or two nights a week, at cruise ship docks and at weddings.

Reggae is tremendously popular in the islands and is played everywhere, all day and all night. There is also a fusion of reggae and soca, known as ragga-soca, which has a faster rhythm than reggae but slower than up-tempo soca.

Soca, which developed in the 1970s, is a blend of calypso story telling and the rhythm of American R&B, an upbeat dance music.

Zouk is a fusion of funk, soca and African music, very popular in the French islands but heard in dance halls all over the Caribbean.

Ringbang, created in 1994, is a mixture of all the varied types of Caribbean music with the emphasis on the beat rather than the melody.

Folk music On many islands you can still hear traditional folk music, usually a string band with instruments looking very home made, which they are.

On Montserrat the string bands play the African shak-shak, made from a calabash gourd, as well as the imported Hawaiian ukelele.

On Nevis a string band uses a washboard and a T-base, a broomstick with a single string on a wooden box, accompanied by a guitarist.

On St-Barth look out for the twins, Henri and Leon, who play traditional music on the accordion and conch shell. The accordion gives a more European feel to the music than you will find in the other French islands of Guadeloupe and Martinique, where slaves introduced African influences.

Alice's Bar, English Harbour Main Rd, **T** 268-4638743. *1900-until the last customer goes, high season only.* *Map 1, F5, p280* A tiny outdoor bar run by Portuguese Alice Vidal, very casual, bare feet are acceptable, no dress code here. A few people can sit at the bar, otherwise there are tables and chairs in the garden. Open very late for burgers and drinks and popular with young crew members.

C&C Wine Bar, Redcliff Quay, **T** 268-4607025. *Mon-Sat 1130-late. Next to the Pottery Shop.* *Map 2, D1, p281* A wine bar serving South African wines and cheese platters, very popular with the local professional crowd as well as tourists.

18 Karat Night Club, Long St and Market St, St John's, **T** 268-5621858, 18karat@candw.ag *Thu-Sun 2200-late, EC$10 cover charge.* *Map 2, B2, p281* A choice of an a/c bar and lounge or an outdoor courtyard. A local club, playing lots of reggae and soca, not many tourists come in to the town at night, but dress smartly.

King's Casino, in Heritage Quay, St John's, **T** 268-4621727. *Mon-Sat 1000-0400, Sun 1800-0400.* *Map 2, C1, p281* On the harbour front, the casino awaits cruise-ship passengers. Drinks free for players. Live entertainment on Friday night, popular with locals.

Last Lemming, Yacht Club Rd, Falmouth, **T** 268-4606910. *Mon-Sat 1100-1500, Sun Brunch 1030-1500 , 1900-2200 daily.* *Map 1, E5, p280* A restaurant and bar right by the mega yachts at the Yacht Club Marina with a great view of how the rich go on holiday. Live reggae and dancing on Friday from 2100, guitarist sings pop and calypso on Saturday nights.

Life, at the entrance to the Dockyard, **T** 268-5624057. *Mon-Sat until late.* *Map 1, F5, p280* Owned by a former London DJ, all types of great music, dancing, casual dining, very lively bar.

Mad Mongoose, Falmouth Harbour, **T** 268-4637900. *Tue-Sun 1500-2300, Nov-May.* *Map 1, E5, p280* Restaurant and bar in a wooden shack overlooking the harbour. Loud music attracts the younger yachting crowd, but there is a deck with outside seating.

Mainbrace Pub, *Copper and Lumber Store Hotel*, in Nelson's Dockyard, English Harbour, **T** 268-4601058. *Daily 0700-2300.* *Map 1, F5, p280* A traditional English pub with beer on tap, the old stone walls and exposed beams of the dockyard buildings. Wednesday night jazz, Thursday karaoke, Friday night two drinks for the price of one. Go for the beer or mixed drinks at US$3.

Miller's by the Sea, Runaway Bay, Fort James, **T** 268-4629414. *Daily 0800-2300.* *Map 1, A2, p280* Serves lunch, dinner or drinks, often has live music (jazz, calypso or reggae bands), owned by a local jazz hero. Beach barbecues on Sundays, dancing on the sand.

O'Grady's, Redcliffe St, St John's, **T** 268-4625392. *Tue-Sat 1000-late.* *Map 2, D2, p281* Irish pub with West Indian flavour, darts and pool. Good pub grub: English breakfast, pies, liver and bacon, fish and chips. Sit on the balcony and watch the world go by. On Wednesdays guitarist and comedian Laurie Stevens performs.

Rush Night Club, Runaway Bay, **T** 268-5627874, hadeedej@candw.ag *Daily 1600-late.* *Map 1, A2, p280* The newest and leading nightclub right on the coast and with a deck overlooking the sea. Very modern decor, fusion music played with something for everyone. Also on site is *Conor's Sports Bar*, on the second floor, with TVs, pool tables, darts, dominoes.

! The Royal Navy Tot Club (members only) meets every night at 1800 at the *Copper and Lumber Store Hotel* for a tot, or a jigger, of rum to signal the end of the working day and a toast, "to wives and lovers – may they never meet – the Queen!"

Shirley Heights Lookout, T 268-4601785, VHF 68. *Sun 1600-
1900 steel pan followed by reggae 1900-2200. Map 1, F6, p280* A
very touristy but fun party on a Sunday, with barbecued burgers,
chicken, ribs and salad at stalls up on the hill overlooking English
Harbour. Bus loads of revellers are brought from hotels all round
the island and while the steel band is good family entertainment, it
can get rowdy by the time the reggae band comes on if people
have been drinking all afternoon.

Cinema

Deluxe Cinema, High St and Cross St, St John's, T 268-4623664.
Map 2, C3, p281 A duplex showing all the latest releases.
Tickets cost EC$15.

Barbuda

Bars and clubs

Green Door, in the centre of Codrington, T 268-5623134. *Daily
0700-2400 or later. Map 3, C6, p281* The island's first bar, run by
Byron Askie and a pivot for social life on the island. Open in the day
for bingo, pool, TV, entertainment in the evenings and a weekend
disco, food on request, you can usually get spicy chicken wings.

Jackie's Seafood Bar, Codrington, T 268-4600408. *1200-the last
customer goes home. Map 3, C6, p281* A lunch spot with evening
food cooked to order, also a bar where you can play cards,
dominoes or watch TV.

Madison's Bar, Madison Sq, Codrington,
T 268-4600465. *Wed-Thu 1400-2400, Fri-Sat 0900-0200, Sun
1700-0100. Map 3, C6, p281* A bar with a wide range of drinks as
well as burgers, chicken, spare ribs and fries to eat in or take away.

> ## Montserrat and the stars

Sir George Martin's famed recording studios, the Air Studios, on the edge of Belham Valley, used to attract rock megastars such as Elton John, the Rolling Stones and Sting to the island, but the studios were closed after Hurricane Hugo. He is now building a Performing Arts/Cultural Centre at Little Bay (to replace the Festival Village). In 1997, Sir George Martin organized a gala fundraising concert for Montserrat at the Royal Albert Hall in London, which included (Sir) Paul McCartney, (Sir) Elton John, Eric Clapton, Sting, Mark Knopfler, Jimmy Buffet and Arrow, who had used Air Studios in the past. At the same time a show was put on at Gerald's Bottom on Montserrat by other musicians who had used the recording studios. The Climax Blues Band reformed for the occasion and Bankie Banks appeared, along with 18 local acts in what was optimistically called 'Many Happy Returns'. A second 'Many Happy Returns' concert was held in 1999 to coincide with St Patrick's Day festivities. Local and London-based bands, choirs and acts attracted a crowd of 3,000, or 75% of the population at that time, and the finale was provided by the king of soca, Arrow and his band (see p194). Lately, some of the touring calypso shows that have played Antigua, such as Shadow and Sparrow, have taken the ferry over to Montserrat and put on memorable shows at the Bitter End Beach Bar in Little Bay.

The Lyme, by the lagoon, Codrington, **T** 268-4600619. *Map 3, C6, p281* The bar and restaurant are open daily throughout the day andevening but at weekends it becomes a night club, with a band and disco for the younger crowd.

Montserrat

Bars occasionally present live music featuring calypsonians and other musicians over from Antigua or other islands; these are advertised on the radio. The veteran **Arrow** (Alphonsus Cassell) is now an international superstar (see p 193) but can still be found on the island, having moved his operation north out of the volcano evacuation zone. In 2003 Arrow received a Goodwill Ambassador Award for *Hot, Hot, Hot* at the Bollywood Music Awards 2003, held at the Trump Taj Mahal in Atlantic City, New Jersey.

Bars and clubs

Howe's Flamboyant Bar, St John's, **T** 664-4913008. *Map 4, B3, p282* Pool table for entertainment with a drink after a meal.

Good Life Night Club, Little Bay, **T** 664-4914576. *Map 4, A2, p282* Newly built on a hillside overlooking the beach, which is only 20 yards away, plantation style with decking receiving a lovely sea breeze. Not open every evening, but he will open for a crowd, eg if a Navy ship comes in, he'll be open all the time they are in port. Great disco for weekend dancing. Open for lunch three to four times a week, with a Caribbean style buffet. The food is OK but it is a better bar than restaurant.

Sint Maarten/St-Martin

St Martin's Week lists what's on where and when for the coming week. *K-Pasa* distributes flyers with what's on. Casinos are a major attraction, most opening from noon to 0300. There are currently 12, all on the Dutch side, half in Philipsburg. The Maho area is very busy at night with restaurants, bars, a strip club and a casino around the plaza. Grand Case has live music Friday-Sunday in high season with beach party entertainment in one of the many bars.

Look out for **Jack** (Irish folk songs) and **King Beau Beau**, the most popular bands of the last few years. Every full moon there is a beach party at Friar's Bay starting around 2100-2200, barbecues on the beach every Friday and Saturday. On Friday evenings and Sunday afternoons (popular with all the family) locals like **Boo Boo Jam**, at Baie Orientale, where there is lots of merengue, salsa and zouk.

Bars and clubs

Bliss, Caravanserai Resort, next to the *Sunset Beach Bar* (Beacon Hill). *Map 5, C2, p283* Restaurant and nightclub, open-air dining and dancing attracts a young crowd. People start to arrive around 0030 and by 0100 it is packed. There is also a martini bar and pool.

Bodeguita del Medio, Marina Port La Royale, **T** 590-(0)590-879841. *1800-late. Map 5, B4, p283* Modelled on the famous bar of the same name in Havana which revels in the atmosphere of the 1950s with screen stars and mob gangsters. Try the selection of Cuban cocktails: they make a great mojito. Gets lively from around 2300, with Cuban music.

Calmos Café, 40 Blvd de Grand Case, Grand Case, **T** 590-(0)590-290185, www.calmoscafe.com *1000-2200. Map 5, A5, p283* A colourful wooden bar on the beach playing classical music during the day and jazz at night. Live music from time to time. Lots of cocktails to choose from or soft drinks, but there is also a range of home-made flavoured rums, such as banana rum.

Casino Royale, at the *Maho Beach Hotel*, **T** 599-5452590, www.mahobeach.com *1300-0400 daily. Map 5, C2, p283* The largest casino on the island. **Q Club** *Daily 2200-late.* Mezzanine level club at the Casino, playing the latest music from Europe, USA, Latin America and the Caribbean. Very busy at weekends and on Wednesdays for Ladies' night. **Showroom Royale**, the theatre at the Casino Royale **T** 599-5452115. Nightly performances of Las Vegas style casino shows with stunning costumes and excellent choreography. Each evening some of the dancers go out onto the street to entertain diners at the restaurants around the square and entice them into the Casino for gambling and the Revue. The theatre seats 1,000 people. In season the Showroom also invites stand-up comedians. You can catch many from HBO or Carsons as well as local comedians or groups. Entry is in the Casino.

Cliffhanger Beach Bar, Cupecoy, no phone. *1130-late. Map 5, C2, p283* Perched precariously on a sandstone cliff with wooden decking around the outside and a walkway down to the sea, this is a great place for a sunset frozen cocktail waiting for the 'green flash'. Usually live entertainment and music in the evenings.

The Greenhouse Bar and Restaurant, next to Bobby's Marina, Philipsburg, **T** 599-5422941. *1100-2400, happy hour 1630-1900. Map 6, H7, p283* A large open-sided restaurant and bar overlooking the bay. Great cocktails, two for one drinks and half-price appetizers during happy hour. Margarita Monday offers half-price margaritas all day and night with Tex-Mex food, DJ on Tuesday with dancing from 2130 with two for one drinks, lobster and party or bingo night on Friday. Good for sunset watching.

The In's, Marina Port La Royale, **T** 590-(0)590-870839. *Map 5, B4, p283* Nightclub and disco playing mostly techno.

Lady C, Simpson Bay, no phone, www.floatingbar.com *1600-late. Happy hour 1600-1800. Map 5, C3, p283* A floating bar which can get wild at night and is very popular with a young crowd. DJ Marco keeps everyone hopping on Tuesday, Wednesday and Friday. The vessel is occasionally taken to other locations or cruises the lagoon, but is usually just east of the bridge. You can get freshly cooked pizza at the *Pizza Galley* and good wines to take away.

The Pub, Blvd de Grand Case, Grand Case. *Map 5, A5, p283*
A cocktail bar which holds a champagne party on Sunday with a free glass to females after 2200. The other side of the road from the *lolos*. Good for late nights with pizza to fill a hole.

Sunset Beach Bar, 2 Beacon Hill Rd, Maho Beach,
T 599-5453998, www.sunsetbeachbar.com *1100-2200*. *Map 5, C2, p283* Popular bar day and night with a very lively crowd but, as the name suggests, this is a great place for sunset watching. You're right at the end of the runway and can see planes at very close range. Take your own laptop and you can hook up to their free wi-fi at the bar or on the deck. Live music or DJ every night.

Cinema

Le Cinéma MJC, Sandy Ground, St-Martin, **T** 590-(0)590-871844. *Map 5, B4, p283* New films shown, tickets US$5.

The Sunset Theatre, Simpson Bay, Sint Maarten, **T** 599-5443630. *Map 5, C3, p283* Recent film releases, tickets US$6.

Anguilla

In high season resort hotels have live music, steel bands, etc; check in the tourist *What We Do in Anguilla* monthly magazine. Look for shows with **North Sound, Mussington Brothers, Happy Hits,** the most popular bands. **Dumpa and the Anvibes** is led by Pan Man Michael (Dumpa) Martin. **Xtreme Band**, formed in 2001 by several musicians who had been involved with the Mussington Brothers, plays a blend of Caribbean, French and Latin rhythms.

Out of season there is not much to do during the week. On Friday the whole island changes, several bars have live music; check the local papers. People on Anguilla get the ferry over to St-Martin to see a movie.

One of the best reggae festivals in the Caribbean is the annual **Moonsplash Music Festival**, a three-day event held in March at Dune Preserve (see below) organized principally by Bankie Banx. His dreadlocks have now gone grey, but Banx has been playing and writing songs since he made his first guitar out of plywood and copper wire at the age of nine. His early influences were the songs of the 1960s, which he heard broadcast from a British frigate off the coast of Anguilla. His first album, *Roots and Herbs*, appeared in 1978 and since then he has gone on to play with all the greats, jamming with Bob Dylan at *Reggae Sunsplash* in Jamaica, touring with Jimmy Cliff, appearing with Paul Simon, Gloria Estefan and Jimmy Buffet in benefit concerts for hurricane relief as well as disaster relief for Montserrat. Some 3,000 people descend on the dunes of Rendezvous Bay for the full moon festival, dancing until the early hours of the morning.

In November, Anguilla hosts the **Annual Tranquillity Jazz Festival**, while in March the **Frangipani Hotel** also holds a jazz festival. (See also Festivals p207.)

Bars

Dune Preserve, at Rendezvous Bay on the beach next to CuisinArt, www.dunepreserve.com *Map 7, C2, p284* Reggae and folk music from the Caribbean, run by the legendary Bankie Banx. The bar is the funkiest on the island, built out of bits of boats and driftwood with a boat in the middle, a great location on the sand dunes. Full moon parties are not to be missed. Home to the annual Moonsplash festival (see p207).

Gorgeous Scilly Cay, T 264-4975123. *1100-1700 Tue-Sun Nov-May; Wed, Fri, Sun Jun-Aug; closed Sep-Oct. Map 7, A5, p284* Live daytime music on Wednesday and Sunday. Sprocka plays and sings on Wednesday with his guitar. An Anguillian band, Happy Hits, sings and plays on Sunday with their ethnic instruments. The place to come for a rum punch and lobster lunch. You can have a massage at the same time. Africa will take you over to the cay by boat from Island Harbour. There is nothing else on the cay, no electricity so the lobsters are stored in natural tidal pools. See p71.

Johnno's Place, Sandy Ground, **T** 264-4972728, www.johnnos.com *Tue-Sun 1100-2200 for food, later for drinks and music.* Map 7, C2, p284 Good on Friday and on Sunday around 1500 for a beach party. A casual place on the sand where barefoot is acceptable. Quite a local institution. Lots of jazz. Bands play at weekends from 2100 to around 0230. When the music dies at Johnno's people go to *Ship's Galley*, for the night shift.

Madeariman Reef, Shoal Bay East, **T** 264-4983833, www.madeariman.com *0830-1900 for food, later for drinks and entertainment.* Map 7, A4, p284 Part of the small and unprepossessing *Madeariman Beach Club* hotel, with pleasant suites and studios. The beach bar is open to all although the sunbeds on the sand are for guests. Soca, calypso, reggae on Friday, Saturday, Caribbean night Wednesday. Live music Sunday afternoons with a party on the sand.

Mirrors Night Club and Bar, at *Swing High*, above Vista Food Market, **T** 264-4975522. *1900-0400 or later, happy hour nightly 1900-2000.* Map 7, C3, p284 Juke box with music from 1960s to now, live entertainment at weekends, dance floor, karaoke, big screen TV, billiards and darts. People come here after *Johnno's* and the *Pump House* close.

The Pump House, Sandy Ground, **T** 264-4975154. *Mon-Sat 1900-0200.* Map 7, C2, p284 In the historic Anguilla Rd Salt Co Factory. Eat, drink, dance or relax; great reggae on Saturday, also soca and calypso. One of the main night spots and usually crowded.

Red Dragon Disco, South Hill, **T** 264-497-2687. *2400-late, weekends only. Map 7, C2, p284* Part of a complex west of the Sandy Ground roundabout. Dance floor outside in a courtyard, bar and disco inside. On the last Friday of the month they host popular over-30s nights, which start earlier at around 2130 with live bands.

Theatre

Anguilla has the **Ruthwill Auditorium**, which is used for drama and concerts. The Anguilla National Creative Arts Association (ANCAA) has a performing arts section, the **National Theatre Group**, which has training workshops and performs at hotels during high season. Visitors with theatre expertise are welcome to participate. Contact the theatre co-ordinator, Ray Tabor, **T** 264-4976685, rbtabor@anguillanet.com. The **Mayoumba Folkloric Theatre**, **T** 264-4976827, puts on a song, dance and drama show at *La Sirena*, Mead's Bay, Anguilla, on Thursday nights.

Saba

Most of the nightlife takes place at the restaurants. On Friday and Saturday nights, the pool room of the *Galaxy* restaurant makes way for a disco, popular with all sections of the community, playing soca, reggae, rap and disco, loud, the only really late-night activity on the island. At weekends there are sometimes barbecues, steel bands and dances. Generally, though, the island is quiet at night.

Bars

Swinging Doors, Windwardside, **T** 599-4162506. *0900-late. Map 8, G4, p284* A bar with a split personality, part English pub, part Wild West saloon with its swinging doors. There is an eclectic menu, but the best meals are the barbecues on Tuesday and Friday nights, with ribs or chicken or a combo. Owner Eddie Hassell is a fount of information and gossip about life on Saba.

Sint Eustatius

Statians like partying and every weekend there is something going on. Quite often you will hear a 'road block' from far away: cars stopped with huge stereos blaring and everyone jumping up in the street. Ask anybody what is going on next weekend, or just wait for the music to start in the evening.

Bars and clubs

Smoke Alley, on the beach by King's Well, **T** 599-3182002. *Wed-Mon, lunch 1130-1400 and dinner 1800-2200. Map 9, E1, p285* Austrian-owned, open-air restaurant overlooking the water, varied menu, Mexican, burgers, etc, and a fun place to be, very popular, lovely place to watch the sunset. Friday night happy hour 1800-2100, usually with a DJ and occasional live music.

St-Barthélemy

St-Barth is known for its gourmet restaurants rather than its discos and many of the bars are attached to restaurants. Baie de St-Jean is busy at night, but there is plenty going on in Gustavia as well, where the yachtsmen are based. You can find a good selection of French wines at no more than you would pay in France, as well as good Martiniquan rums. Many places make their own digestifs, flavoured rums, delicious with coffee after a meal. There are no casinos, no formal cinema, but check the weekly flyers for what's on where. Most places close at midnight, at least during the week.

Bars and clubs

Bar Le Select, rue de la France with rue Gén. de Gaulle, Gustavia, **T** 590-(0)590-278687. *Mon-Sat 1100-2400. Map 12, C8, p286* Also known as *Cheeseburgers in Paradise*, this bar and burger place is famous for being the subject of the Jimmy Buffet song of the same name. Open for burgers and snacks during the day and good for lunch, it is best visited at night, when live music is often performed. Jimmy Buffet has been known to play here.

Baz Bar/Bete a Z'Ailes, rue Samuel Fahlberg, Gustavia, **T** 590-(0)590-297409. *Mon-Sat 1100-2400. Map 12, E7, p286* Lovely position on the waterfront with a boardwalk for outdoor seating, a great place to watch the boats. Lively at night with a variety of music including zouk, occasional live bands.

La Créole, Villa Créole Shopping Centre, St-Jean, **T** 590-(0)590-276809. *0700-2200. Map 11, D2, p286* A brasserie and bar in the heart of St-Jean, busy with people popping in for lunch, dinner or a pizza to take away. The bar is lively and doubles as a track-betting centre.

Le Petit Club, Gustavia, **T** 590-(0)590-276633, lepetitclub@ saint-barths.com *From 2200. Map 12, E9, p286* Popular with the yachting crowd, this disco close to the harbour doesn't get going until after midnight and is often still thumping at 0300. Dress smartly, no jeans.

Le Repaire des Rebelles et des Emigrés, rue de la République, Gustavia, opposite where the *Voyager* docks, **T** 590-(0)590-277248. *Lunch, dinner and takeaway. Bar open all day until 2400. Map 12, B8, p286* Known simply as *Le Repaire*, the bar/restaurant overlooks the ferry and the harbour and is a pleasant spot to watch boats during the day or at night for an after-dinner drink . There is a billiards room. Well-prepared Creole food, salads, fish and lobster, the daily special costs €19.

Le Ti St-Barth, Pointe Milou, **T** 590-(0)590-279771. *1930-late daily in high season, closed Sun Apr-Nov. Map 11, C4, p286* A bistro and bar with a party atmosphere and entertainment which changes nightly. Monday, live acoustic music, Tuesday, Italian specialities, Wednesday, plastic boots party, Thursday, sexy fashion show, Friday, theme party, Saturday Ti St-Barth Saturday night, Sunday, Gourmet Delights. Barbecue food, lots of music and often dancing on the tables.

Wine and Dinner Club, Colombier, **T** 590-(0)590-298022. *1700-2400. Map 11, C1, p286* An elegant dining room and cocktail bar, decorated with liberal use of leather, the main attraction here is the wine list. You can choose from a list of 40 wines served by the glass, or 360 by the bottle, including several grand cru wines. Tapas are available to accompany your drink if you don't want to eat a full meal.

Cinema
On St-Barth most Saturday nights everyone goes to the AJOE tennis court in Lorient to watch a movie dubbed in French. It is projected onto a huge concrete wall, there is a popcorn stand and you help yourself to a chair from a stack. St-Barth also has an annual film festival the week after Easter, see p208

St Kitts

The club scene has no set hours; doors open around 2200 with people arriving at around 2300-2400 and leaving at 0500 when the sun comes up. Most dance floors provide a wide variety of music and entrance costs US$3.50-18.50, depending on the occasion, with overseas performers commanding the upper limit. Nightclubs have a great mix of calypso, soca, salsa, hip-hop, reggae, dance hall, R&B, house, techno and other types of music. For the real local experience you may want to visit another of the dance clubs or dance spots out in the country area: *BCA*, **T** 869-4657606/7, at Saddlers; *Manhattan Gardens*, **T** 869-4659121, and *Sprat Net*, in Old

Road, *Off Limit*, in Cayon, **T** 869-4669821, and the *Inner Circle Club*, at St Paul's, where action takes place by announcement. These venues are frequented by some of the region's top DJs as well as local bands playing local music.

On St Kitts a band to look out for is **Nu-Vybes** which has been going since 1987 (www.nu-vybes.com) and has won international acclaim for its soca, reggae and calypso, while also borrowing from traditional rhythms of popular Caribbean music to create 'street style'. Several times they have won *Best Carnival Album* and have been the Road March Champions producing the best Carnival music. Their latest album, released in 2004, is *Reloaded*. If you can't make Carnival, St Kitts holds a music festival at the end of June for four nights (see p.209)

Bars

Bobsy's, Sugar's Complex, Frigate Bay Rd, **T** 869-4666138. *1200-late, see p. Map 13, E3, p287* A breezy rooftop bar and restaurant on a hill above Frigate Bay with a panoramic view over the island to the sea and Nevis in the distance. Tables outside in the sunshine or under cover. In the evening the clientele ranges from the happy-hour crew to the intimate dinner romantics and the nightlife enthusiasts, up for **salsa classes**, karaoke and dancing at weekends.

Dolce Cabana, Frigate Bay Beach, **T** 869-4651569. *Club Fri 2200-0400, restaurant Wed-Mon 1600-2200, bar Wed-Mon 1600-0200. Map 13, E3, p287* Currently the most popular club, open Fridays only and getting going around 0030, with music well mixed to suit everyone. A good mix of locals and visitors and everybody has a blast. There are tables under cover and picnic benches outside if you want to eat there. They cook pizzas in a wood burning oven until 0400 on Friday. Steps lead down to the beach, where lots of people end up, dancing under the stars. On other nights there is karaoke (Thursday, Sunday) or theme nights such as salsa (Saturday), with pizza until 0200.

Malloy's Irish Pub, at Baker's Corner, Basseterre, **T** 869-4666519. *Map 13, D2, p287* Close to the bus stop for buses going up the west side, not picturesque, but easy to find, painted green with a shamrock on the outside. Trying to be an Irish pub, but more like a regular bar really, friendly atmosphere.

Moon Dance, at the *Angelus Hotel*, Frigate Bay, **T** 869-4666224. *Map 13, D3, p287* It's a fair walk from the hotel next to the *Marriott* down to the beach, but worth it. They even have their own natural snorkelling reef with lots of fish where visitors have caught their own lobsters to cook on the grill, so bring your snorkelling gear for a daytime visit. On Friday night they have a beach bonfire and grill, with local reggae and steel pan. At weekends there is beach volleyball, with four courts set up, while Sunday is an official Beach Lime for relaxing, listening to local music, eating and drinking.

OTI, Basseterre, **T** 869-4652754, www.oceanterraceinn.com *Daily 1900-2300*. *Map 13, D2, p287* Friday night is Caribbean night, when a Caribbean buffet is served in the *Waterfalls* restaurant, calypso music is played and you can dance. There are fountains, tropical plants and beautiful landscaping in the gardens and there is a view down to the sea and Basseterre.

The Pumpkin, Newton Ground. *Map 13, B0, p287* Looks like an orange pumpkin but very small so you should expect to be very 'intimate' with other guests. Visitors should go with a local if they are interested, it's not a place for softies, nor for lovers of R&B, hip hop, jazz and the like. Expect wild Caribbean music which calls for a knowledge of hip giration or a great passion to learn. Lots of fun and dancing with the local crowd, hot on Friday and Saturday, DJs and occasionally local bands perform.

Nevis

Nevis is quiet and most visitors content themselves with a good meal in the evening and maybe an after-dinner drink. However, there is entertainment for visitors and locals, particularly at the weekends. Hotels organize activities on different nights in high season. The *Nisbet Plantation* (see p148), **T** 869-4699325, has live music on Thursday, *Four Seasons Resort* on Pinney's Beach, **T** 869-4691111, has live music on Friday and Saturday nights. The *Old Manor* at Gingerland, **T** 869-4693445, hosts steel pan on Friday nights, *Oualie Beach Hotel* (see p150), **T** 869-4699735, has a Saturday buffet with live string band, and the *Golden Rock* (see p149) **T** 869-4693346, also has a string band on Saturday nights. Look for posters, radio announcements or ask what's on at the tourist office.

Bars and clubs

Rumours Bar, Newcastle Village near the airport, **T** 869-4698412. *Daily lunch and dinner. Map 15, B3, p288* A new, very local bar, casual with live music occasionally. Restaurant serves local dishes.

The Spotlight, Bath Village. *Weekends 2200-late in season. Map 15, F1, p288* A trendy club featuring live local entertainment as well as popular artists from the Caribbean. Full bar and local food served and a popular location for private functions and parties. Dress code smart casual.

Tequila Sheilas, Cades Bay, **T** 869-4698633. *Thu-Sun lunch and dinner. Map 15, C1, p288* A circular restaurant and bar on the beach with a disco on Saturday night for romantic dancing on the sand late into the night. Seafood and Caribbean style menu options but most popular for Sunday jazz brunch. Themed evenings throughout the year with a popular steak night.

Festivals and events

January

2 weeks mid-Jan (7-25 Jan 2005)

St-Barthèlemy – **Festival de Musique** Classical, folk, jazz music and ballet performed by both school children and guest artists, from abroad.

February

Pre-Lent

(4-9 Feb 2005)

St-Martin – **Carnival** Calypso and beauty contests at the Carnival Village, Marigot and a grand parade.
St-Barthèlemy – **Carnival** Children's parades, a Grand Parade through Gustavia for *Mardi Gras*, a black-and-white parade to Shell Beach on Ash Wednesday when Vaval, Carnival King, is burned.

March

17 Mar

Montserrat – **St Patrick's Day** A national holiday, celebrated on the 'Emerald Isle' with concerts, masquerades, festivities.
Sint Maarten/St-Martin – **The Heineken Regatta** Yacht racing and a big party.
Anguilla – **Annual Jazz Festival** held at the *Frangipani Hotel* and at *Johnno's Bar* on the beach - musicians from abroad and locally. **John T Memorial Cycle Race** Annual showpiece for cyclists from all over the Caribbean. Locals Ronnie and Charles Bryan, Kris Pradell represented the island at the 2002 Commonwealth Games.

April

Anguilla – **Moonsplash Music Festival** A three-day event when there is a full moon at Dune Preserve, Rendezvous Bay, organized by Bankie Banx. www.dunepreserve.com

	Easter Monday Boat Racing A fun day of activities and picnics, Mead's Bay.
Mid-Apr	Sint Maarten – **Carnival** Lasts for three weeks, with up to 100,000 people taking part, culminating in the burning of King Mo-Mo. Most events are held at Carnival Village, next to the university.
In the 2nd half of Apr	Antigua – **The Classic Regatta** Spectacular, with yawls, ketches, schooners and square-masted vessels, contact the Antigua Yacht Club, **T** 268-4601799. You can ride on a Classic yacht in the regatta by donating US$100 to charity (The Hourglass Foundation), contact Hans Smit at the *Gold Smitty* in Redcliff Quay, **T** 268-4622601.
Late Apr	St-Barthélemy – **Caribbean Film Festival** Films by Caribbean film makers, with subtitles.
Last week of Apr or early May	Antigua – **Antigua Sailing Week** **T** 268-4628872, www.sailingweek.com. A huge regatta with participants from over 30 countries, fun events, live music.Nelson's Dockyard.
30 Apr	Saba/Sint Eustatius – **Queen's Birthday** Ceremonies commemorating the coronation of Queen Beatrix and Queen Juliana's birthday.
	May St-Barthélemy – **Transat AG2R Race** Arrives every other year (2004, 2006, 2008) from Lorient in Brittany, France, after a stopover in Madeira. All boats are 33-foot, single hull, Figaro Beneteau, with same sails, safety equipment and two sailors.
	Barbuda – **Caribana** Carnival or jump-up, talent competitions, horse racing and a beach bash.
(6-8 May 2005)	Anguilla – **Anguilla Yacht Regatta** Three days with international yacht crews and traditional Anguilla boat racing; then they swap

over: locals man the yachts, the professionals the traditional boats; www.anguillaregatta2005.com.

2nd Sun in May St Kitts – **The St Kitts Triathlon** An ITU international race, www.stkittstriathlon.com. The grandstand is at *Timothy Beach Hotel*.

30 May Anguilla – **Anguilla Day** Commemorates the beginning of the Anguillian Revolution in 1967, parades, boat races and sporting competitions. Events through the month with live concerts.

June

End of the month St Kitts – **Music Festival** Four nights of calypso, reggae, R&B, jazz, street-style, gospel, country and western and rap, with local and famous artists.

July

1 Jul Sint Eustatius – **Emancipation Day** Celebrations of the abolition of slavery.

2nd week of Jul Sint Maarten/Saba/Sint Eustatius – **The Antillian Games** Sporting competitions between islands of the Netherlands Antilles.

(11-14 Jul 2005) St-Barthélemy – **St-Barth Open Fishing Tournament** Organized by Océan Must.

14 Jul St-Martin – **Bastille Day** Live music, jump-ups and boat races; the celebrations move to Grand Case (more fun) for **Schoelcher Day** on 21 July.

(30-31 Jul 2005) St-Barthélemy – **Fête des Quartiers du Nord** Music, volley ball, dancing, fireworks at Flamands.

End of Jul till first Tue in Aug Antigua – **Carnival** The main event is 'J'ouvert', or 'Juvé' when from 0400 people come into town dancing behind steel and brass bands. There are competitions for the Calypso Monarch with sections for women and children as well as beauty pageants. Hotels and airlines tend to be booked up well in advance. For information contact the

Carnival Committee, High St, St John's, **T** 268-4624707.

A week near the end of Jul
Saba – **Carnival/Saba Summer Festival** Celebrated with jump-ups, music and costumed dancing, shows, food and contests including the Saba Hill Climb. Parades on the last weekend and Carnival Monday is a public holiday.

10 days in Jul and Aug
Sint Eustatius – **Carnival** The main event of the year with steel bands, sports, contests and a Grand Parade on the last Sunday of the month.

End-Jul and finishing on the 1st Mon in Aug
Nevis – **Culturama** Is a version of Carnival. There is a Queen show, calypso competition, local and guest bands and many 'street jams'.

August

1st week
Anguilla – **Carnival/Anguilla Summer Festival** The island comes to life with street dancing, Calypso competitions, the Carnival Queen Coronation, the Prince and Princess Show, parades, nightly entertainment in The Valley and beach barbecues, www.festival.ai. **J'ouvert Morning** is on the Monday at crack of dawn, when people from all over the island dance in the streets of The Valley until noon. There are also the **Heineken Cup Boat Race**, the **August Monday Boat Race** and the **August Thursday Boat Race** at Sandy Ground. Handmade racing boats compete every day for the grand prize.

August Monday weekend
Montserrat – **August Monday weekend** Another national knees-up, connected to Emancipation Day on 1 August, commemorating the abolition of slavery in 1834. Beach barbecues and picnics all weekend. **Cudjoe Head Day** on Saturday starts with a big

	breakfast and carries on into the night, St Peter's Anglican Fete is held at the village rectory on Monday.
6-7 Aug	St-Barthèlemy – **Fête du Vent** Held in Lorient with a regatta, music and fireworks.
20 Aug	**Festival of Gustavia** Dragnet fishing contests, dances and parties.
24 Aug	Day of the island's patron saint, **St-Barthélemy**, when the church bells ring, boats are blessed, there are regattas, fireworks and a public ball.
25 Aug	**Feast of St Louis** Celebrated in the village of Corossol, with a fishing festival, pétanque, belote, dancing and fireworks.

October

21 Oct	Saba/Sint Eustatius – **Antillian Day** Flag ceremonies, games and fetes.
	Antigua – **Heritage Day** Builds up for two weeks in October with schools and offices preparing decorations for judging and various events leading up to **National Dress Day** on 31 October with a Food Fair and Exhibition, followed by a ceremonial parade on 1 November.

November

1 Nov	St-Barthélemy – **All Saints Day** A public and religious holiday. At dusk thousands of candles are lit in the cemeteries. **All Souls Day** on 2 November is also a public holiday.
11 Nov	Sint Maarten/St-Martin – **Discovery Day** Celebrated by both sides of the island on 11 November, together with the **Armistice** and there are celebrations in French Quarter.
2nd week	Anguilla – **Tranquillity Jazz Festival** Lots of bands playing on the beach, www.anguillajazz.org.

16 Nov	Sint Eustatius – **Statia/America Day** Festivities commemorating the First Salute to the American Flag by a foreign government in 1776.
24 Nov	St-Barthélemy – **Swedish Marathon Race/ Gustavialoppet** With distances of 3 and 12 km for children, women and men.

December

1st week	Anguilla – **Anguilla International Arts Festival** Arts competition, www.artfestival.ai.
3-5 Dec	St-Barthélemy – **Mondial Billes** A marbles competition qualifying the winner to participate in the next regional heat before joining the international players.
1st weekend	Saba – **Saba Days** A mini-carnival when donkey races are held, with dancing, steel bands, barbecues and other festivities.
12 Dec – New Year's Day	Montserrat – **Christmas** Is the island's main festival, shows, concerts, calypso competitions, jump-ups and masquerades and of course lots of festivities and parties on New Year's Eve, helped down with lots of goat water.
Christmas/ New Year	St Kitts and Nevis – **Carnival** With parades, calypso competitions and street dancing. St Kitts and Nevis are very proud of their masquerade traditions. Spirits are high and there is never a dull moment. For details, contact the Ministry of Culture, www.stkittscarnival.com.
26 Dec	Sint Eustatius – **Boxing Day** Celebrated with local actors playing (Nigger business), depicting the social, cultural and political happenings (gossip) of the year just finished. They make stops at homes and are rewarded with money, food and drinks.

Opportunities for shopping vary considerably between islands. Sint Maarten is known for its duty-free shops on Front Street, Philipsburg, with imported china, jewellery, electrical goods and clothing. Residents of other islands come here especially to shop for things which are unavailable at home. In addition to its gourmet food, St-Barth is famous for its chic designer shops where you can find all the top labels for clothes, shoes, watches and jewellery, and to a lesser extent St-Martin is following in its footsteps but with a less affluent clientele. There are arts and crafts to be bought on other islands such as St Kitts and Nevis and always a good selection of condiments, jams and jellies in Antigua to remind you of your visit, but little of anything memorable. Statia and Barbuda barely have a shop between them, while Saba is limited to lace and glass. Anguilla has some art work, carvings and sculpture and Montserrat has postage stamps. Throughout the region, however, you can buy the ubiquitous T-shirt to announce to the world that you've been there, done that.

Island artists

There are many art galleries on Anguilla, St-Martin, St-Barth, St Kitts and Antigua which display works by local and ex-patriate artists.

The most notable artist is **Roland Richardson**, who was born in Marigot, St-Martin, in 1944 and is the father of impressionism in the region. He works in oil, water colour, etching, charcoal and pastels. He studied in the USA and has exhibited worldwide, but still lives in St-Martin and has a gallery in Marigot although you can also visit his studio at his house, see p216.

The sculptor **Courtney Devonish** was born in Barbados but trained in the UK and Italy before settling in Anguilla and specializing in wood and clay. He has exhibited in North America, Europe and the Caribbean and has a gallery in Anguilla displaying other local artists' works as well as his own.

Rosey Cameron-Smith paints local views and customs and her gallery in Basseterre contains a wide selection of her prints and paintings as well as other artists' work .

Kate Spencer, also on St Kitts, paints portraits, still life and landscapes in bright tropical colours in oils, watercolours and on silk.

Art galleries

Antigua
Harmony Hall, Brown's Bay Mill, near Freetown.
T 268-4604120. *Daily 1000-1800, Nov-Apr. Map 1, D7, p280* An art gallery and gift shop, exhibiting and selling paintings, sculpture and crafts from leading Caribbean artists, popular for a lunch stop at the restaurant while touring by car or yacht.

St-Martin

Roland Richardson, rue de la République, Marigot, **T** 590-(0)590-873221. *Map 5, B4, p283* In Orléans you can visit the home of Roland Richardson, the only well-known native artist on St-Martin, **T** 590-(0)590-873224, *open Thu 1000-1800*.

Marigot has a large crop of art galleries, including **Camaïeu**, rue Kennedy, **T** 590-(0)590-872578, **Galerie Valentin**, 112 Les Amandiers, **T** 590-(0)590-870894, **Galeries Gingerbread**, Arrière Port de Galisbay, **T** 590-(0)590-877321, and **Graffiti's** at Les Amandiers, **T** 590-(0)590-879533.

Anguilla

Jo-Anne Mason has produced a map of all the art galleries in Anguilla which gives a brief description of each gallery and is available in hotels and galleries www.anguillaart.com.

Devonish Art Gallery, West End Rd, The Cove, **T** 264-4972949, www.devonishgallery.com *Map 7, C1, p284* Local deposits of clay have been found and pottery is now made on the island. The work of Barbadian potter and sculptor in wood, stone and clay, Courtney Devonish, his students and other artists, is on display. Courtney is the founder of the Anguilla International Arts Festival and a mover and shaker on Anguilla's art scene.

Cheddie's Carving Studio, opposite Devonish Art Gallery, West End Rd, The Cove, **T** 264-4976027, www.cheddieonline.com *Map 7, C1, p284* Cheddie Richardson is a wood sculptor who uses the driftwood roseberry roots found among the rocks on the shore. He highlights a feature of the wood to carve and polish animals, birds, fish and people, leaving the rest of the wood untouched. He also works in coral and stone and limited edition bronzes.

L'Atelier, North Hill, **T** 264-4975668. *Daily 1000-1730.*
Map 7, B3, p284 Michèle Lavalette, a French artist and
photographer who specializes in flowers, in oil, acrylic and pastels,
has her studio here. She has designed postage stamps.

Loblolly Gallery, on the road from The Valley to Crocus Hill,
T 264-4972263, www.loblollygallery.com *Tue-Sat 0900-1700.*
Map 7, B7, p284 Features eight local artists working in oil
and acrylic.

Mother Weme (Weme Caster), Sea Rocks, near Island Harbour,
T 264-4974504 for an appointment. *Map 7, A5, p284*
Mother Weme sells originals and limited edition prints of her
paintings of local scenes from her home. Prices for prints start from
US$75 and for her acrylic and oil paintings from US$300.

Saba

Peanut Gallery, Lambee's Place, Windwardside, **T** 599-4162509,
judysaba@hotmail.com *Tue-Fri 1000-1700, Sat 1000-1600,*
Sun 1100-1500. Map 8, G3, p284 Local and regional art and a
few crafts.

There are several art galleries in Windwardside where local
artists have their studios and sell their watercolours, oil paintings,
prints and sculptures. Ask the tourist office for a leaflet.

St Kitts and Nevis

The Plantation Picture House, at Rawlins Plantation,
T 869-4657740. *1100-1700. Map 13, B1, p287* Kate Spencer's
studio and gallery of portraits, still life and landscapes in oils and
watercolours. Her designs are also on silk. She has a shop in
Basseterre, on Bank St, just off The Circus, called **Kate**, with
paintings, prints, silk sarongs, hats by Dale Isaac, and another shop
in Main St, Charlestown, Nevis.

Bookshops

Antigua
The Best of Books, Benjies Mall upstairs, Redcliffe St, St John's, **T** 268-5623198, bestofbooks@yahoo.com *Map 2, D1, p281* It really does have the best selection of Caribbean and international books, newspapers and magazines in the Leewards.

Anguilla
National Bookstore, in the Social Security Complex next to Cable and Wireless, The Valley. *Mon-Sat 0800-1700. Map 7, B4, p284* Wide selection of novels, magazines, non-fiction, children's books, tourist guides, Caribbean history and literature, managed by Mrs Kelly. A *Dictionary of Anguillian Language* is a 34-page booklet, published by the Adult and Continuing Education Unit.

Clothing

Montserrat
Arrow's Manshop, Salem, **T** 664-4913852, or **Sweeneys**, **T** 664-4916355. *Mon, Tue, Thu 0800-1630, Wed 0800-1400, Fri, Sat 0800-1800. Map 4, E1 and B3, p282* The *Manshop* is owned by Arrow, see p194, and stocks clothing for men and boys, as well as shoes, hats, luggage, hair products, CD players, mobile phones and music, mainly gospel, reggae and calypso. Don't forget your volcano T-shirt.

St Barthélemy
St-Barth is the place to find designer labels such as *Armani, Louis Vuitton, Cartier, Hermès* and *Ralph Lauren*, most of which are in shops in Gustavia.

St Kitts and Nevis
Brown Sugar, Upper Central St, Basseterre, St Kitts,
T 869-4664664. *0800-1600 Mon-Fri, 0800-1300 Sat. Map 14, E7, p287* Judith Rawlins, a young local designer, owns this clothing line, which is very attractive, Caribbean style without the bright colours, all designed and sewn by Judith herself.

The Island Hopper Boutique, The Circus, Basseterre, St Kitts,
T 869-4652905. *0800-1600 Mon-Fri, 0800-1300 Sat. Map 14, E7, p287* Stocks the Caribelle Batik range of cotton fashions and also carries clothes from Trinidad, St Lucia, Barbados and Haiti; also at The Arcade, Charlestown, Nevis, **T** 869-4691491.

Crafts

Antigua
The Pottery Shop, Redcliffe Quay, St John's, **T** 268-5621264, fullerj@candw.ag *Map 2, D1, p281* Lovely pottery and interesting designs by Sarah Fuller, hand crafted using local clay. You can visit the studio on the beach, two miles north of the airport, well signposted, where they will make anything to order.

Saba
The Saba Artisan Foundation, in The Bottom. *Map 8, H2, p284* Local crafts have been developed by the Foundation and include dolls, books and silk-screened textiles and clothing.

The typical local, drawn-thread work 'Saba lace' is sold at several shops on the island. Taxi drivers may make unofficial stops at the houses where Saba lace, dolls, pillows, etc, are made.

!
● Saba lace is also known as 'Spanish work' because it was learned by a Saban woman in a Spanish convent in Venezuela at the end of the last century.

Jobean's Hot Glass Studio, Windwardside, **T** 599-4162499, www.jobeanglass.com *Map 8, H4, p284* Hand made coloured glass skilfully crafted into beads, mermaids, tiny frogs and lizards. Watch the artists at work or sign up for a tutorial and have a go yourself. An excellent alternative to diving and hiking. Jewellery, ornaments, glassware for sale.

St Barthélemy
Made in St-Barth I, Villa Créole Shopping Centre, St-Jean, **T** 590-(0)590-275657, madeinstbarth@wanadoo.fr *Map 11, D2, p286* and **Made in St-Barth II**, rue Général de Gaulle, Gustavia, **T** 590-(0)590-275745. *Map 12, C8, p286* Local art and crafts in two outlets.

There are several other art galleries in Gustavia and St-Jean.

Nevis
Nevis Handicraft Co-operative, Main St, Charlestown, **T** 869-4691746. *Map 15, E1, p288* A good collection of local artisans' work.

There are also several local craft shops in town.

Newcastle Pottery, Newcastle, Nevis. *Mon-Fri 0900-1600. Map 15, B3, p288* The pottery makes red clay artefacts including bowls and candleholders. You can watch potters at work. The kilns are fired by burning coconut husks.

Markets

Antigua
Market day in St John's, Antigua, is Saturday but the main market is open Monday-Saturday. The market building is at the south end of Market St but there are goods on sale all around. In season, there is a good supply of fruit and vegetables, which are easy to obtain on the island.

St-Martin
Every morning in the market place on the waterfront next to Marigot harbour. Clothing and souvenirs available as well as the usual fruit and vegetables and best on Wednesday and Saturday

St Kitts and Nevis
The public markets in Basseterre, St Kitts, and Charlestown, Nevis, are busiest Saturday morning, good for fruit and vegetables, also fish stalls and butchers.

Music

Anguilla
Ellie's Record Shop, at Fairplay Commercial Complex, **T** 264-4975073. *Mon-Sat 1000-1800. Map 7, B4, p284* Sells Caribbean and international music.

St Kitts
Walls Deluxe Record and Bookshop, Fort St, Basseterre. *Mon-Thu 0800-1700, Fri 0800-1800, Sat 0800-1630. Map 14, E7, p287* A good selection of music and Caribbean books, maps, cards, games.

Shopping centres

Antigua
Heritage Quay and Redcliffe Quay, St John's. *Map 2, C0/1 D0/1, p281* Shopping complexes with expensive duty-free shops (has public toilets) in the former, and boutiques. The latter has bars and restaurants and a parking lot, free if you are shopping there. Some tourist shops offer 10% reductions to locals; they compensate by overcharging tourists.

Duty-free shops at the airport are more expensive than normal shops in town.

Woods Center. *Map 1, B3, p280* A modern shopping mall with a wide variety of shops including *The Epicurean Supermarket*, the most modern, well-stocked supermarket on the island, a drugstore, post office, dental clinic and dry cleaners.

St Barthélemy
St-Jean. *Map 11, D2, p286* There are six small shopping centres in Saint-Jean: *La Savane*, *Les Galeries du Commerce*, *La Villa Créole*, *Le Pélican*, *Vaval* and *Centre Commercial de Neptune*, with boutiques, food shops and restaurants.

Stamps

Montserrat
Montserrat Philatelic Bureau, Salem, Montserrat, **T** 664-4912996. *Map 4, D1, p282* Montserrat's postage stamps have traditionally been collectors' items. There are six issues a year and a definitive issue every four or five years, Montserrat having issued its own stamps since 1876. The volcanic eruption is featured, as is the eclipse of the sun.

St Kitts and Nevis
Nevis Philatelic Bureau, Charlestown, Nevis. *Mon-Fri 0800-1600*. *Map 15, E1, p288* and **St Kitts Philatelic Bureau**, Pelican Shopping Mall, Basseterre, St Kitts. *Mon-Wed, Fri-Sat 0800-1200, 1300-1500, Thu 0800-1100*. *Map 14, F7, p287* St Kitts and Nevis are famous (the latter more so) for their first-day covers of the islands' fauna and flora, undersea life, history and carnival.

The Leeward Islands have a range of activities for all tastes. In the Anglo islands, cricket is the number one sport and Antigua is the best place to watch a match, whether an international Test match or a local game. On the water, Antigua is also number one for sailing, with English Harbour hosting the world-famous Racing Week in May and receiving yachts making the trans-Atlantic crossing. There are also major events in Sint Maarten and St-Barth drawing fleets and crowds. Diving is excellent around the unspoilt islands of Saba and Statia, and there are exciting historical wrecks to explore at St Kitts, but diving and snorkelling are good everywhere in the group. Off most of the islands where the trade winds give a reliable breeze and the water is shallow, particularly around St-Martin, you can windsurf. Kite surfing is becoming more popular where there is enough room. Hiking trails are well developed in Saba, Statia and St Kitts, where you can hike up to the summit of dormant volcanoes, and there are paths on Antigua, Nevis, Montserrat, St-Martin and all other islands.

Cricket

Cricket is the national sport in Antigua and the island has produced many famous cricketers, including captains of the West Indies team, Sir Viv Richards and Richie Richardson, and fast bowlers, Andy Roberts and Curtly Ambrose, Kenneth Benjamin, Eldine Baptiste and Winston Benjamin. Test matches are played at the Antigua Recreation Ground, ARG to locals. Matches are helped along by DJ Chickie's Hi Fi and characters like Gravy, the cross-dressing cheerleader who entertains during intervals, now retired but occasionally puts in a cameo performance. Brian Lara scored his world record 375 runs here in 1994 and again in 2004 with 400 not out, both times against England. There are also good cricket pitches at the *Sticky Wicket* by the airport, home of the Leeward Islands team, and at the *Jolly Beach Hotel* (where the teams usually stay), which are used as practice grounds during an international match. Local matches can be seen in St John's near the market and all over the island in the evenings and at weekends. The West Indies Cricket Board has information on Test matches, **T** 268-4605462. The cricket season runs from January to July.

St Kitts and Nevis are also cricket-mad and have produced four players, all from Nevis, to play in the West Indies team in Test matches. In July 2004 the sister islands were delighted to be picked (along with Antigua and six others) to host matches in the 2007 Cricket World Cup. Warner Park in St Kitts will be the venue for Australia's opening matches, while Antigua will host three of the biggest Super Eight matches in the next round. First-class cricket is played at the Salem Cricket Ground, Montserrat and at the Ronald Webster Park on Anguilla, including international matches. Call the Sports Officer, **T** 264-4972317, for information on fixtures.

! Anguilla produced its first international cricketer in 2003 when 20-year-old Omari Banks played for the West Indies against Australia at the Kensington Oval, Barbados.

Cycling

Several of the islands have good off-road cycling or roads which are quiet with little traffic. Tours are available and equipment hire.

Antigua
The *Antigua & Barbuda Amateur Cycling Association* can be contacted through **Cycle Krazy** on Pope's Head St, St John's, **T** 268-4629253, for races, information as well as hire of equipment.

Sint Maarten/St-Martin
Trisport, Airport Road, Simpson Bay, Sint Maarten, **T** 599-5454384, *Map 5, C3, p283* hire out mountain bikes and offer guided tours of the island as do **Authentic French Tours**, Marigot, St-Martin, **T** 590-(0)590-870511, www.authenticfrenchtours.com *Map 5, B4, p283* and **L2R Location 2 roues**, Galerie Commerciale Baie Nettlé, St-Martin, T 590-(0)590-872059, contact@L2R-rentascoot.com *Map 5, B3, p283*

St Kitts and Nevis
Blue Water Safaris, St Kitts, **T** 869-4664933, waterfun@caribsurf.com *Map 14, E7, p287* Offer mountain biking tours (US$15), island biking tours and beach outings.

St Kitts on Wheels, next to Cable TV office on Cayon St, Basseterre, St Kitts, **T** 869-4663912. *Map 14, D6, p287* They hire 21-speed mountain bikes, with helmet, lock, touring information.

Windsurf'n'Mountainbike and **Wheel World** cycling shop, at the *Oualie Beach Club*, Nevis, **T** 869-4699682, www.mountain bikenevis.com *Map 15, B2, p288* Winston Crooke organizes races, triathlons, tours, bike hire (US$20-35 a day, US$120-195 a week) and a cycle club, *The Trailblazers*; often competitions going on.

Diving

There are barrier reefs around most of Antigua which are host to lots of colourful fish and underwater plant life. Diving is mostly shallow, up to 60 ft, except below **Shirley Heights**, where dives are up to 110 ft, or **Sunken Rock**, with a depth of 122 ft where the cleft rock formation gives the impression of a cave dive. Popular sites are **Cades Reef**, which runs for 2½ miles along the leeward side of the island and is an underwater park; **Sandy Island Reef**, covered with several types of coral and only 30-50 ft deep; **Horseshoe Reef**, **Barracuda Alley** and **Little Bird Island**. There are also some wrecks to explore, including the *Andes*, in 20 ft of water in **Deep Bay**, but others have disappeared in the recent hurricanes. Diving off Barbuda is for certified divers only with wrecks to explore as well as reefs. The water is fairly shallow, so snorkelling can be enjoyable. You can take your own scuba gear or hire it from Byron Askie see p231.

Montserrat has a modest reputation as an undiscovered destination. The volcano has had an unexpected benefit for Montserrat's underwater life, as the 2-mile exclusion zone has created a marine reserve, with no one going into the area for some years. The waters are teeming with fish, coral and sponges and their larvae have drifted with the currents to the reefs of the north where the best dive sites are. Shore diving is good from **Lime Kiln Bay**, where there are ledges with coral, sponges and lots of fish; **Woodlands Bay**, where there is a shallow reef at 25-30 ft; at **Carr's Bay** where there are some excellent coral and interesting fish about 400 yards from the shore; and at **Little Bay**. There are some shallow dives from boats, suitable for novices or a second dive, but also deep dives for experienced divers. **Pinnacle** is a deep dive, dropping from 65 ft down to 300 ft, where you can see brain coral, sponges and lots of fish.

Reefs surround Sint Maarten/St-Martin providing habitats for a variety of fish while marine turtles nest on the beaches.

Wreck Alley, on Proselyte Reef, has several wrecks which can be explored on one dive. *HMS Proselyte* is a 200-year-old British frigate (mostly broken up and covered in coral, although cannon and anchors are visible), while *The Minnow* and *SS Lucy* are modern ships deliberately sunk as dive sites. Diving the east side is recommended in good weather, either from the shore or drift diving from a boat. The coral barrier reef is undamaged by silt run-off and there are lots of fish, fed by Atlantic currents. There are about a dozen dive centres offering a full range of courses. Boats are often small with no shade.

The Government of Anguilla is introducing a **marine parks** system, installing permanent moorings in certain areas to eliminate anchor damage. Designated marine parks include Dog Island, Island Harbour, Little Bay, Prickly Pear, Sandy Island, Seal Island and Shoal Bay. Mooring permits are required. Do not remove any marine life such as coral or shells from underwater. Spear fishing is prohibited. **Stoney Bay Marine Park Underwater Archaeological Preserve** was opened in March 1999. The park is protecting the wreck of a Spanish ship, *El Buen Consejo*, which ran aground on 8 July 1772 off the northern tip of Anguilla while on its way to Mexico with 50 Franciscan missionaries bound for the Philippines. It now lies about 100 yards offshore at a depth of 30 ft, with cannon, anchors and historical artefacts. Nine wrecks have been deliberately sunk as dive sites around the island, the most recent in 1993. **Paintcan Reef** at a depth of 80 ft contains several acres of coral and you can sometimes find large turtles there. Nearby, **Authors Deep**, at 110 ft, has black coral, turtles and a host of small fish, but this is more for the experienced diver. On the north side of the **Prickly Pear Cays** you can find a beautiful underwater canyon with ledges and caves where nurse sharks often go to rest.

Saba is known for its superb dive sites, protected by a well-established marine park. Not much fishing is done in these waters, so there is a wide range of sizes and varieties of fish to be seen. Tarpon and barracuda of up to 2½ m are common, as are giant sea turtles. From January to April **humpback whales** pass by on their migration south and can be encountered by divers, while in the winter dive boats are often accompanied by schools of porpoises. Smaller, tropical fish are not in short supply, and, together with bright red, orange, yellow and purple giant tube sponges and different coloured coral, are a photographer's delight. Divers are not allowed to feed the fish as it has been proved to alter fish behaviour and encourage the aggressive species. The **marine park office** is at Fort Bay, **T/F** 599-4163295, www.sabapark.com. Dive operators collect the mandatory visitor fees of US$3 per dive or US$15 per year to help maintain the park which is now self-financing. The *Guide to the Saba Marine Park*, by Tom Van't Hof, published by the Saba Conservation Foundation, is highly recommended, available at dive shops, the museum and souvenir shops, US$15. Saba has a four-person recompression chamber at Fort Bay, operated by medical school people.

Statia's waters offer a wonderful combination of coral reefs, marine life and historic shipwrecks. Diving is excellent, with plenty of corals, sea fans, hydroids and big fish such as groupers and barracudas, as well as rays, turtles and the occasional dolphin, but unlike some other Caribbean diving destinations, you will not bump into any other divers underwater. Water visibility can be over 100 ft and diving and snorkelling are very good. **Sint Eustatius Marine Park** was established in 1996 and became operational in 1998. STENAPA has identified four protected areas: the southern part from Crooks Castle to White Wall is a restricted fishing zone; the wreck sites in Oranje Bay, STENAPA Reef (a modern wreck site) and the northern marine park are open for fishing and diving. Marine park fees are US$3 per dive, US$3 per snorkelling trip when using the park buoys, US$35 for a non-resident annual pass. You may not anchor anywhere in the park; spear guns and spear fishing are prohibited in all waters around Statia; nothing may be removed, whether animals, plants or historical artefacts; you may not touch or feed marine life. You must by law dive with a local company.

There is very good snorkelling and scuba diving off **St Kitts and Nevis**. Most dive sites are on the Caribbean side of the islands, where the reef starts in shallow water and falls off to 100 ft or more. Between the two islands there is a shelf in only 25 ft of water which attracts lots of fish, including angel fish, to the corals, sea fans and sponges. There is black coral off the southeast peninsula, coral caves, reefs and wrecks with abundant fish and other sea creatures of all sizes and colours. Off **St Kitts** good reefs to dive include **Turtle Reef** (off Shitten Bay) which is good for beginners and snorkelling, **Coconut Reef** in Basseterre Bay and **Pump Bay** by Sandy Point. Much of the diving is suitable for novices and few of the major sites are deeper than 70 ft. The waters around St Kitts are the resting place of several shipwrecks. The Anglo-Danish Maritime Archaeological Team (ADMAT) set up a field school in 2003, the largest of this sort ever carried out in the Caribbean. The aim is to record two pre-1760s shipwrecks, uncovered by recent hurricanes in White House Bay, a time when the Caribbean was a battleground and a burial ground. Several wrecks and some other sites are actually shallow enough for very rewarding snorkelling although the very best snorkelling around St Kitts is only accessible by boat.

Snorkelling off **Oualie Beach**, Nevis, is excellent and also good at **Nisbett Beach** and Tamarind Bay. Good dive sites include **Monkey Shoal**, where you can find angel fish, black durgons, octopus, flying gurnard and maybe nurse sharks in the overhangs, crevices and grottos of this densely covered reef. **Devil's Caves** are another series of grottos, where you can see lobster and squirrelfish and often turtles riding the surge. **Nag's Head**, just off Oualie Beach, is a schooling ground for big fish such as king mackerel, barracuda, jacks and yellowtail snappers. Some dive operators will take you as far as Redonda, where diving is superb and untouched.

Antigua and Barbuda
Byron Askie, Barbuda, **T** 268-5623234. *Map 3, D6, p281* For two-four people (certified divers only) US$80 per person (US$150 for a single diver), including gear, boat and three dives.

Deep Bay Divers, Redcliff Quay, St John's, Antigua, **T** 268-4638000, www.deepbaydivers.com *Map 2, D0/1 p281* Catching the cruise ship market and surrounding hotels, they cater for beginners as well as advanced divers, taking up to 14 divers on the boat and going to Sandy Island, Cades Reef and Ariadne Shoal. There are several other dive operators based at hotels.

Octopus Divers, English Harbour, Antigua, **T** 268-4606286, octopusdivers@candw.ag *Map 1, F5, p280* Concentrating on the south coast, they have a comfortable boat and offer diving and accommodation packages.

Montserrat
Sea Wolf Diving School, Woodlands, **T** 664-4917807, www.seawolfdivingschool.com *Map 4, D1, p282* Diving and kayaking are offered. A shore dive costs US$40, a single-tank boat dive US$60, two tanks US$80, scuba equipment hire US$30, snorkel gear rental US$10. They also offer kayak diving, US$60, PADI courses, snorkelling tours and boat trips. Wolf and Inge Krebs started the dive operation in 1992 and there is little they don't know about Montserrat underwater.

Sint Maarten/St-Martin
Ocean Explorers Dive Centre, Simpson Bay Beach, Sint Maarten, **T** 599-5445252, www.stmaartendiving.com *Map 5, C3, p283* Dominique and LeRoy French run this friendly outfit, offering PADI and NAUI courses for all levels, two dives daily except Sunday, US$45 per dive, no more than eight divers on the boat or six for resort courses, English, French, Spanish and German spoken.

Sports

Blue Ocean, Baie Nettlé, St-Martin, **T** 590-(0)590-878973, www.blueocean.ws *Map 5, B3, p283* They have a fast boat for no more than 12 divers. As well as local sites they also go to Anguilla, St-Barth and Tintamarre. A snorkelling trip costs €23, a single dive €42 and a PADI Open Water course, €375.

Anguilla

Anguilla Divers, based at La Sirena, Mead's Bay and Island Harbour, **T** 264-4974750, axadiver@anguillanet.com *Map 7, C1, p284* They dive the east end of the island and offer PADI courses, in English, French, German or Spanish.

Shoal Bay Scuba & Watersports, Anguilla, **T** 264-4974371, http://shoalbayscuba.ai *Map 7, A4, p284* Spacious boat with plenty of shade and ladder for getting out of the water. Full service, towels, drinks and fruit provided, friendly and helpful. Single dive US$50, PADI Open Water course US$375.

Saba

Saba Deep, Fort Bay, **T** 599-4163347, www.sabadeep.com *Map 8 just off H2 p284* NAUI, PADI, SSI, TDI and IANTD instructors and a full-service dive centre with Nitrox and Drager Rebreathers. Three dives daily and return to the harbour between dives for the surface interval. All your gear is washed and taken care of during your stay or there is well-maintained rental equipment. Dive rates are US$56 single dive, US$101 double, US$141 triple, US$82 night, all including equipment, Marine Park fees and taxes. Dive packages, with accommodation and transfers, are available.

Saba Divers, Fort Bay, **T** 599-4163840,www.sabadivers.com *Map 8 just off H2, p284* Run by Wolfgang and Barbara Tooten, of Germany, who also run *Scout's Place* hotel. PADI, SSI, DAN, CMAS courses offered in several languages, diving and accommodation packages available. This is a NRC facility with a Nitrox compressor and the only dive shop in the Caribbean offering Nitrox for free. Three dives a day at 0930, 1130, 1330 and night dives on request, US$41 per dive with tank and weights. Other equipment US$10 a day. Special prices for yachties, who can be picked up from their boat, contact the office or boats, *Big Star* and *Big Blue*, on VHF Ch 16.

Sea Saba Dive Centre, office and extensive retail shop at Lambee's Place, Windwardside, Saba, **T** 599-4162246, www.seasaba.com *Map 8, G3/4 and off H2, p284* Fort Bay harbour depot for all rental equipment and compressors. They offer PADI and NAUI courses from beginner to divemaster and also Nitrox diving at US$59 a week, unlimited. Sea Saba has two large 40-ft boats but limits groups to 10 divers. Two dives between 0930 and 1330 with surface interval spent at Well's Bay for sunbathing, snorkelling or ocean kayaking. US$90 for two dives, including tax and equipment. Night dives on request.

Sint Eustatius

Dive Statia, Lower Town, Oranjestad, **T** 599-3182435, www.divestatia.com *Map 10, C5, p285* Run by Rudy and Rinda Hees, who have a comfortable, 26-ft catamaran for diving and a 14-ft rigid boat for training or special dives. A full range of courses and hotel/dive packages is offered at this Gold Palm five-star PADI operation, including Nitrox certification. Families with children of 12 and above are welcome. Three dives a day with night dives on request, all dives fully guided. A package of dives is the best value; a single tank dive costs US$35. Equipment rental is available, PADI Open Water four-day course US$350, snorkel trips US$25 with equipment.

Golden Rock Dive Centre, Lower Town, Oranjestad, **T/F** 599-3182964, www.goldenrockdive.net *Map 10, F6, p285* Owned by Glen Fairs, US$45 per dive, hotel/dive packages, PADI Open Water course US$350. Charter fishing and boat trips to Saba.

Scubaqua, *Golden Era Hotel*, Lower Town, Oranjestad, own pier, **T/F** 599-3182160, scubaqua@goldenrock.net *Map 10, C5, p285* One boat, taking 12 divers, and an inflatable for dive courses (PADI, SSI, CMAS). No more than six per instructor, captain stays on board. Drift diving for whale watching between end-January and April. Also waterskiing, wakeboards and fishing trips. A single dive costs US$29, equipment rental US$20, snorkelling trips with lunch on the beach US$25, full Open Water certification course, US$350.

St Barthélemy
Plongée Caraïbes, Gustavia, **T** 590-(0)590-275594, www.plongee-caraibes.com *Map 12, D7, p286* A single dive is about US$50, or there are packages of five or 10 dives for US$220 or US$400. PADI Open Water certification costs US$480.

St Kitts and Nevis
Kenneth's Dive Centre, Bay Rd, Basseterre, St Kitts, **T** 869-4652670. *Map 14, F8, p287* Kenneth Samuel, a PADI-certified Dive Master (friendly and helpful), offers courses, dive packages (single-tank dive US$50, US$75 two-tank dive, four-day package US$245) and all equipment. There are facilities for people with disabilities.

Pro-Divers, at *Ocean Terrace Inn*, Basseterre, St Kitts, **T** 869-4663483, prodiver@caribsurf.com *Map 13, D2, p287* Large boat and takes large parties diving, PADI instruction, Dive gear for rent, dive packages available, single-tank dive US$45, two-tank dive US$70, three-hour snorkelling US$35. Ocean kayaks for hire.

Scuba Safaris, Oualie Beach, Nevis, **T** 869-4699518, scubanev@caribsurf.com *Map 15, B2, p288* Five-star operation run by Ellis Chaderton. Diving costs US$45 for a single-tank dive, US$80 for two tanks, PADI and NAUI instruction and equipment rental. Trips to see dolphins and humpback whales can be arranged.

Fishing

Marlin, swordfish, tuna, mackerel and dorado (locally called dolphin fish) abound in these waters. In the reefs and shallows there are big barracuda, tarpon and bonefish. Although most fish run between November and March, there is no real off-season and local captains will know where to find the best fishing grounds. **Sport fishing** tournaments are held on several islands, such as Antigua (Whitsun weekend in May) and Sint Maarten (all year round). **Deep-sea fishing** boats can be chartered for a half or full day and some on a weekly basis. English Harbour is the best place to start in Antigua; in Sint Maarten/St-Martin, boats are based at Bobby's Marina, Pelican Marina, Great Bay Marina, the Marina Port Royale, Marina Anse Marcel or Marina Oyster Pond. Arrange through the hotels or contact the tourist offices for a current list of operators. Fishermen should beware of eating large predators, such as barracuda and others, which accumulate the ciguatera toxin.

Antigua
Nightwing, Falmouth Harbour, **T** 268-4638779, www.fishantigua.com *Map 1, E5, p280* A 31-ft Bertrum, US$450 for four hours, US$650 for eight hours, plus tip, maximum six people, split charters, good for beginners or experienced fishermen.

Overdraft, English Harbour, **T** 268-4644954, www.antiguafishing.com *Map 1, F5, p280* A 40-ft fishing boat leaves from Nelson's Dockyard, US$400 for four hours, US$500 for six hours, or US$600 for eight hours.

Montserrat
Danny Sweeney, Olveston, **T** 664-4915645, mwilson@candw.ag *Map 4, D1, p282* Long-time fisherman Danny Sweeney can take you fishing or organize any number of watersports.

Sint Maarten/St-Martin

Taylor Made, Simpson Bay, Sint Maarten, **T** 599-5527539, www.st-maarten-st-martin.com/taylormade *Map 5, C3, p283* The captain, Dougie, has been fishing since he was nine and is experienced at finding mahi mahi, wahoo, or tuna. Also trips for non-fisherfolk.

St-Barthélemy

Marine Service, Quai du Yacht Club, Gustavia, **T** 590-(0)590-277034, VHF 74. *Map 12, C7, p286* Deep-sea fishing trips and watersports and boat rentals. The price depends on the type of boat (four-eight people) and ranges from US$470-640 for a half day to US$780-1,100 for a full day with open bar and picnic lunch.

Océan Must Marina, La Pointe, Gustavia, **T** 590-(0)590-276225, VHF 10. *Map 12, A7, p286* Deep-sea fishing, also charter boats for cruising, diving, waterskiing.

St Kitts and Nevis

Nevis Water Sports, Oualie Beach, Nevis, **T** 869-4699060, www.fishnevis.com *Map 15, B2, p288* The *Sea Brat* and *Sea Troll* can be chartered for fishing or leisure tours. October to December is peak wahoo season, February to April is best for tuna and wahoo, June to August for billfish, all of which are released.

Oliver Spencer, Old Rd, St Kitts, **T** 869-4656314. *Map 13, D1, p287* A fisherman who is happy to take visitors deep-sea fishing.

Golf

Golf is a growing industry in the islands and several excellent courses have been built in the last 10 years. A regular supply of fresh water is always a problem, but new strains of grass and desalination plants are overcoming the difficulties.

Antigua
Cedar Valley, near St John's, **T** 268-4620161. *Map 1, A3, p280*
An 18-hole, par 70 championship course which sometimes gets dried out but has pleasant coastal views. Green fees are US$35 for 18 holes. The *Antigua Open* is played at Cedar Valley in November.

Jolly Harbour, **T** 268-4623085. *Map 1, D2, p280* A par-71 championship course in a parkland setting with seven lakes, designed by Karl Litton. Clubhouse, pro-shop, rental, restaurant.

Sint Maarten
Mullet Bay Resort, **T** 599-5453069. *Map 5, C2, p283*
An 18-hole par 70 championship golf course stretches along the shores of Mullet Pond and Simpson Bay Lagoon. The Resort is still closed after hurricane damage. Green fees are high for what you get, at US$111 for 18 holes for a non-resident; busy at weekends.

St Kitts and Nevis
Royal St Kitts Golf Club, Frigate Bay, St Kitts, **T** 869-4662700, www.royalstkittsgolfclub.com *Map 13, D3, p287* An 18-hole international championship golf course. Completed in 2004, built on 125 acres, with two holes on the Caribbean and three holes on the Atlantic. Brackish water is used to irrigate the special grass which can tolerate salt. Green fees are US$150 for 18 holes, US$100 for nine holes, reduced rate for juniors and discounts in summer.

Golden Rock, St Kitts, **T** 869-4658103. *Map 13, D3, p287* Nine-hole course; a fun day is held on the last Sunday of the month.

The Four Seasons, Nevis, **T** 869-4691111. *Map 15, D1, p288*
An excellent 18-hole, par 71 championship course designed by Robert Trent Jones Jr. People fly in from other islands just to play golf here. It is beautifully maintained and offers beautiful views, but green fees will set you back US$175.

For something completely different, the **Nevis Golf Course** costs only US$15 and has two holes with six different approaches, while the **Cat Ghaut Course** opposite the entrance to the *Mount Nevis Hotel*, **T** 869-4699826, costs US$10.

Hiking

Organized hikes to historical and natural attractions can be a good way of seeing any island, but apart from some very out of the way places, there is no problem in setting off on your own with a map or local directions, plenty of drinking water, sunscreen and a hat.

Antigua

In the Nelson's Dockyard National Park there are five trails up to 1½ miles long in the hills, past fortifications and with fantastic views. Pick up a copy of *A Guide to the Hiking Trails in the National Park* at the museum or entrance to the dockyard.

Hikes are arranged frequently to historical and natural attractions. Once a month the **Historical and Archaeological Society** organizes free hikes. **Hash House Harriers** arrange hikes off the beaten track every other Saturday at 1600, free of charge, contact Bunnie Butler **T** 268-4610643 or David Crump **T** 268-4610686. The **Environmental Awareness Group** offers monthly excursions, **T** 268-4626236.

The **Hiking Company**, **T** 268-4601151, run by Peter Todd, takes groups of six minimum (0900-1700) for moderate hikes in the southwest, with lunch on a beach for swimming afterwards.

Mac's Tracks, run by Brian MacMillan, St John's (home **T** 268-4627376), explore the countryside for two- to four-hour hikes on special request, from US$10 per person, lunch and transport to the start arranged, to Boggy Peak, Mount McNish, Monterose Hill, Signal Hill Green, Castle Hill.

Tropikelly Trails, St John's, **T** 268-4610383, www.tropikellytrails.com *Mon-Fri 0800 and 1500*. Tours for US$65 per person include drinks, lunch, water and walking sticks, hotel pick-up, five-six hours to Body Pond, Monk's Hill, the government pineapple farm, Fig Tree Drive, Boggy Peak and silk cotton tree at Cades Bay, where 10 people can stand inside the trunk.

Montserrat

There are some excellent mountain walks in the north of the island. Contact the **Montserrat National Trust**, **T** 664-4913086, as they maintain the trails and advise on guides. Hiking with a forest ranger is usually US$20 per person depending on the size of group.

Sint Maarten/St-Martin

There are 40 km of trails for hiking, most of which are old paths used by settlers and slaves. They vary in length from 1 km to 6½ km through inland or coastal scenery. Contact **Association Action Nature**, **T** 590-(0)590-879787, which has a booth at the top of Pic Paradis, or the **Dutch Hiking Club**, **T** 599-5424917.

Saba

Saba has fantastic hiking on the old roads up and down the mountains built before there were any vehicles and steps were acceptable for people and horses, see p75. The **Saba Trail Shop**, Windwardside, **T** 599-4162630 (*Tue-Fri 0930-1530, Sat-Sun 1000-1400*) collects the US$3 fee for park maintenance and you receive a disk entitling you to hike on any trail. US$1 for hire of walking stick, recommended. There are maps and information here and a trail guide: *Saban Trails…A Walking and Hiking Guide*, published by the Saba Conservation Foundation, 1998. Trails are classified as easy, moderate or strenuous, but even easy ones usually require climbing steps and negotiating steep and/or slippery parts. Wear hiking boots or good trainers, take a sweater and waterproof jacket if you are going up into the clouds, as well as suntan lotion and water. **James Johnson**, **T** 599-4162630, a local man and the trails manager, does guided tours after 1500 weekdays and all day at weekends, US$40-50 per group, maximum eight people. He knows the island intimately and local plant and animal names.

Sint Eustatius

There is a trail up to the Quill and several around it as well as trails up the Boven, see p85. Some trails are overgrown and difficult to follow. STENAPA is in the process of restoring and extending Statia's trail system. Quill hikes with local guides are available with a voucher system from the tourist office or participating hotels.

St Kitts and Nevis

St Kitts has comparatively clear trails including Old Road to Philips, the old British military road, which connected the British settlements on the northeast and southwest coasts without going through French territory when the island was partitioned. There are also trails from Belmont to the crater of Mount Liamuiga, from Saddlers to the Peak, from Lamberts or the top of Wingfield Heights to Dos d'Ane pond. There are excellent hiking tours to the volcano and through the rainforest on St Kitts, and over old sugar plantations and through the forested hill of Nevis.

St Kitts **Greg's Safaris**, **T** 869-4654121, www.skbee.com/safaris, pleasant and informative, US$40-80; **Kriss Tours**, **T** 869-4654042, US$50 per full day, overnight camping US$90; **Periwinkle Tours**, **T** 869-4656314, offers guided walks, US$30-35.

Nevis **Eco-Tours**, **T** 869-4692091, droll@caribsurf.com David Rollinson is very knowledgeable; he offers 'eco rambles' over the 18th-century Coconut Walk and New River Estates, a 'Sugar trail' Mountravers hike over the old Pinney Estate (US$25 per person), Sunday morning strolls around historic Charlestown (US$10).

Heb's Nature Tours run by Michael Herbert, Rawlins village, Gingerland, **T** 869-4692501, offers Mount Nevis hike (five hours, US$35-40), rainforest hike (four hours, US$25-30), Saddle Hill hike (three hours, US$20-25), medicinal plants (two hours, US$15) and Camp Spring (2½ hours, US$15-20), price depends on numbers.

Sunrise Tours, **T** 869-4692758, trips to Nevis Peak (four hours round trip, US$35 per person), Saddle Hill (1½ hours, US$30) or the Water Source (three hours, US$40).

Top to Bottom, **T** 869-4699080, run by biologists Jim and Nikki Johnson, organize walks to suit you, including a night-time, star-gazing walk, two-three hours, US$25, children half price, snacks of fruit and coconut.

Horse riding

Horse riding is available for all levels on most islands, whether you just want a beach ride, a swim with your horse, a trek up into the hills, or flat work and show-jumping lessons.

Sint Maarten/St-Martin
Bayside Riding Club, Route du Galion, Orient Bay, St-Martin, **T** 590-(0)590-873664 (Dutch side **T** 599-5576822), bayside-riding-club@wanadoo.fr *Map 5, B6, p283* Beach rides and riding lessons.

Lucky Stables, 2 Tray Bay Drive, in Cay Bay, Sint Maarten, **T** 599-5445255. *Map 5, D4, p283* Takes groups on a two-hour trail and beach ride, three rides a day at 0930, 1500 and 2030, US$50 per person, children under 12 US$30.

Anguilla

Cliffside Riding Stables, **T** 264-2353667. *Map 7, B3, p284* Beach and trail rides, 0930, 1½hours, US$50, 1100 and 1415, 1 hour, US$40, 1630, sunset ride US$50, private rides for experienced riders (English or Western saddles), US$60.

Spring Hill Riding Club, on the road to Rendezvous Bay, **T** 264-4607787. *Daily from 0730 Map 7, C3, p284* Fully insured tuition from BHS qualified instructors, English style, show jumping, dressage, horses and ponies, beach rides, swimming on horseback, forest rides.

St-Barthélemy

St-Barth Equitation, Flamands, **T** 590-(0)690-629930, www.st-barth-equitation.com *Map 11, C1, p286* Contact Coralie Fournier for lessons or beach and countryside rides.

Nevis

Hermitage Plantation, **T** 869-4693477. *Map 15, F3, p288* Horse-drawn carriage tours, US$50 per 30 mins, and horse riding US$45 for 1½ hours. Nevis horses are thoroughbred/Creole crosses, mostly retired from racing on Nevis, where it is the second most popular sport after cricket.

Nevis Equestrian Centre, Main Rd, Clifton Estate, Cotton Ground, Nevis, **T** 869-4698118, guilbert@caribsurf.com *Map 15, C1, p288* Run by John and Ali Jordan Guilbert and Erika Guilbert-Walters. They offer 10 different rides from US$50 with a combination of trail and beach, English or Western saddles, for novice or experienced riders, and have an arena for lessons, US$20-30. They even have a six-hour cross island ride, but don't try that if you're not used to sitting in a saddle.

▸▸ *For information on horse racing on Nevis see p115*

Running

The Road Runners Club, Sint Maarten (contact Rose), **T** 599-5567815. *Map 5, D3, p283* A fun run of 5-10 km every Wednesday at 1730 and Sunday at 1830, starting from the *Pelican Resort & Casino* car park. On Sunday at 0700 there are two 20-km runs. There are monthly races with prizes and an annual relay race around the island to relive the legendary race between the Dutch and the French when they divided the island.

Sailing

Antigua

For cruisers or bare-boat charters Antigua offers good provisioning and marine supplies with facilities to haul out boats at Antigua Slipway or Jolly Harbour. There are several marinas. Charter fleets include **Sun Yacht Charter Services**, **T** 268-5622893, charterservices@candw.ag, and **Nicholson's Yacht Charters**, **T** 268-4601093, nicholsoncy@ candw.ag.

Adventure Antigua, **T** 268-7273261, www.adventure antigua.com *Map 1, A2, p280* Eco tour by boat exploring the North Sound islands, snorkelling, lunch and drinks for US$90.

Antigua Yacht Club, English Harbour. *Map 1, F5, p280* Holds races every Thursday. Anyone wishing to crew should listen to English Harbour Radio at 0900 on VHF 68/06 that morning.

Jolly Harbour Yacht Club, Jolly Harbour Marina, **T** 268-4626042, www.jollyharbour-marina.com *Map1, D1, p280* Holds Saturday races as well as the *Red Stripe Regatta* in February and *Jolly Harbour Regatta* in September. There are 159 slips (103 fully serviced) for yachts of up to 260 ft and 12 ft draft, with a mega yacht facility.

Jolly Roger, **T** 268-4622064. *Map 1, D1, p280* A wooden sailing ship used for entertaining would-be pirates, with Wednesday and Friday lunchtime cruises, Thursday cocktail cruises and Saturday night barbecue and dancing cruise.

Kokomo Cat, **T** 268-4627245, www.kokomocat.com, and **Wadadli Cats**, **T** 268-4624792, www.wadadli cats.com *Map 1, D1, p280* Trips round the island with stops at smaller islands such as Bird Island, Prickly Pear Island, or even Barbuda or Montserrat, can be arranged for US$60-90 on these catamarans.

Sentio, **T** 268-4647127. *Map 1, F3, p280* A luxury 50-ft sailing yacht (operating from Curtain Bluff in winter and English Harbour in summer) for small groups, honeymooners, families: special trips, beach exploring, overnight to Barbuda or instruction.

Sint Maarten/St-Martin
Bobby's Marina, Philipsburg, **T** 599-5422366. *Map 6, H6, p283* A popular excursion is match racing on *Canada II*, *True North*, *True North IV* or *Stars and Stripes*, boats from the Americas Cup, US$70, races daily, three hours.

St Maarten Yacht Club, Simpson Bay, **T** 599-5442079. *Map 5, C4, p283* A race to Nevis and back is held in mid-June with a day for resting/parties. Other regattas held are for catamarans, match racing with charter boats, windsurfing, etc. For information contact Mirian Leffers, or ask Robbie Ferron at Budget Marina in Cole Bay, **T** 599-5443134.

St-Barthélemy
Marine Service, Gustavia, **T** 590-(0)590-277034, www.st-barths .com/marine.service *Map 12, C7, p286* A range of craft for hire, motorboats, catamarans, jet ski, scuba diving.

Yannis Marine, Gustavia, St-Barthélemy, **T** 590-(0)590-298912, www.yannismarine.com *Map 12, D7, p286* Motor boat rentals, island tours, sunset cruises, jet ski, diving, waterskiing, bare-boat charters and sailing trips. Sailing and snorkelling cruises are offered by several catamarans. They go to Colombier Beach, Fourche Island, Tintamarre, Anguilla or St-Martin. Half-day cruises cost US$55-60, whole day with lunch US$90-95, sunset cruises US$46.

St Kitts and Nevis

Blue Water Safaris, St Kitts, **T** 869-4664933, waterfun@ caribsurf.com *Map 14, E7, p287* Has one boat, *Caretaker* (38 ft) and two catamarans, *Falcon* (55 ft) and *Irie Lime* (65 ft), offering fishing (US$60 per person), moonlight cruises (US$25), party cruises (US$25), Nevis day tours (US$60), sunset cruises (US$35) and snorkelling trips (US$35), private snorkelling, sailing and fishing charters (US$360 half day).

Leeward Island Charters, office next to the *Ballahoo* restaurant above the Circus, Basseterre, St Kitts, **T** 869-4657474. *Map 14, E7, p287* *Caona ll*, a 47-ft catamaran, 67-ft *Eagle*, or *Spirit of St Kitts*, a 70-ft catamaran for a sail, snorkel and beach barbecue.

St Kitts-Nevis Boating Club, **T** 869-4658766. *Map 13, E3, p287* Organizes sunfish races, check the bulletin board for details at *PJ's Pizza Bar* (**T** 869-4658373), Frigate Bay, the *Ballahoo* (**T** 869-4654197) in Basseterre, or Dougie Brookes who manages the boatyard *Caribee Yachts* (**T** 869-4658411).

Tennis

Many of the large hotels have courts, although they are often reserved for guests only. If you buy a day pass to an all-inclusive hotel, all their sports facilities are included in the price.

Antigua

Temo Sports, English Harbour, **T** 268-4601781, VHF Channel 68. *Mon-Sat 0700-2200 Map 1, F5, p280* A tennis and squash club open to the public with floodlit tennis courts, glass-backed squash courts, bar/bistro, equipment rental, no credit cards.

BBR Sportive, Jolly Harbour, **T** 268-4626260, VHF Channel 68. *0800-2100. Map 1, D1, p280* Lit tennis and squash courts (US$20 per 30 minutes) and a 25-m swimming pool.

Anguilla

Ronald Webster Park, Anguilla. *Map 7, B4, p284* Public tennis courts. Several hotels have tennis courts but some are for guests only; *Cinnamon Reef* has two at a cost of US$25 per hour for non-residents; *Carimar Beach Club*, US$20 per hour; *Masara Resort*, US$10 per hour; *Rendezvous Bay*, US$5 per hour; *Spindrift Apartments*, US$5-10 per hour.

St-Barthélemy

ASCCO, Colombier, St-Barth, **T** 590-(0)590-276107. *Map 11, C1, p286* Two lit courts. Also *AJOE* in Lorient, **T** 590-(0)590-276763. Tennis at several hotels, guests take priority.

Watersports

Waterskiing, windsurfing, parasailing, snorkelling, kayaking, kite surfing are available on most islands and, in Antigua, swimming with stingrays. Dickenson Bay, Antigua, is the only beach with public hire of watersports equipment, some hotels will hire to the public, especially out of season. *Sandals* on Dickenson Bay will admit outsiders, at US$150 per couple 1000-1800 or US$130 for the evening, giving you the use of all sports facilities, meals, bar. Most watersports operators offer hotel transfers.

Antigua

Kayak Antigua, T 268-4801225, tropad@candw.ag *Map 1, B6, p280* Kayaking through the mangroves in the northeast.

Kite Antigua, Jabberwock Beach, T 268-7273983, *0900-1700*, T 268-4603414 *after 1800*, www.kiteantigua.com *Dec-Aug Map 1, A5, p280* Kitesurfing lessons, rentals, sales by an IKO-approved school. Try a 30-minute orientation class on land for US$30.

Paddles, T 268-4631944, www.antiguapaddles.com *Map 1, B6, p280* An excellent half-day eco tour of the mangroves and islands off the northeast shore with snorkelling and hiking.

Patrick's Windsurfing School, Dutchman's Bay north of the airport, T 268-4619463, windsurfingantigua@hotmail.com *Map 1, A5, p280* Instruction to beginners (guarantee to achieve in two hours or no charge), intermediate and advanced windsurfers. Patrick will travel to any hotel requested.

Sting Ray City, Seatons, T 268-5627297, stingray@candw.ag *Map 1, C6, p280* Modelled on the Grand Cayman experience of snorkellers interacting with stingrays, wading or swimming with them and feeding them. Here the rays are confined in a spacious pen on a sand bank in the sea so they are available for visitors.

Sint Maarten/St-Martin

Club Nathalie Simon, Orient Bay, St-Martin, T 590-(0)590-294157, www.wind-adventures.com *Map 5, A6, p283* Windsurfing, kitesurfing and hobie cats on the east coast.

Kontiki Watersport, Orient Bay, St-Martin, T 590-(0)590-874689, www.sxm-game.com *Map 5, A6, p283* Wave runners, jet ski, parasailing, snorkelling equipment, banana boat and water taxi service to offshore islands.

St-Barthélemy
Carib Water Play, Baie de Saint-Jean, **T** 590-(0)590-277122.
Map 11, D2, p286 A BiC Centre, windsurfing lessons and rental.

Wind Wave Power, Grand Cul de Sac, **T** 590-(0)590-278257.
Map 11, C5, p286 Windsurfing school with Mistral gear.

St Kitts and Nevis
Fantasy Parasailing, Frigate Bay, St Kitts, **T** 869-4668930,
bentels@caribsurf.com *Map 13, E3, p287* Takes up to six up in the
air with optional dips in the sea.

Mr X Watersports, next to *Monkey Bar* in Frigate Bay, St Kitts,
T 869-4654995. *Map 13, E3, p287* Rents windsurfing and
snorkelling equipment, and offers fishing trips and weekly
all-inclusive packages. Also jet skis, waterskiing, windsurfing. In
summer there is a race for windsurfers and sunfish to Nevis.

Under the Sea, Oualie Beach, Nevis, **T** 869-4691291,
www.undertheseanevis.com *Map 15, B2, p288* A small aquarium
run by Barbara Whitman as an excellent educational venture for
children and adults alike. She takes groups snorkelling after a
hands-on talk about the contents of her aquarium and you learn to
look out for smaller creatures underwater. Highly recommended
Touch and Go snorkelling US$50 (US$35 children 5-11), snorkel
gear included but if you want to hire it separately it is US$10 per
day. Snorkelling lessons US$25, or US$15 for trip participants.

Windsurf'n'Mountainbike Nevis, Oualie Beach, Nevis,
T 869-4699682, www.windsurfingnevis.com *Map 15, B2, p288*
Windsurfing, rentals and lessons: beginners US$50 for two hours,
intermediate and advanced US$30 for one hour, rentals US$65-95 a
day, US$20-30 an hour. Sea kayaks for US$15 per hour single, US$20
for a double, hobie cats are US$45-95 an hour, no credit cards.

Airline offices

Antigua Airline offices are either in St John's or at the airport. **LIAT** has its regional headquarters here, **T** 268-4620700. **Caribbean Star**, **T** 268-4802550. **BWIA**, **T** 268-4620260. **Carib Aviation**, **T** 268-4623147, is a charter airline which will meet any incoming flight in Antigua and fly you to another island without you having to clear Antiguan customs. Sint Maarten Most offices are on the Dutch side at Juliana airport. **American Airlines**, **T** 599-5452040. **Air France**, **T** 599-5454212, **T** 590-(0)590-510202. **BWIA**, **T** 599-5454646. **Continental**, **T** 599-5453444. **KLM**, **T** 599-5454747. **LIAT**, **T** 599-5454203. **US Airways**, **T** 599-5454344. **Winair**, reservations, **T** 599-5454230, flight information, **T** 599-5454210, **T** 800-6344907. **Dutch Caribbean Airline**, ticket office at Cannegieter St 93, Philipsburg, **T** 599-5421564, www.flydce.com. Anguilla Airline offices are at the airport. **American Eagle**, **T** 264-4973500. **LIAT** (at Gumbs Travel Agency), **T** 264-4972238. **Caribbean Star**, **T** 264-4978698. **Winair**, **T** 264-4972238. St-Barth There are several charter airlines as well as **Winair**, **T** 590-(0)590-276101. St Kitts and Nevis **Caribbean Star Airlines** has its regional headquarters at the RL Bradshaw airport, St Kitts, **T** 869-4655929. **USAir**, Kisco Travel, Central St, Basseterre, **T** 869-4654167. **LIAT**, TDC Airline Services, Basseterre, **T** 869-4652511/2286. Evelyn's Travel, on Main St, Charlestown, Nevis, is the general sales agent for **BWIA**, **LIAT**, **American Airlines** and **British Airways**, **T** 869-4695302/5238. **BWIA**, **T** 869-4652286 on St Kitts, **T** 869-4695238 on Nevis. **American Eagle**, **T** 869-4658490 (St Kitts). **Winair**, Sprott St, Basseterre, **T** 869-4652186, **T** 869-4695583 on Nevis. **Carib Aviation**, **T** 869-4653055 (The Circus, Basseterre and R L Bradshaw Airport, St Kitts), **T** 869-4699295 (Vance Amory Airport, Nevis).

Banks and ATMs

Most banks take Mastercard and Visa, Cirrus and Plus. An ATM will dispense the local currency, eg EC$ rather than US$. **Scotia Bank**,

FirstCaribbean International Bank (formerly Barclays Bank), Royal Bank of Canada, Canadian Imperial Bank of Commerce, Antigua and Barbuda Investment Bank, Antigua Commercial Bank, all in the centre of St John's, Antigua. American Express is at Antours near Heritage Quay. Banks on St-Martin include Banque des Antilles Françaises (BDAF) and Banque Française Commerciale (BFC). There are exchange houses for changing from euros to dollars in rue du Kennedy, Marigot, and in the Marina Royale complex. In Philipsburg on Sint Maarten, Scotiabank, Windward Islands Bank, FirstCaribbean, RBTT Bank, Antilles Banking Corporation. There are lots of ATMs, including one at the airport taxi rank dispensing guilders, US$ or €. FirstCaribbean, National Bank of Anguilla and Scotiabank are in The Valley, Anguilla. On Saba there are FirstCaribbean and RBTT in Windwardside. In Oranjestad, Sint Eustatius, FirstCaribbean, Centrale Hypotheek Bank, Windward Islands Bank. On St-Barth, Banque Nationale de Paris (BNP), Banque Française Commerciale (BFC), Crédit Agricole. The BFC ATM at Galeries du Commerce, St-Jean, dispenses both US$ and €. The bank here is open Sat morning. On St Kitts, St Kitts-Nevis-Anguilla National Bank, FirstCaribbean, Royal Bank of Canada, Scotia Bank. On Nevis all banks are in Charlestown: the Bank of Nevis, FirstCaribbean, Scotia Bank.

Bicycle hire
See Sports, p226. Many hotels also have bicycles for guests' use.

Car hire
Prices for a small car generally range from US$30-55 a day plus insurance depending on the season and length of hire. In peak season it is often difficult to hire for just one day; your hotel may be able to help. Tourist offices have full lists. The international companies are well-represented, www.hertz.com, www.avis.com,

www.budget.co.uk, www.europcar.co.uk, www.nationalcar.com, www.dollar.com, www.thrifty.com. Antigua **Oakland Rent-A-Car**, **T** 268-4623021. Barbuda **Linton Thomas**, **T** 268-4600081, has a pick-up truck for US$50 a day or US$65 overnight; **Byron Askie T** 268-5623134 rents jeeps at US$60 a day, negotiate longer rental; **Discount**, **T** 869-4690343; **Striker's**, **T** 869-4692654; **Nevis Car Rental**, **T** 869-4699837. Montserrat **Be-Peep's Car Rentals**, **T** 664-4913787; **Ethelyne's Car Rental**, **T** 664-4912855; **KC's Car Rentals**, **T** 664-4915756; **Montserrat Company Ltd T** 664-4912431; **Neville Bradshaw Agencies**, **T** 664-4915270; **Zeekies Rentals**, **T** 664-4914515. Sint Maarten/St-Martin **Cannegie Car Rental**, **T** 599-5422397; **Empress Rent-a-Car**, **T** 599-5443637; **Safari Rentals**, **T** 599-5453185, safari@ sintmaarten.net; **Paradise**, **T** 599-5453737. Anguilla **Island Car Rentals**, **T** 264-4972723, islandcar@anguillanet.com; **Summer Set Car Rental**, **T** 264-4975278, summerset@anguillanet.com; **Highway Rent-a-Car**, **T** 264-4972183, www.rentalcars.ai. Saba **Caja's Enterprises NV**, **T** 599-4163460. Statia **Brown's**, **T/F** 599-3182266; **Rainbow**, **T** 599-3182811; **ARC**, **T** 599-3182595; **Lady Ama's Services**, **T** 599-3182712. St-Barth **Gumbs Rental**, **T** 590-(0)590-277532; **Island Car Rental**, **T** 590-(0)590-277001; **Questel**, **T** 590-(0)590-277322; **Soleil Caraïbes**, **T** 590-(0)590-276718; **Turbe**, **T** 590-(0)590-277142. St Kitts **Caines Rent-A-Car**, **T** 869-4652366; **Sunshine Car Rental**, **T** 869-4652193; **A & T Car**, **T** 869-4654030; **Courtesy Car Rentals**, **T** 869-4657804; **G & L**, **T** 869-4658040/1, www.gandlcarrentals.com. Nevis **Nisbett Rentals Ltd**, **T** 869-4699211.

Credit card lines

American Express, **T** 1-800-3271267. **Mastercard**, **T** 1-800-8472911. **Visa**, **T** 1-800-3077309. For other credit cards without a local or regional contact number, make sure you bring details from home for a number to call if your card is lost or stolen.

Dentists

Antigua **Dr SenGupta BDS**, **T** 268-4629312, **T** 268-4649738 for emergencies. www.antiguasmiles.com **Dr Bernie Evan-Wong T** 268-4623050. **Gentle Dental Services**, **T** 268-4622000. Anguilla Dental clinic, **T** 264-4972343.

Disabled

A few of the larger hotels have a room or two adapted for wheelchair users, but generally facilities are limited. Pavements and sidewalks can be narrow and intermittent, while shops and restaurants are often reached via steps.

Electricity

Antigua 220V usually, but 110V in some areas. St-Martin 220V, 60 cycles. Sint Maarten, Saba/Statia 110V 60 cycles, Saba has 220V on request. Anguilla 110V AC, 60 cycles. St-Barth 220V, 50 cycles. St Kitts and Nevis 230V usually but some hotels have110V.

Embassies and consulates

The **British High Commission**, 11 Old Parham Rd, St John's, Antigua, **T** 268-4620008. No diplomatic representation on the other islands, other than a **Swedish Consulate** on St-Barth. Anguilla and Montserrat are British Dependent Territories, so embassies are in the UK, similarly for St-Martin and St-Barth in France and the Dutch islands in the Netherlands.

Emergency numbers

T 911. Sint Maarten Fire, **T** 599-5426001; ambulance, **T** 599-5422111. St-Martin Fire, **T** 590-(0)590-875008. Saba Fire, **T** 599-4162222. St-Barth Gendarmerie, **T** 590-(0)590-276012 or 17; fire, **T** 590-(0)590-276231 or 18. St Kitts Fire, **T** 869-4652515. Nevis Fire, **T** 869-4693444.

Gay and lesbian

Attitudes to gays vary throughout the islands but even where homosexuality is accepted openly, there are few specifically gay venues. The islands are too small to be able to afford a distinction between the pink dollar and any other dollar. Local people tend to hide any gay tendencies. Saba is very gay friendly, gay dive groups come several times a year and some businesses are run by gays, but they are open to all. Sint Maarten is also gay tolerant, with the 12-room hotel **Delfina**, (see p131), run primarily for gay travellers, but no bars devoted entirely to gays. However, Statia is not so free-thinking and the local people prefer discretion. St-Barth and St-Martin are free and easy and happy to accept the tourist dollar of couples of whatever persuasion, but there are no specifically gay bars. On the Anglo islands, the *Golden Lemon Inn* on St Kitts is gay friendly, see p144, as is the *Hermitage Plantation Inn* on Nevis, see p149, but nearly all hotels accept same sex couples.

Hospitals

Antigua **Holborton Public Hospital**, T 268-4620251, in poor state of repair. A new Mount St John's Hospital is being built but lacks financing for completion. **Adelin Medical Centre** is a private practice, T 268-4620866. Montserrat The hospital is in St John's, for most routine and surgical emergencies, T 664-4912802. Private doctors and a dentist are also available. Serious medical cases are taken by helicopter to Antigua or Guadeloupe. Sint Maarten **Cay Hill**, T 140, or T 599-5431111. 60 beds, all basic specialisms, a haemodialysis department and 24-hr emergency services. A helicopter airlift to Puerto Rico is available for extreme medical emergencies. St-Martin **Concordia Hospital**, T 590-(0)590-295757. Ambulance, T 590-(0)590-292934. Anguilla The **Princess Alexandra Hospital**, T 264-4972551. Saba Hospital, T 599-4163288, doctor Ms Anita Radix, T 599-4163289. **Saba Marine Park Hyperbaric Facility**, T 599-463295, serving the Eastern Caribbean.

Statia The **Queen Beatrix Medical Centre** is on Prinsesweg, **T** 599-3182371 for Nurses Station, an ambulance, or **T** 599-3182211 for a doctor. Doctors are on 24-hr call. St-Barth Hospital, **T** 590-(0)590-276035, doctor on call, **T** 590-(0)590-277304. St Kitts **Joseph N France General Hospital**, **T** 869-4652551. Nevis **Alexandra Hospital**, **T** 869-4695473.

Internet/email

Marinas and yacht clubs have internet access and most hotels offer access for guests. Antigua You can set up internet access for your own computer before arriving through www.cwantigua.com with charges billed to a credit card. **Cable and Wireless Cybercafé** at Antigua Yacht Club (bring your own computer, or use theirs). **Internet Café**, Upper Church St, St John's; **Cyber Stop II**, Falmouth Harbour, **T** 268-4603575, *Mon-Fri 1000-1800, Sat 1000-1400*, EC$20 for 35 mins, EC$30 for 1 hr, EC$10 each subsequent 30 mins; **Comnett Ltd**, upstairs above Fedex in Redcliffe Quay, St John's, **T** 268-4621040, www.comnett-online.com, good machines, US$3 for 15 mins. Montserrat **CompuGET**, cybercafé in Brades, **T** 664-4919654, granten@candw.ag; **Jim Lee's Computer Services**, St Peter's, **T** 664-4918499, leej@candw.ag. Sint Maarten/St-Martin **Tel Net**, Front St, Philipsburg, *0730-1200*, internet US$3 per hr, also phones and phone cards. **Cyberzone**, Emmaplein, Philipsburg, opposite *Jump Up* casino, internet café upstairs, lots of computers, good comfy seats, US$2.50 per hr. Anguilla **Internet Café Voyage**, Caribbean Commercial Centre, The Valley, **T** 268-4985551, benjc@hotmail.com, *Mon-Sat 0900-1800, Sun 1400-1800*, US$2 for 15 mins, US$7 for 1 hr, printing US$1 per page. **Bits & Bites**, Sandy Ground, next to *Johnno's*, is a breakfast and internet café, also rooms to rent. Saba **Island Communication Services Business Centre**, next to RBTT, Windwardside, opposite Scout's Place and Post Office, *Mon-Fri 1000-1900, Sat 1000-1700*, US$5 per 30 mins, also video rental.

Statia **Computers & More Internet Club**, Fort Oranjestraat 20, **T** 599-3182596, *Mon, Tue, Thu, Fri 1000-1800 or 1900, Wed, Sat 1000-2100*, three computers in a small building, US$5 per hr. St Kitts **Leyton's Internet Café**, at the Amory Mall, **T** 869-4667873, EC$0.25 per min or EC$15 per hr. **Dot Com** internet café on The Circus, Basseterre, *Mon-Fri 0900-1630, Sat 0900-1300*. Nevis **Connexions Internet Café** on Main St, **T** 869-4699675, EC$0.50 per minute, or EC$50 per day, *Mon-Sat 0900-2100 occasionally Sun if cruise ship in port.*

Motorcycle hire

Sint Maarten/St-Martin **Super Honda**, Bush Rd, Cul-de-Sac, **T** 599-5425712; **Moped Cruising**, Front St, **T** 599-5422330; **OK Scooter Rental**, at *Maho Beach Hotel and Cupecoy Resort*, **T** 599-5442115; **Concordia**, **T** 590-(0)590-871424, from US$20 per day including helmets and insurance. If you have a heavyweight motorcycle licence, you can rent a Harley-Davidson for US$112 a day at **Super Bikes**, 71 Union Rd, Cole Bay. St-Barth Scooters can be rented from **Rent Some Fun**, **T** 590-(0)590-277059; **Chez Beranger**, **T** 590-(0)590-278900; **Saint Barth Moto Bike**, **T** 590-(0)590-276789. **Denis Dufau**, Saint-Jean, **T** 590-(0)590-275483, is a Harley-Davidson shop.

Pharmacies

Antigua **Woods Pharmacy**, Woods Centre, **T** 268-4629287, *Mon-Fri 0900-2200, Sun 1100-1800*.
Sint Maarten **Philipsburg Pharmacy**, 4 Vogessteeg, **T** 599-5423001, www.stmaarten-pharmacy-outlet.com, is a duty-free pharmacy, *Mon-Fri 0730-1900, Sat 0900-1300, Sun and holidays 1000-1200*. Anguilla **T** 268-4972366.

Directory

Police

Antigua **T** 268-4620125. Sint Maarten **T** 599-5422222.
St-Martin **T** 590-(0)590-875010. Saba **T** 599-4163237.
St-Barth Gendarmerie, **T** 590-(0)590-276012, Police
T 590-(0)590-276666. St Kitts **T** 869-4652241.
Nevis **T** 869-4695391.

Post offices

Antigua Long St, St John's, opposite the supermarket, *Mon-Thu 0815-1200, 1300-1600, until 1700 on Fri*; also at the *Woods Shopping Centre*, the airport and English Harbour. A postcard to the USA costs EC$0.75. Montserrat *Mon-Fri 0815-1555*, **T** 664-4912457. Sint Maarten Two safe places for holding mail are **Bobby's Marina**, PO Box 383, Philipsburg and **Island Water World**, PO Box 234, Cole Bay. No parcels by sea, only airmail which is expensive. St-Martin 25 rue de la Liberté, Marigot, will hold mail, but only for two weeks. Letters sent c/o Capitainerie Marina Port La Royale, Marigot, will be kept four -six weeks. Anguilla The Valley, **T** 268-4972528, *Mon-Fri 0800-1530*. Commemorative stamps and collections sold. Saba Airmail takes about two weeks to the USA or Europe. The post office in Windwardside is open *0800-1200, 1300-1700*, **T** 599-4162221, in The Bottom, **T** 599-4163217. Statia Fiscal Rd, Oranjestad, **T** 599-3182207, *Mon-Fri 0730-1600*. Airmail letters to the USA, Canada, Holland, US$1.25, First 10 g, to the Caribbean US$1, postcards US$0.62 and US$0.51, aerograms US$0.71. Express mail is available as are limited banking services. Special stamp issues and first day covers for collectors. St-Barth In Gustavia there are three post offices, *Mon, Tue, Thu, Fri 0730-1500, Wed, Sat 0730-1200*, **T** 590-(0)590-276200; in Saint-Jean, *Mon, Tue, Thu, Fri 0800-1400 Wed, Sat, 0730-1100* , **T** 590-(0)590-276402; in Lorient, *Mon-Fri 0700-1100, Sat 0800-1000*, **T** 590-(0)590-276135. St Kitts Bay Rd, Basseterre, *Mon-Sat 0800-1500 except Thu when it closes at 1100 and Sat at 1200*. Nevis Main St, Charlestown, *0800-1500 except Thu, closes at 1100, and Sat at 1130*.

Public holidays

All the islands have holidays at **New Year's Day**, **Easter** and **Christmas**. 1 May (or the first Mon) is **Labour Day/May Day** everywhere. Antigua **Whit Monday** (end May), **Queen's Birthday** (second Sat in Jun), **Caricom Day** (beginning of Jul, whole island closes down), **Carnival** (first Mon and Tue in Aug), **Independence Day** (1 Nov). Sint Maarten **Carnival Monday** (Apr), **Queen's Day** (30 Apr), **Ascension Day/Sint Maarten Day** (11 Nov). St-Martin/St-Barth **Ascension Day/Whit Monday** (end May), **VE Day** (8 May), **Slavery Abolition Day** (27 May), **National/Bastille Day** (14 Jul) , **Schoelcher Day** (21 Jul), **Assumption Day** (Aug), **All Saints' Day** (1 Nov), **All Souls' Day** (2 Nov), **Armistice Day** (11 Nov). Anguilla **Whit Monday** (end May), **Anguilla Day** commemorates Anguilla Revolution which began 30 May 1967, the **Queen's Official Birthday** (Jun, the first Mon and the first Thu in Aug), **Constitution Day** (Aug), **Separation Day** (19 Dec). Saba **Queen's Birthday** (30 Apr), **Ascension Day/Saba Days** (1st week in Dec). Statia **Queen's Birthday** (30 Apr), **Ascension Day, Statia/America Day** (16 Nov). St Kitts and Nevis **Carnival Day/Las' Lap** (2 Jan), **Whit Monday** (end of May), the **Queen's Birthday** (Jun), **Aug Mon/Emancipation Day** (beginning of the month), **National Heroes Day** (16 Sep), **Independence Day** (19 Sep).

Taxi firms

See p30 for fares and tours. Antigua In St John's there is a taxi rank on St Mary St, or outside the supermarket. If going to the airport early in the morning, book a taxi the night before as there are not many around. Montserrat **Reuben Furlonge**, **T** 664-4914376. Anguilla **Brod's**, **T** 264-4972592. At the airport (**T** 264-4975054) and ferry (**T** 264-4976089). Sint Maarten/St-Martin In the square next to the Courthouse in Philipsburg, **T** 599-5422359, Juliana Airport, **T** 599-5454317, or dispatch office **T** 147, in Marigot, **T** 590-(0)590-875654, in Grand Case, **T** 590-(0)590-877579.

Saba Taxis at the airport. St-Barth At the airport,
T 590-(0)590-277581, and in Gustavia, **T** 590-(0)590-276631.
St Kitts Taxis at the airport, by the ferry and at the large hotels.
Nevis **TC Taxis**, **T** 869-4692911, tctaxi@caribsurf.com

Telephone

Antigua **Cable and Wireless Ltd**, Long St, St John's, the Woods
Mall and at English Harbour. Prepaid cards are available for
overseas calls and for cell phones. GSM tri-band handsets can be
used by purchase of a SIM card from **Apua**, Long St, St John's,
T 268-7272782, www.apuatel.com. Montserrat **Cable &
Wireless (West Indies) Ltd**, at Sweeneys, **T** 664-4912112,
Mon-Fri 0800-1600. Phone cards are available, as are credit card
service, toll free 800 service and cellular phones. St-Martin/Sint
Maarten To call the Dutch side from the French use the
international code 00599 followed by the 7-digit number. To call
the French side from the Dutch use the international code
00590-590 followed by a 6-digit number. To call the French islands
from France, **T** 0590 followed by the 6-digit number, to call from
the USA, **T** 011-590-590 and the 6-digit number. Calls from one
side of the island to the other are expensive. When calling within
the Netherlands Antilles, dial 0 before the 7-digit number. There
are several telephone booths on the French side but they only take
phonecards: 120 units for €13.7, sold at the post office and at the
bookshop opposite. Phonecards for the Dutch side of the island
can be bought at **Landsradio (Tel em)** telecommunications
office in Cannegieter St, *0700-2400*, or at Landsradio's offices at
Simpson Bay, Cole Bay and St Peter's. Note that card phones at
Juliana Airport, although marked as 'téléphone' and displaying
instructions in French, do not work with French phonecards. The
GSM network covers both the Dutch and French sides. **Tel Cell**,
T 599-5424155, and **ECC**, **T** 599-5422100, provide roaming
services and ATT calling cards. Anguilla **Cable and Wireless**,
T 268-4973100, *Mon-Fri 0800-1700, Sat, Sun, holidays 0900-1300*.

There are two AT&T USA direct telephones by C & W office in The Valley and by the airport. For credit card calls overseas **T** 1800-8778000. Saba Most hotels have direct dialling worldwide, otherwise overseas calls can be made from Landsradio phone booths in Windwardside or The Bottom. Statia Phonecards of US$10 and US$17 can be used at phone booth outside near police station and at the corner of Korthalsweg, at the airport, at the harbour and the road to the airport, for local or international calls. St-Barth There are phone booths on the Quai de Gaulle, at the airport, Galeries du Commerce and Flamands, among other places. There are some phones which take coins but most take phonecards. USA Direct phone at the airport. St Kitts and Nevis **Cable & Wireless** main office on Cayon St, Basseterre. Credit card calls, **T** 1-800-8778000. USA Direct public phones available at C & W office. Phonecards are sold in denominations of EC$10, 20 and 40. Coin boxes take EC quarters minimum and EC dollars. Call charges are from US$5 for 3 mins to USA, Canada or UK. **Boat Phone Company**, Victoria Rd, Basseterre, **T/F** 869-4663003, offers cellular phone service for yachts.

Time
Atlantic Standard Time, 4 hrs behind GMT, 1 hr ahead of EST.

A sprint through history

1493	Columbus names most of the Leeward Islands during his second voyage in 1493.
1623	St Christopher becomes the first British colony in the West Indies, later important for its sugar industry, with the importation of large numbers of African slaves. A rival French group arrives and they divide the island, the French taking the north and the south, the British taking the centre.
1626	Reports that the Caribs, under the leadership of their chief Tegramond, were about to attack the colonists in St Kitts, led the French and the British to join forces and massacre some 2,000 Caribs at Bloody Point.
1629	French colonists arrive in the north of St-Martin.
1630	Dutch colonists are attracted to the salt ponds in the south of Sint Maarten, called Sualiga, land of salt, by the original Amerindian settlers.
1632	The English colonize Antigua and its dependencies, Barbuda and uninhabited Redonda. Some shipwrecked Englishmen land on Saba, finding it uninhabited. In 1635 the French claim Saba but in the 1640s the Dutch settle it, building communities at Tent Bay and The Bottom.
1632-48	Spain occupies St-Martin/Sint Maarten, fending off an attack by Peter Stuyvesant in 1644 which costs him his leg.
1636	The Dutch colonize Sint Eustatius and build Fort Oranje.

1645	St-Barthélemy is settled by Frenchmen from Dieppe.
1648	Dutch and French settlers return to Sint Maarten/ St-Martin and divide the island between them in the *Treaty of Mount Concordia*. The island later changes hands 16 times but the accord has been honoured since 1839.
1649	Oliver Cromwell sends some of his Irish political prisoners to Montserrat. The Irish settle, import slaves and start to grow sugar.
1650	Anguilla is colonized by the British, remaining British despite invasions by Caribs in 1656 and by the French in 1745 and 1796.
1672	After a brief possession by the Order of the Knights of Malta, and ravaging by the Caribs, St-Barth is bought by the Compagnie des Îles and added to the French royal domain.
1674	Sir Christopher Codrington establishes the first large sugar estate in Antigua and leases Barbuda to raise provisions for his plantations. Forests are cleared and African slaves imported. In the 17th and 18th centuries, Antigua is important for its natural harbours, where British ships can be refitted safe from hurricanes and from attack. The Dockyard and the many fortifications date from this period.
1690	A severe earthquake struck St Kitts, Nevis and Redonda, followed by a tidal wave which destroyed Nevis' first capital, Jamestown.
1713	The Peace of Utrecht awards St Kitts to England.

1768	A slave rebellion on Montserrat on St Patrick's Day leads to all the rebels being executed.
1776	On 16 November the cannon of Fort Oranje, Statia, unknowingly fires the first official salute by a foreign nation to the American colours. Statia is a major trans-shipment point for arms and supplies to George Washington's troops taken by blockade runners to Boston, New York and Charleston.
1781	Statia is taken without a shot being fired by troops under the British Admiral Rodney, who captures 150 merchant ships and £5 million of booty in retaliation for the island's support for the USA, before being expelled by the French in 1782.
1784	France cedes St-Barth to Sweden in exchange for trading rights in the port of Göteborg.
1816	Saba becomes definitively Dutch after 12 changes in sovereignty with the Spanish, French, Dutch and English all claiming it. St Christopher, Nevis, Anguilla and the British Virgin Islands are administered as a single colony.
1834	Emancipation of the slaves on Antigua. Freed labourers are limited by a lack of surplus farming land, no access to credit, and an economy built on agriculture rather than manufacturing. Conditions for black people are little better than under slavery.
1863	Abolition of slavery in the Dutch islands. The plantation system on Sint Maarten and Sint Eustatius breaks up as ex-slaves leave the island to look for work elsewhere.

1871	The Leeward Islands Federation is formed for the administration of all British colonies in the region.
1878	St-Barthélemy is handed back to France after a referendum.
1935	Sugar workers on St Kitts strike and there are riots. A warship arrives to impose order after several people are killed. Robert L Bradshaw emerges as a labour leader and trade unionist, with the newly formed St Kitts-Nevis Trades and Labour Union the main vehicle for protest.
1939	In Antigua, workers protest against low wages, food shortages and poor living conditions. The Antigua Trades and Labour Union is formed.
1943	Vere Cornwall Bird becomes the Antigua Trades and Labour Union's president and with other trade unionists forms the Antigua Labour Party (ALP).
1946	The ALP wins the first of a long series of electoral victories, being voted out of office only in 1971-76.
1949	Salt industry on Sint Maarten ends. Emigration leads to sharp decline in population which survives on subsistence farming and fishing.
1956	Vere Cornwall (Papa) Bird becomes Antigua's first Chief Minister.
1958-62	St Kitts-Nevis and Anguilla belong to the West Indies Federation.
1967	St Kitts-Nevis-Anguilla becomes a State in Association with the UK, gaining internal independence. Robert L Bradshaw is the first

1967 (cont'd)	Premier of the Associated State. Anguilla repudiates government from St Kitts. Ronald Webster of the People's Progressive Party (PPP) leads a breakaway movement. Antigua becomes a State in Association with the UK with full internal self-government. Vere C Bird becomes the first Premier.
1968	British forces invade Anguilla to install a British Commissioner. The London Metropolitan Police control the island until 1972.
1980	Dr Kennedy Simmonds, People's Action Movement (PAM) is elected Prime Minister of St Kitts and Nevis and holds office until July 1995.
1981	Antigua and Barbuda, as a single territory, become independent. Vere C Bird is the first Prime Minister.
1983	Nevis' local council is keen to become a Crown Colony but the British government opposes it. Eventually, on 19 September 1983, St Kitts and Nevis become independent as a single nation.
1990	Antigua is rocked by an arms smuggling scandal involving arms shipments from Israel to the Medellín cocaine cartel in Colombia. Vere Bird Jr is implicated and loses his cabinet appointment.
1992	Demonstrations in Antigua seek the resignation of the Prime Minister amid allegations of corruption.
1993	Fresh allegations concerning property development contracts and misuse of public funds in Antigua are published by opposition newspaper, *Outlet*, edited by Tim Hector, the most outspoken critic of the Bird administration until his death in 2002.

1993   In St Kitts, elections in November are highly controversial. A state of emergency is declared for 10 days because of rioting. Negotiations fail between the two main parties for a caretaker government for six months.

1994   A constitutional referendum in Dutch islands on whether they want to remain part of the Netherlands Antilles. In Sint Maarten, 59.8% vote for the status quo, in St Eustatius 90.6% and in Saba 86.3%. Vere Bird retires as Prime Minister of Antigua at the age of 84. His son, Lester Bird, leads the ALP into the general elections and wins with a reduced majority. In St Kitts, more clashes greet the budget presentation in February with the SKNLP boycotting parliament in support of fresh elections. A corruption scandal links senior political officials to drugs trafficking, murder and prison riots. The crisis provokes a new general election. The result is an overwhelming victory for the SKNLP, winning seven seats. Dr Denzil Douglas becomes Prime Minister.

1995   The volcano blows on Montserrat. Over the next few years the south is covered in ash and the capital, Plymouth, destroyed. Thousands of people are evacuated to other islands or to the UK. Those left are relocated to the north. With over £250 mn of British funding they build new communities.

1996   Efforts are made to clean up Antigua's poor reputation for illicit drugs and money laundering. Eleven offshore banks are closed. New legislation in 1998 close loopholes in banking regulations.

1997	Nevis' Assembly votes unanimously for secession from St Kitts but a referendum in 1998 fails to get the approval of two-thirds of the electorate.
1999	The ALP wins another election. Vere Bird Jr is reappointed to the Cabinet. Corruption and fraud are still endemic.
2000	The Dutch islands hold another referendum on status, with around 60% of the electorate on Sint Maarten voting for Status Aparte. General elections in St Kitts and Nevis return the SKNLP to power with eight seats. Dr Kennedy Simmonds retires and is replaced as leader of the opposition by Lindsey Grant.
2001	General elections on Montserrat are won by the New People's Liberation Movement (New PLM), led by John Osborne, with seven seats of the total of nine in the Legislative Council. The National Progressive Party (NPP), led by Reuben T Meade, win the other two seats.
2004	General elections are held in Antigua and Barbuda which result in an overwhelming vote for change. The ALP is beaten into second place with only four seats, while the UPP wins with 12 seats. Stanley Baldwin takes office as Prime Minister, vowing to get rid of corruption and nepotism. Lester Bird loses his seat. Optimism sweeps the country.

Books

Three island-born novelists stand out as eminent in their field with worldwide respect for their work, none of whom now lives in the islands. **EA Markham** was born in Montserrat in 1939 and moved to Britain to study in 1956. He has since lived in various countries all round the world working as a theatre director and a magazine editor, while also writing short stories, plays, a travel book and six collections of his poetry. Despite his international career and many years living in the UK, his childhood memories of Montserrat are a recurring topic in his work. **Jamaica Kincaid** was born in St John's, Antigua, in 1949 as Elaine Potter Richardson. As a young woman she moved to the USA to work as a children's nanny, later becoming a journalist and author. Many visitors regard Antigua as the ideal Caribbean holiday destination. The role of tourism in Antigua is, however, one of the objects of a vehement attack in Jamaica Kincaid's first book, *A Small Place*. Addressed to the foreign visitor, the essay proposes to reveal the realities underneath the island's surface. What follows is a passionate indictment of much of Antiguan government, society, the colonists who laid its foundations and the modern tourist. It is a profoundly negative book, designed to inspire the visitor to think beyond the beach and the hotel on this, or any other, island. Memories and images from her childhood, together with the problems of race and gender faced by black women, figure strongly in her other books , including *Annie John* (1985), *Lucy* (1990) and *Autobiography of My Mother* (1996). **Caryl Phillips** was born in St Kitts in 1958 but brought up in Leeds and educated at Oxford University. He has a prolific output of screenplays, radio and theatre plays, fiction and non-fiction. His novels reflect the West Indian concern with alienation and isolation and deal with slavery, emigration, poverty and longing. *Crossing the River*, about slavery and the African diaspora, was shortlisted for the Booker Prize in 1993.

Fiction

Markham, EA, (ed), *The Penguin Book of Caribbean Short Stories* (1996) Penguin Books. A collection of stories from authors around the English-speaking Caribbean.

Phillips, C, *The Final Passage* (1985) Faber and Faber, London. Traces the anxieties and tension before a young couple decide to emigrate from St Kitts to London and subsequent disillusionment.

Phillips, C, *A State of Independence* (1986) Faber and Faber. A novel about a fictional St Kitts and a man who returns to his native land after 20 years living in London, to witness the independence celebrations and decide whether to return for good.

Sekou, LM, *Love Songs Make You Cry* (1989) House of Nehesi, Philipsburg, Sint Maarten. Sekou is a newspaper editor, poet and short story writer. This book of short stories takes local issues and characters as its theme, decrying the commercialization of the island and attempting to get back to African cultural roots.

Non-fiction

Coram, R, *Caribbean Time Bomb: the United States' Complicity in the Corruption of Antigua* (1993) William Morrow and Company, New York. US journalist Robert Coram exposed the corruption of Vere C Bird and his sons, their illegal activities, arms shipments, drugs running for the Medellín cartel and sex scandals – a dynasty propped up by the US administration with millions of dollars of aid.

Jane, CWE, *Shirley Heights, The Story of the Red Coats in Antigua* (1982) the Reference Library of Nelson's Dockyard National Park Foundation at English Harbour, Antigua. A detailed account of the military history of the island and the building of the fortifications.

Kincaid, J, *A Small Place* (1988) Virago, London. Kincaid's essay is a fierce attack on government, colonialism, society and tourism.

Hubbard, V, *Swords, Ships and Sugar – A History of Nevis to 1900*. Available in St Kitts and Nevis bookshops.

The Kingdom of Redonda 1865-1990 (1991) The Redonda Cultural Foundation in association with Aylesford Press. The Foundation is an independent association of people interested in Redonda, its history and monarchs, which tries to steer through the minefield of Redondan politics. Established in 1988 by the late Reverend Paul de Fortis, it exists to promote the writings of MP Shiell, John Gawsworth and other authors of the realm's 'intellectual aristocracy'. It celebrates Redonda as 'the last outpost of Bohemia'.

Petty, CL, and **Hodge, N,** *Anguilla's Battle for Freedom, 1967* (1987) Petnat, Anguilla. The eminent local historian, Colville Petty, and Nat Hodge have documented the breakaway movement of Anguilla from St Kitts and the farcical gunboat diplomacy of the British in response to Anguilla's 'revolution'.

Smith, KB, and **Smith, FC,** *To Shoot Hard Labour (The Life and Times of Samuel Smith, an Antiguan Workingman 1877-1982)* Karia Press, London, and Edan's Publishers, Toronto. A graphic account of the terrible conditions in which black people lived and worked during slavery and its aftermath.

Poetry

Markham, EA, *Human Rites* (1984) Anvil Press, London. A collection of poems by Montserrat's leading poet, including *Late Return*, about returning to Montserrat after years spent living abroad.

Index

Credits

Footprint credits

Text editor: Rachel Fielding
Map editor: Sarah Sorensen
Picture editor: Robert Lunn
Production assistant: Jo Morgan
Publisher: Patrick Dawson
Series created by Rachel Fielding
In-house cartography: Claire Benison,
Kevin Feeney, Angus Dawson
Proof-reading: Tim Jollands

Design: Mytton Williams
Maps Footprint Handbooks Ltd

Photography credits

Front cover: colourful Anguillan shack,
Image State
Inside: Alamy; Montserrat Volcano:
  Rob Huibers, Panos Pictures
Cut-out images: Alamy, Powerstock
Generic images: John Matchett
Back cover: Tropical fish, Martha Gilks

Print

Manufactured in Italy by LegoPrint

Footprint feedback

We try as hard as we can to make each
Footprint guide as up to date as possible
but, of course, things always change. If
you want to let us know about your
experiences – good, bad or ugly –
then don't delay, go to
www.footprintbooks.com and
send in your comments.

® Footprint Handbooks and the Footprint
mark are a registered trademark of
Footprint Handbooks Ltd

Publishing information

Footprint Antigua & Leeward Islands
1st edition
Text and maps © Footprint Handbooks
Ltd December 2004

ISBN 1 904777 09 0
CIP DATA: a catalogue record for this
book is available from the British Library

Published by Footprint Handbooks
6 Riverside Court
Lower Bristol Road
Bath, BA2 3DZ, UK
T +44 (0)1225 469141
F +44 (0)1225 469461
E discover@footprintbooks.com
W www.footprintbooks.com

Distributed in the USA by
Publishers Group West

Publishing stuff

Complete title list

Latin America & Caribbean

Argentina
Barbados (P)
Bolivia
Brazil
Caribbean Islands
Central America & Mexico
Chile
Colombia
Costa Rica
Cuba
Cusco & the Inca Trail
Dominican Republic (P)
Ecuador & Galápagos
Guatemala
Havana (P)
Mexico
Nicaragua
Peru
Rio de Janeiro (P)
St Lucia (P)
South American
  Handbook
Venezuela

North America

New York (P)
Vancouver (P)
Western Canada

Middle East

Dubai (P)
Israel
Jordan
Syria & Lebanon

(P) denotes pocket
Handbook

Africa

Cape Town (P)
East Africa
Egypt
Libya
Marrakech (P)
Marrakech &
  the High Atlas
Morocco
Namibia
South Africa
Tunisia
Uganda

Asia

Bali
Bangkok & the Beaches
Bhutan
Cambodia
Goa
Hong Kong (P)
India
Indian Himalaya
Indonesia
Laos
Malaysia
Myanmar (Burma)
Nepal
Northern Pakistan
Pakistan
Rajasthan
Singapore
South India
Sri Lanka
Sumatra
Thailand
Tibet
Vietnam

Australasia

Australia
New Zealand
Sydney (P)
West Coast Australia

Europe

Andalucía
Barcelona
Berlin (P)
Bilbao (P)
Bologna (P)
Cardiff & South Wales (P)
Copenhagen (P)
Croatia
Dublin (P)
Edinburgh (P)
England
Glasgow
Ireland
London
London (P)
Madrid (P)
Naples (P)
Northern Spain
Paris (P)
Reykjavik (P)
Scotland
Scotland Highlands
  & Islands
Seville (P)
Spain
Tallinn (P)
Turin (P)
Turkey
Valencia (P)
Verona (P)

Lifestyle guide

Surfing Europe

of the Caribbean

BWIA's A340 has the largest seat and legroom ever, as well as the quietest cabin in the sky.

Cross the atlantic in luxurious comfort and style on our A340. You can enjoy up to a staggering 60" seat pitch in business class and up to a really generous 38" in economy. Add to that our renowned friendly and professional service, it's no wonder we fly more people to the Caribbean than any other.

For more information please call 0870 499 2942 or visit our website at www.bwee.com.

SHARING OUR WARMTH WITH THE WORLD

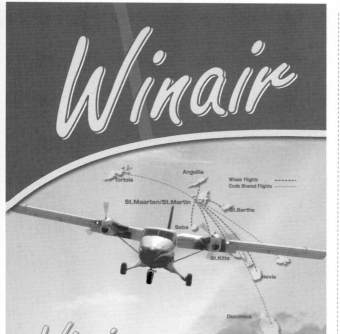

Winair

Your dependable airline

Throughout

Anguilla • Nevis • Saba • St. Barths • St. Eustatius • St. Kitts
St. Maarten • Tortola • Antigua • Dominica

For Reservations Call: (599) 545-4237•(599) 545-4230
(599) 545-4210• (599) 545-2002

Or book on line at www.fly-winair.com

Visit our website for specials or contact your local travel agent

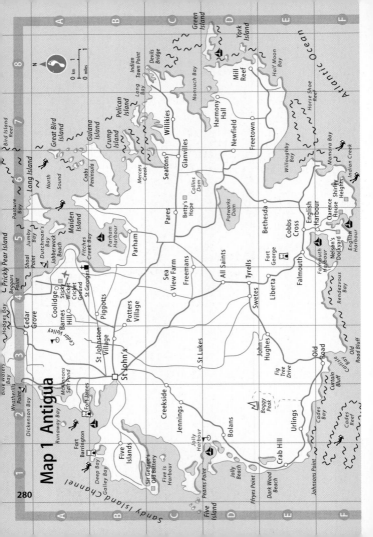

Map 1 Antigua

280

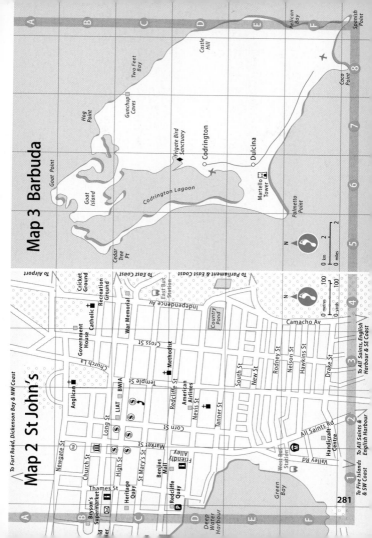

Map 3 Barbuda

Goat Point

Goat Island

Hog Point

Cedar Tree Pt

Gunchup Caves

Two Feet Bay

Castle Hill

Pelican Bay

Spanish Point

Coco Point

Frigate Bird Sanctuary

Codrington Lagoon

Codrington

Dulcina

Martello Tower

Palmetto Point

N

0 km 2
0 miles 2

Map 2 St John's

To Fort Road, Dickenson Bay & NW Coast

To Airport

Cricket Ground

Recreation Ground

Government House

Catholic

War Memorial

Church La

Anglican

BWIA

LIAT

Methodist

Cross St

East Bus Station

Independence Av

Country Pond

Camacho Av

To Parliament & East Coast

To East Coast

American Airlines

Temple St

Redcliffe St

Nevis St

Corn St

Tanner St

South St

New St

Rodney St

Nelson St

Hawkins St

Drake St

To All Saints, English Harbour & SE Coast

Newgate St

Church St

Long St

High St

St Mary's St

Market St

Redcliffe Quay

Benjies Mall

Friendly Alley

All Saints Rd Centre

Handicraft Centre

West Bus Station

Valley Rd

To All Saints & English Harbour

Thames St

Heritage Quay

Bryson's Supermarket

Deep Water Harbour

Green Bay

To Five Islands & SW Coast

N

0 metres 100
0 yards 100

281

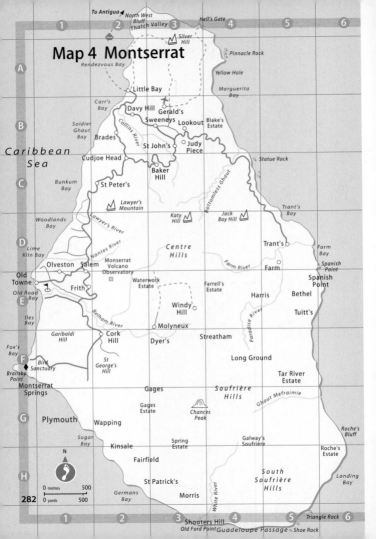

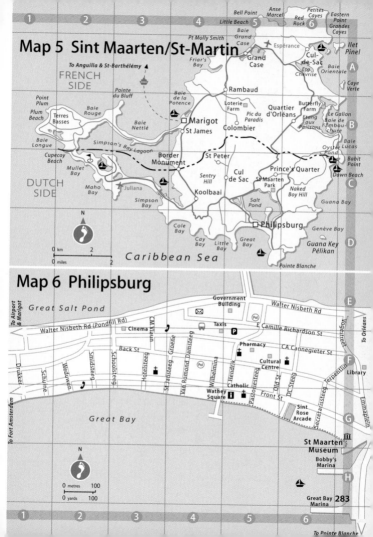

Map 5 Sint Maarten/St-Martin

To Anguilla & St-Barthélémy

FRENCH SIDE

DUTCH SIDE

Bell Point
Little Beach
Anse Marcel
Petites Cayes
Red Rock
Eastern Point Grandes Cayes
Ilet Pinel
Pt Molly Smith
Baie Grand Case
Esperance
Cul-de-Sac
Etg Chevrise
Baie Orientale
Caye Verte
Friar's Bay
Grand Case
Rambaud
Butterfly Farm
Le Galion
Baie de l'Embouchure
Point Plum
Plum Beach
Terres Basses
Pointe du Bluff
Baie de la Potence
Loterie Farm
Pic du Paradis
Quartier d'Orléans
Etang aux Poissons
Baie Rouge
Baie Nettlé
Marigot
St James
Colombier
Baie Lucas
Oyster Pond
Babit Point
Baie Longue
Simpson's Bay Lagoon
Border Monument
St Peter
Dawn Beach
Cupecoy Beach
Mullet Bay
Maho Bay
Juliana
Simpson Bay
Sentry Hill
Cul de Sac
Koolbaai
St Maarten Park
Prince's Quarter
Naked Boy Hill
Guana Bay
Salt Pond
Cole Bay
Cay Bay
Little Bay
Great Bay
Philipsburg
Genève Bay
Guana Key Pélikan
Pointe Blanche

N

0 km 2
0 miles 2

Caribbean Sea

Map 6 Philipsburg

To Airport & Marigot

Great Salt Pond

Government Building
Walter Nisbeth Rd
To Orleans
Walter Nisbeth Rd (Pondfill Rd)
Cinema
Taxis
E Camille Richardson St
Back St
Pharmacy
CA Cannegieter St
Cultural Centre
Catholic
Wathey Square
Library
Front St
Sint Rose Arcade
To Fort Amsterdam
Great Bay
St Maarten Museum
Bobby's Marina
Great Bay Marina 283

Drukkerij
Schurse
Weduwah
Smidsteeg
Schoolsteeg
Hofelsteeg
CM Vlaun
St Janssteeg
Groene
Van Romond Damsteeg
Wilhelmina
Hendrik
Pistolesteeg
DC Steeg
Secretalissteeg
Terpentin
Emmaplein

N

0 metres 100
0 yards 100

To Pointe Blanche

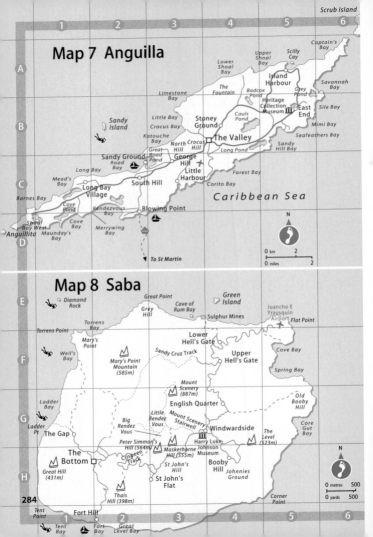

Map 7 Anguilla

Scrub Island

Captain's Bay

Lower Shoal Bay

Upper Shoal Bay

Scilly Cay

Island Harbour

Savannah Bay

Grey Pond

Sile Bay

The Fountain

Badcox Pond

Heritage Collection Museum

East End

Limestone Bay

Cauls Pond

Mimi Bay

Little Bay

Crocus Bay

Stoney Ground

The Valley

Seafeathers Bay

Sandy Island

Katouche Bay

North Hill

Crocus Hill

Long Pond

Sandy Hill Bay

Great Road Pond

Sandy Ground

Road Bay

George Hill

Little Harbour

Mead's Bay

Long Bay

Long Bay Village

South Hill

Forest Bay

Cove Pond

Rendezvous Bay

Blowing Point

Corito Bay

Barnes Bay

Caribbean Sea

Shoal Bay West

Cove Bay

Maunday's Bay

Merrywing Bay

Anguillita

N

0 km   2
0 miles   2

To St Martin

Map 8 Saba

Diamond Rock

Great Point

Green Island

Cave of Rum Bay

Grey Hill

Sulphur Mines

Juancho E Yrausquin Airport

Flat Point

Torrens Point

Mary's Point

Lower Hell's Gate

Upper Hell's Gate

Cove Bay

Torrens Point

Well's Bay

Sandy Cruz Track

Spring Bay

Mary's Point Mountain (585m)

Mount Scenery (887m)

English Quarter

Old Booby Hill

Ladder Bay

Little Rendez Vous

Mount Scenery Stairwell

Windwardside

Ladder Pt

The Gap

Big Rendez Vous

Peter Simmon's Hill (564m)

Harry Luke

Johnson Museum

The Level (523m)

Core Gut Bay

Crispeen Track

Maskerhorne Hill (555m)

Booby Hill

Great Hill (431m)

The Bottom

St John's Hill

St John's Flat

Johnnies Ground

Thais Hill (398m)

Corner Point

284

N

0 metres   500
0 yards   500

Tent Point

Fort Hill

Tent Bay

Fort Bay

Great Level Bay

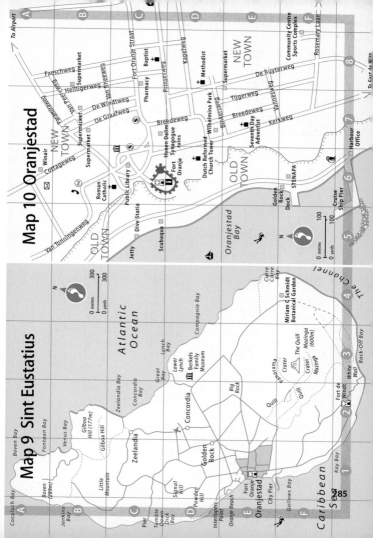

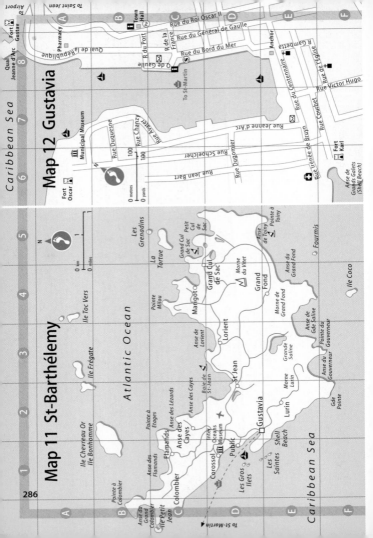

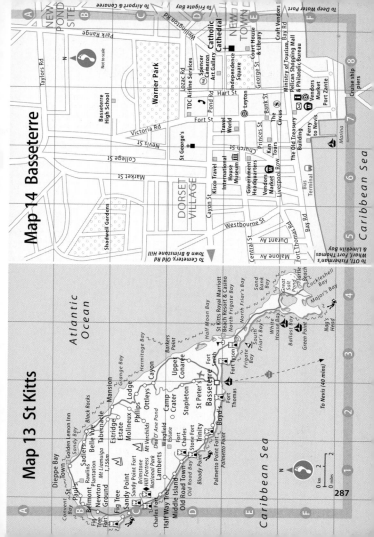

Map 15 Nevis

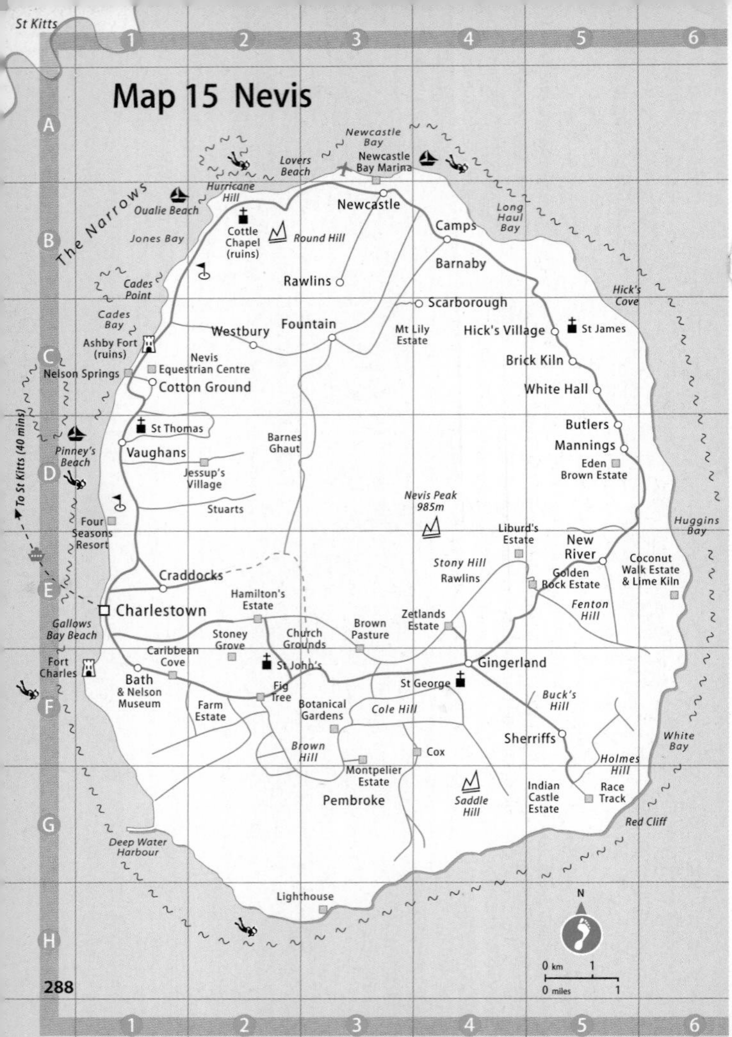

St Kitts

The Narrows

Lovers Beach
Newcastle Bay
Newcastle Bay Marina
Newcastle Bay

Oualie Beach
Hurricane Hill
Jones Bay
Cades Point
Cottle Chapel (ruins)
Round Hill
Newcastle
Camps
Long Haul Bay

Cades Bay
Ashby Fort (ruins)
Nelson Springs
Nevis Equestrian Centre
Cotton Ground
Westbury
Fountain
Rawlins
Mt Lily Estate
Scarborough
Barnaby
Hick's Village
Brick Kiln
White Hall
St James
Hick's Cove

Pinney's Beach
St Thomas
Vaughans
Jessup's Village
Stuarts
Barnes Ghaut
Butlers
Mannings
Eden Brown Estate

To St Kitts (40 mins)
Four Seasons Resort
Craddocks
Nevis Peak 985m
Liburd's Estate
New River
Huggins Bay
Coconut Walk Estate & Lime Kiln

Gallows Bay Beach
Charlestown
Hamilton's Estate
Stony Hill Rawlins
Golden Rock Estate
Fenton Hill

Fort Charles
Caribbean Cove
Stoney Grove
Church Grounds
Brown Pasture
Zetlands Estate
Gingerland

Bath & Nelson Museum
Farm Estate
St John's
Fig Tree
Botanical Gardens
Cole Hill
St George
Buck's Hill
Sherriffs
Holmes Hill
White Bay

Brown Hill
Montpelier Estate
Pembroke
Cox
Saddle Hill
Indian Castle Estate
Race Track
Red Cliff

Deep Water Harbour
Lighthouse

N

0 km   1
0 miles   1